Journeys through the Rabbit Hole

धर्म

A life of Beyond Philosophy

Sanvik Virji

Journeys through the Rabbit Hole

Sanvik Virji is, these days, best known as the Founder & Director of a group of companies called the WeComeOne Group.

His first degree and Masters was in Aerospace Engineering for which he had won a prestigious scholarship programme with the MoD. In 2002, he was an ardent anti-war protest organiser, for which, he was later dismissed from his fast track management programme. Sanvik went onto study Philosophy, a life long passion, and completed his thesis on a *Critique of Liberalism* in 2005. He has also studied a Post Graduate Diploma in Christian & Islamic Theology at Oxford.

He is known to many for his 'Thought of the Day' broadcasts on the BBC, and has appeared in several documentaries.

This is his first book.

Sanvik lives in Leicester, UK.

Acknowledgements

My Parents
&
And to all those who came into my life as guides & teachers.

Preface
धर्म

IF you're anything like me then you'll be reading this preface after you've read the book! I'm usually far too impatient to get to the *soul* of any book I read. If, for some obscure reason, you're actually reading this book in the logical order that it should be read, then you've already shown an attribute I still have to nurture – namely *patience*.

I should tell you how the idea for this book was coined. In early 2007, I attended an annual fundraising dinner at Oxford University. On my table, there sat a representative of Oxford University Press, of whom I had no knowledge. We never spoke once that evening. Instead, I spent my evening talking to an extraordinarily inquisitive bright PhD student, who was happening to construct a *critique* of my thesis; and thought it'd be completely appropriate to find out my life story.

As I drivelled on, the chap from the University Press must have been eavesdropping intently. He acknowledged that I had an unusual childhood – not materially you understand, but rather, *philosophically*. He rang me a few days later and suggested that we meet for a coffee at Merton College, Oxford; a place that I knew only too well. It was here that he proposed the schematics of this book, and so some credit must go to *Charles*, without whom I would never have written such an audacious account of my journeys.

This book is first and foremost a book on Philosophy. Many, I suspect, will take it to be a biography, albeit, an unusual one. I firmly believe that I'm in no position to be writing a biography, especially because materially I've achieved nothing of any great value! Rather this book is an introduction to not only some of the most powerful, audacious, perplexing philosophy that's ever been written, but also an insight into *living philosophically*.

For too long, I believe, has philosophy been hijacked by 'professional philosophers' who claim great satisfaction on being the only kids on the block to be able to explore and *know truth*. Believe me; I've spent long enough with these great masters of trivia and needless over complication. No doubt professional philosophers have their place well within the ivory tower of academia, but have no exclusive jurisdiction on *knowing truth*! Philosophy is for everyone. By this I mean that philosophy is something that each of us has, albeit often unknowingly. Philosophy is meant to be lived, not merely read, debated and criticised.

This book is my *mediocre* attempt to liberate philosophy from its chains and to introduce you to it. In order to show the tangible benefits, and often if I were to be honest, *the pain*, of living philosophically, I have shared my most powerful life evolving experiences as a reflective medium for you to ponder on long after you've switched the lights off and shut your eyes waiting to fall into a deep slumber. The biographical nature of this book is meant to provide a much needed narrative, and context, to the deep underlying philosophy I write about.

I should also share my hopes about this book.

I have no intention of making you into philosophers; *far from it*; I want people who read this book, to know of the great minds humanity has created; these minds provide each of us a *rough sketch* of how to find that little solace, and happiness we all seek in our lives. My hope is that having read this book, many of you will go and seek out the *actual* works of some of these great minds, and enrich your own lives. For those who are well versed in philosophical concepts, this book, I hope, becomes a template from which you can begin to *live the ideas* that you may already *know*.

For me personally, this book has been a revelation. I have always been a keeper of personal diaries ever since I was an adolescent teenager. My diaries have been my treasure chest, my gospels, to writing this book. The experiences I share have, in the metaphorical sense, '*unclothed*' my being. Many who claim to know me will be surprised, and maybe even a little shocked at my revelations. I've changed many names in order to conceal their identity, and those names that I have kept, I've much to thank them for. Some key individuals who have shaped my *intellectual Self* have asked me to make no mention of them; I've respected their wishes.

I hope you find the philosophy as much of a revelation as I've had in writing it.

Sanvik Virji
December, 2008

SANVIK VIRJI

One
धर्म
Spectres in the Past

I woke up early on the morning of 29th May 2005. It was my last day in England. I was due to fly out to India the following day, for what was going to be a seven weeklong trip. Not usually a landmark event, one might think, especially because I had been to India before in 2001 for two weeks, plus I was born there and had lived there on and off until the age of five, when my family finally decided to settle in England. My father had a British passport as he was born in Uganda in 1952 and had moved to India when he was 16, apparently to study, but I have a sneaky suspicion that he, in actual fact had wanted to move far away as possible from his parents. Of course he has never admitted this. I was drowsily aware that this time the cliché was true; tomorrow was going to be the first day of the rest of my life. In two days time I would be in India completely lost – by my own choice. I didn't call it lost, of course. I was *'re-forging myself'* I would say, proudly using the term I had coined a couple of weeks earlier to describe the kind of travelling experience I was hoping to have. People gazed at me, smiling awkwardly every time I used the phrase, I could never figure out a way to respond to the awkwardness, usually I ended up breaking eye contact and wishing I had not sounded like a *nut*. But this was a re-occurring phenomenon in my life ever since I was young.

    My childhood is something of a blur to me now, but there are several episodes that stand out. I believe these episodes are important to understand. It would be pleasing to think that the future was a blank screen on which we could design our future. The reality, as Charles Handy once said quoting Ernest Hemingway, is that seeds of our life are there from the beginning – if we bother to look. In using my own life as a case study I needed to start by recognising that 'the past is a prologue', as Shakespeare put it. I aimed to do exactly that – understand the prologue, thereby being in a better position to write the future. The problem was to understand the prologue of ones own life was no easy task. I knew little about my father's upbringing and the key episodes in his life that helped shape his worldview, I knew even less about my mother's upbringing. I realised early on that one should always begin by understanding ones own prologue first.

I remember only flashes of my life in India. My conscious memory seems to begin when we landed in Heathrow, London for the first time. I remember it being a frosty March night, and I was introduced for the first time to Manish, my cousin who was only six months older. I remember connecting with him instantly and in a profound way, as if we were meant to be emotionally and intellectually bound, that connection still remains today. He has influenced my worldview greatly and completely unintentionally.

My brother, seven years my senior was determined to make me independent. When I was seven years old, he made my father stop the car a few miles away from our house and made me find my own way home. On another occasion he once woke me up in the dark one December morning and took me out running. He packed my rucksack with stones, put it on my back and made me run five miles. At the end of the run he decided that it would be better for me to make my own way home while he went to meet a friend. Of course he knew very well that I had no idea where home was. Home seemed like an eternity away. I had never been running prior to that morning, I was not particularly a sporty child and I lacked confidence. I vividly remember the pain, my legs felt like *jelly*, my shoulders ached and I was cold. I cried for the first five minutes after my brother had left me at the entrance gate to the park. I was only seven years old, but my brother had thought that it would teach me the importance of toughness and a sense of direction. I have no idea how I found my way back to the house, or how I carried the rucksack full of rocks, but I do remember walking into the kitchen like a conquering hero, feeling tremendously proud of my marathon and expecting a huge welcome.

"Well done San", my brother greeted me in the kitchen, where he was helping Dad fix the washing machine. "Was that fun? Do a favour and go to the shop, we need some milk."

I disliked him intensely at these moments. He always seemed to set me the tasks I hated most. He would set me physical challenges rather than academic, but soon I was setting them for myself.

I have an early memory of learning kickboxing at a local centre above a Burger King. I must have been either seven or eight. We had been on a family outing with Dad's friend, and his family, everyone was older than me and so I was pretty bored. I was particularly found of dogs back then and had decided to go and pat a puppy that was passing by, when suddenly I felt a short sharp pain at the back of my neck forcing me to my knees. Tears sweltered immediately in my eyes. A boy who was probably younger than me had decided that he didn't like me patting his puppy and in order to communicate that point, he hit me. As I turned I don't remember seeing the boy, his face seems a blur, but I remember my brother just watching. I was furious inside, I couldn't figure out how he could watch me get whacked and do or say nothing.

"Never mind, San," my brother said hours later when we had returned home. "There's always the next bully", he continued.

He had said those words with such smugness that I couldn't hold it in any longer. His infuriating runs, his cruel jokes and the general power he possessed over me had come to their eventual logical conclusion. I threw a right hook and caught him clean on the chin with a heavy contact. There was a moment while my fist was on its way to making contact with his chin that I had felt victorious, proud and confident. Moments later, I found myself roaring my eyes out as my brother dragged me by my feet to the garden. He had violently pulled me onto Mum's precious lawn.

"Get up" he shouted. "Come on, fight, let's see what you got" he roared, in what looked like an epiphanal rage.

I remember lying still, unable to move. I think that was the first time I tasted fear in all its glory, and it was a pivotal few seconds that to this day I haven't forgotten. I believe this to be my first *re-forging* experience. Interestingly, I cannot remember what happened next; I probably received a small beating, which my ego has totally suppressed. What I do remember however is that that night he spoke to me as a wiser, concerned older brother.

"San, how could you cry when that six year old hit you but then strike me?" he gently asked.

"I don't know", I replied.

We ended our day with him sombrely but authoritatively saying "tomorrow you're learning kickboxing".

I continued to learn kickboxing for ten years thereafter.

I cannot remember a moment in my life when I have not felt the love of my family. We were a family that would have killed for each other – we still are. My parents adored each other, and in my childhood there was barely a cross word said between them. My father was the galvanising force and my mother, Sarla was the driver of the household. As I grew up I realised that my house was unique in that my mother was the one in charge, while my father allowed her to get on with it, always being the peace maker whenever their were rifts, normally between my mother and my brother most of the time over my welfare. My brother wanted me to be tough and confident, while my mother wanted me to remain gentle and concentrate on my studies. My mother was the carer of the family. She wasn't educated having been born in an extremely orthodox Indian family in 1954. She was intelligent in worldly terms, but couldn't speak English, which restricted her exposure to the English way of life. She worked in a near by hosiery factory which was full of women who were in identical situations to that which my mother had faced. My mother's life consisted of working eight-hour shifts and overtime on the weekends. She cooked for the family when she got back from work; she tidied up after dinner, spoke to my father for a while, checked up on my welfare and then went off to bed by 10.30pm sharp, straight after the 10 o'clock news with Trevor McDonald. She had great confidence in my brother, she always expected him to do the right thing, she gave little attention to him, yet the bond between them was far stronger than I had realised.

My mother was a simple lady; she was innocent to the way of the new world. She had longed to return back home, for her this was India, a place where she was apart of something, she understood the way things worked and most of all where her family lived. What my mother did not realise for a long-time was that her sons were growing up as British. We were bi-lingual. We lived in India when we were at home and in England when we were at school or with our friends. We spoke Gujarati at home and English everywhere else. We were familiar with Indian food as well as English, Mexican and Italian. My mother had little to no exposure to white, English people. Come to think of it, she had very little exposure to anyone outside the Indian community. This was not out of any particular bad feeling towards other cultures but simply because she could not speak the language, resulting in a desperate lack of confidence.

My mother was also very religious in the sense that she followed traditions thoroughly. She would fast once a week, a tradition that she follows today. She would pray before leaving the house every morning. She would pray before she ate in the evening. She would know the dates of all the Hindu festivals and would prepare for them accordingly. My mother had once told me that when she was expecting me, she would read the Bhagvad Gita every night to make sure that she always thought of things that were beyond the here and now. She did this to keep herself happy and to begin teaching me the way of Brahma even before I was able to kick. She has always been convinced that I have turned out the way I have because of those very early days. She would read philosophy, which she didn't understand. She would listen to people talk about God in ways that she could not comprehend, all in the hope that I would be listening while inside her. I have grown up watching my mother feed the birds every morning before she fed any of us, no matter how late we all were, we could not eat until my mother had distributed the daily rations to the birds. I have been annoyed by this tradition several times and have questioned it by asking her why she does it. She has never properly replied.

Recently, I asked her "mum I understand why it is that you feed the birds every morning, but why have you never explained it to me?"

She simply replied, "if you cannot know by looking, you'll never know it by words".

It is only now that I appreciate her humanity and her worldly intelligence. My father, Prakash had met her once, and knew she was the one for him. He had fallen for my mother instantly and asked her at their first meeting whether she would be willing to get married with him when the time came. My father tells me that she said yes immediately. My mother however, has a different story. When my mother's orthodox family realised that there was a young man from Africa who was interested in their daughter, one of four, by the way, they immediately sent out the inquisition. My father has always been a networking 'guru' and within no time he had impressed my mother's brother. They got married in 1973. My mother was 18 and my father 20, a year later Vikas was born – my older brother.

Unlike my mother who had a strict but stable upbringing in a middle class Indian family, my father had been born in a severely dysfunctional family in Uganda, Africa. My father was one of ten; in fact he was the fourth one in the 'pecking' order. My grandfather worked in a PowerStation, he was a big man, and incredibly aggressive. Life, it seems had made him that way. My grandfather had run away from home at the age of twelve and ended up migrating from India to South Africa before moving to Kenya and then Uganda. He led a nomadic existence for most of his childhood. He had run away from home, convinced that his stepmother had tried to poison him. His real mother had died when he was very young. My grandfather had the look and style of a mafia 'Godfather', with a temper that had apparently killed people according to family folklore. He was one never to be messed with.

We lived five minutes away from my Grandfather who had moved to England when Edi Amen had caused the great Indian exodus of Uganda. His eldest son, Arvind had moved to England in the early 70's with his wife and four children. My Grandfather followed suit but he had decided to buy a house with his life savings in Leicester, whereas Arvind uncle had settled for East end of London.

My father decided to follow his father and settle in Leicester rather than London. I remember being about ten years old; I would make special trips to my Grandfathers house and listen to him talk for hours on end about when he was young and tough.

Most children at ten see their grandparents as aliens or at best a little boring. I, on the other hand had found my grandfather fascinating. I don't really know why. Maybe it was his presence, or his spiced-up tales of adventure, being lost in jungles, being chased by mobs, rebelling against the authorities and finding forbidden love. My Grandfather seemed completely different to everyone else I had known. He reminded me of my brother, but a nicer version because he would never pack my rucksack with rocks and send me on early morning runs. I admired his strength; he was resilient, brave and had lived an exciting life.

My Grandfather was the backbone of the family. He had commanded respect and obedience. As a child I was very sensitive to people. I could always accurately second-guess them. I would know what they were thinking or about to do, simply by watching them. I knew from my observations that my uncles and aunts did not think much of my Grandfather as a caring personality, but everyone knew where his loyalty lay. It was this that I found above all else that gave him respect. I realised from watching my Grandfather that people were slaves to strength. He possessed abundance of strength and no matter what his trespasses were, people always respected him. My first lesson in human dynamics came from this observation; strength of character equals respect from others.

My father was nothing like my Grandfather. He was gentle, sensitive to other people's feelings and had the natural ability to get along with anyone. He was and still is the best networker I know. His influence on me has been profound in several ways. Whereas my mother was carer of the family, my father was the trendsetter. I often like to think of my household as a country. My mother was the economist, my father was the legislator, and my brother was the army and police while I was the citizen. When I was young, I hated being the citizen. I was the slave on whose behalf everyone made decisions. Later, I realised that to be citizen is to be in a privileged position, one of strength rather than weakness, if only one knew how to manoeuvre oneself. The economist, the legislator and the army all work for the betterment of the citizen. I have become the person I am precisely because I had three equally powerful, intellectual and compassionate individuals, each in their own way, who had put me at the centre of their everyday household duties.

My father was an excellent household politician. Even though he earned more money than mum, he was better educated and he understood the world better, he could accept that my mother had an aptitude for finances. She was meticulous with the pennies, whereas my father liked to spend and live a little even if we couldn't afford it. I admired my father's lack of ego. He could accept other people for who they were without seeing them as a threat. He could always accept reality. Whenever there was an argument between Vikas and mum, I remember he never took sides. At first he would just ignore the situation and see if they could resolve it themselves. He would then wait for a cue and precisely at the required moment he would step in which gave legitimacy in him resolving the argument. Both sides trusted him to understand. My mother would leave the argument thinking she had got her message across to Vikas and that he had listened to her. Vikas would leave feeling that mum was right in her own way but she understood his position also. My father was the sustainer of democracy in my household. He always made sure that everyone had a voice. He would listen and make sure everyone felt as if they were heard. I firmly believe that any person who can manage his or her own family in this way is guaranteed to be a successful manager in business. Recently, I have begun to advise firms that if you really want team players who have the ability to communicate, lead, listen, be sensitive to others, delegate responsibilities to the right people, an expert in conflict resolution and many other such leadership qualities you must first understand their relationship with their immediate family. The way in which a person manages their household can be an excellent insight into their natural management ability.

My father was a passionate patriot. He adored all things Indian. His patriotism had rubbed off on my brother. Both of them would discuss politics and religion passionately over dinner while, mum and I got on with the task of eating and then clearing up. I remember asking my first political question over dinner when I was about eight. They were discussing the role NATO was playing in some conflict or another, when I suddenly asked "where is NATO?"

They both looked at me bemused and didn't quite know how to answer. I had thought NATO was a country and yet had never been able to locate it on an atlas. Vikas gave me an awkward glance and carried on his discussion with dad. To this day, the dinner table is the debating area for the family, with dad being the speaker of the house, always setting the agenda and making sure no body breaks the rules or gets too heated. My father had always made a point of eating together. Everyone had to be there and only under exceptional circumstances would we be allowed to eat separately. I believe this brought the family closer together. The dinner table was the perfect place to find out what everyone had been up to that day, or to resolve arguments and for me personally, it was always the perfect time to report my brother's mean behaviour to the authorities of the house.

My father inculcated his values in us from a very early age. We were never to swear in the house or to anyone in the family. We would always take our shoes off at the front door and we always greeted each other whenever we entered the house with a *'Jai Shree Krishna'* (hail lord Krishna), a typical north Indian Gujarati greeting. But above all, I remember that no body was allowed to be selfish, or self-centred, we were not meant to allow our emotions to run wild. My father always created and maintained a sombre atmosphere in the house, at least when he was in it. I can't remember a time when we got over excited, or laughed uncontrollably or became so angry at each other that we fought. I'm not sure how father maintained such a balanced household, he never even once, stopped us from laughing or getting excited or for that matter he never stopped arguments either. It was simply the unspoken understanding we all had, when dad was in the house everyone was controlled.

The same could have been said of the atmosphere around my grandfather, but with him it was blind fear that made everyone check themselves. But my father was gentle, polite and understanding, it wasn't fear that made us check ourselves, it was more of the example he would set us, including the example he would set to my sometimes over the top, emotionally charged mother. This was another example of my father's leadership, he wouldn't set the rules and then enforce it through fear or strength; instead he led by example and left it to us to make our decision whether to follow him or not. I learnt at a very early age that one should lead through example. People respected those that did as they preached rather than the vast majority of so called leaders who practiced the all too easy art of *'do as I say, not as I do'*.

My father also had some weaker tendencies. He could never say "no" to anyone. I remember his conversations on the phone with colleagues where he would commit to things that he knew farewell he didn't want to take on. I often felt that people saw this as a weakness and delegated allsorts of jobs to him, which they didn't want. My mum would often complain and argue whenever dad was rushed off his feet doing other peoples jobs. She would often say "if you can't say no, I'll say it for you".

Of course she never did. She accepted his weaknesses as well as his strengths. Another tendency my father suffered from was tangentiality, the act of digressing from a topic under discussion. He would start talking about one point, stray from it and ramble on about another, which he thought, was connected but no body else thought so. He would often describe events and conversations to the most excruciating detail, often boring the listener to the point where no body cared what the point of the conversation was. These tendencies and his blatant lack of focus on any one topic at a time was often his biggest weakness and undermined his strengths.

Having a spongy mind helps. I absorbed my fathers' strengths and his weaknesses. I learnt that people inherently look for flaws in others. People feel insecure and inadequate when in front of someone who comes across as faultless or more superior to themselves. A good leader or manager needs to understand that people will drive relentlessly to find faults in them and if they fail to find anything significant, they'll make something up. People do this almost subconsciously. They are often not aware that they are doing it. The reason for this relentless pursuit of faults in others who are in superior positions is so that we can see them as simply ordinary, which make us feel adequate and more secure in ourselves. We narrow the gulf between them and us. We accept our own weaknesses and label them as *'normal'*. This way, we manage to feel superficially secure by finding reasons to lower the person onto the level we feel we are on. I learnt during my later days as a teenager that if you wanted to survive as a respected member among a tight circle of friends, you had to show some flaws in your personality. You have to give some food for the *piranhas* that will satisfy their hunger to find flaws in you but at the same time not undermine your leadership. I have used this tactic in managing all group dynamics ever since my teenage days. I used to let my friends know that I wasn't good at everything. I would openly claim that I had a poor dress sense or that I didn't know much about music. I fed the group with these flaws because they were true and as a sign of imperfection, consciously aware that they prided themselves on dressing and music. This 'tit bit' of information allowed them to accept my strengths because it satisfied their hunger to find my flaws. It gave them one area in which they could feel comfortable in knowing more than I did. This allowed me to influence them in all other areas, my strengths were acknowledged without breeding insecurity in anyone. It has taken years for me to develop this skill and I am yet to perfect it.

I learnt this as a direct consequence of observing my father and how people behaved around him. I enjoyed people watching. I always have. I used to notice how his strengths were used by others but also undermined when it suited them because they had noticed his weaknesses without him having done so. Consequently he didn't know how to deal with certain types of people or manage conflict that occurred outside the family. The difference, I realised in latter life, was that in the home, his family had valued his strengths more than his weaknesses. I found out that this was not so outside the home. People only saw his strengths as a commodity that they could use as and when they wanted to. This meant that others were in charge, not my father. This used to upset me immensely. I even tried to explain my observations to my father. He would acknowledge them but then fail to resolve the situation because of his passivity and his habit of always seeing the good in people. It was through this that I learnt, *'too much of anything is bad for you'*. In my fathers case he was too kind, he saw the good in everyone and consequently, people took advantage of him.

Some of the experiences I have described profoundly influenced me. My parents began forging my character well before I was even born, hoping that I would have the values to deal with the challenges life would throw my way. My father especially had a terrible upbringing. So did all of my father's siblings, relatively speaking. They were determined as every parent in every generation is that their children should not have to face the hardships of life, which they had to suffer. Life however, always has other plans.

16th November 1995 – my 15th birthday

I can't remember what I did on my 15th birthday. In actual fact, birthdays were never celebrated in my family much. They have never been regarded as a significant event. In the morning mum and dad would cheerfully greet me as I woke up with a "happy birthday", followed by a hug and blessings. I remember that until my 10th birthday, I was encouraged to say the *'Gayatri Mantra'* in front of our homemade shrine. But by my 15th birthday I was a full blown rebellious teenager and rules and traditions meant as little as Arsenal winning the Worthington Cup.

Even though I didn't care much for prayers and rituals, I was still an inquisitive teenager. I always wondered about God, the universe & everything. *"What did it all mean"*, I asked myself.

By thirteen I had realised that much of the life's deep questions lead to infinite regresses or circularity. Of course at that age I had no idea what that meant, but nevertheless pursued all matters to their eventual ends. I remember asking the question *"if God made everything, what made God?"* People would just blow off the question and say that God was always there, he is infinite. What I couldn't get my head round was that everything seemed to have a beginning and an eventual end, everything except God that is, *"why? How is God any different to any other thing in the universe?"* I mused.

I remember once asking the question to my science teacher, to which he replied, "There is no God".

That was the first person in my life that had out rightly told me there was no God. I liked him immediately, not because I agreed with him, but because he gave me a clear answer.

The next day I asked him "Sir, if there is no God and you say that the universe is infinite, what is the universe in?" Before he answered, I went on "if it's more space, then what is that more space inside?"

I can't remember what he said, but I am sure it wasn't of any great value. The outcome of that conversation was that he became interested in me. I was a troubled child by this age, and my school work had suffered. Mr Clutton took me under his wing for the next few years helped me to stay away from trouble and advising me on my future career. We had many fantastic conversations thereafter.

It was from this experience that I realised the importance of distinguishing oneself in front of any person of significant authority. Mr Clutton helped me immensely through some difficult times, not because he thought I was bright, but because I stood out from others. People in authority have a natural tendency to help those who they can relate to or can sympathise with and can benefit from their influence. It gives their influence meaning by making it worth while. Mr Clutton's classes were renowned across the school for their undisciplined nature and every loud mouth teenager got their way in his class. His influence was negligible at the best of times, so when he connected with me and saw that I was ready to listen and take him seriously, his position as a teacher of science became meaningful. He wasn't getting paid any extra to sit with me after school and play chess, while we discussed the existence of God and how I could stay focused on my studies. I noticed that when a person in any authority has meaning to their work, they seldom care for the monetary benefits that they might gain. It's a wonderful aspect of all human beings. Give them meaning to their work and everything else will fall away into the background.

The mid 1990's were a time when every able teenager wanted to become an optometrist, pharmacist, dentist, software programmer or an accountant. At least that was the case in my school. Soar Valley College was a well-spaced out school with open green fields surrounding every side. It was an urban school with a 50% ethnic Indian student population. It was the 3rd highest achieving school in Leicester closely following two private schools in the city. It certainly didn't feel like a successful school. Most students took their studies seriously enough never to miss classes but the average student, of which I was one, didn't seem to care much for high academic achievement. We all seemed to think that things would just happen, we would just fall into a career, it was just accepted that we would all go onto college and then university to get a degree, get a well paid professional job, get married, have children, watch them grow old and eventually call it a day with this life. Looking back on those days I realise that most of my fellow students were from working class backgrounds, as I was. We all lived in a small world where everyone lived in similar houses, had a similar family structure, a similar cultural background *(in our case it was predominately Hindu)*, everyone had similar aspirations and held identical values. Since moving back to Leicester in 2006, at the age of 25, I had begun to bump into some of these people who used to be in my class, or study groups, or we used to play football together. Nearly everyone that I have met who used to attend Soar Valley College is living the life that I have just highlighted. Nearly everyone has some degree or another, either in some business related field or in the area of science and engineering. Most, if not all of them, have jobs. The ones that did exceptionally well at university and attended decent ones have landed jobs that have propelled them from working class background to middle class over night. With this extra income, they have become more self assured, better travelled, live in middle class areas, have got married and some have kids who go to private Montessori schools. Their children will grow up as the offspring to Britain's new successful Middle class – the driving force behind any economy. *The rules of the game are changing because the key players have changed!*

Even though nearly everyone that I have met, since my secondary school days have excelled materially, I found to my surprise that their thinking and view of the world hadn't changed at all. So many of my student friends are now accountants, solicitors, optometrists, IT technicians or programmers and all of them started working immediately after graduating. They still all held the same values of buying a house, getting married, having children, getting a promotion at work and retiring comfortably in old age. Along the way most of them want to travel and see as much of the world as possible – by *the world* they mean family resorts and other tourist spots. It seemed to me that their thinking hadn't changed significantly from when we were fifteen. Most of my friends from Soar Valley have a typical 21st century life style. Wake up at 6am, get to work by 8am, have lunch in the afternoon *(if they're lucky)*, leave the office by 5 or 6, have dinner with the wife, go out for a few drinks down the local, and come home to sleep. This type of lifestyle had always frightened me. I think it was to escape this lifestyle that I wanted to join the Air Force – I wanted to travel *(not to resorts but to backpack and see the world for what it really was)*; I wanted to be independent; I never wanted a *nine to five*; I didn't really want any kids; I didn't want a mortgage as soon as possible; I didn't want to start earning as much as I could as soon as I could! My mind was always pre-occupied with questions of God – *what is it? Does it exist? If so where and how? What is reality? What is the meaning of life? Why am I here? Why is our society rich and most of Africa so poor? Why do people behave the way they do? Why do I behave the way I do? Why am I not motivated by money? What is war? What does it mean to be happy?* I can go on and on listing moral and metaphysical questions, but I won't. As a rebellious fifteen year old I was deeply engrossed in questions that no one else seemed to be asking and if they were, they weren't apparent. I vividly remember several puzzling questions that consumed me at that age.

After I had switched the lights to my bedroom off, to fall asleep, I remember always trying to *catch* myself falling asleep. It was always the same: one moment I was thinking in the dark, and the next I was waking up in the morning sunshine having slept the entire night. Yet I knew that every night there must have come a time when I stopped thinking and settled down to sleep. It was baffling that I could not experience that, and never remembered it. I also wondered about time. I would lie awake in my bed, thinking something along the following lines. I know there was a day before yesterday, and a day before that, and a day before that, and so on, as far back as I can remember. But there must have been a day before the last day in my conscious memory. I was born on 16th November 1980. There must have been a day before this day too. Before everyday there must have been a day before. So it must be possible to back like that forever and ever – yet is it? The idea of going back forever was something that I couldn't get hold of; infinity was not graspable to my mind. So perhaps I thought there must have been a beginning to the universe. There must have been a point which was the first day. But if this is true, what was before the first day? Logically, I would say *'nothing'* was before the first day. But if there was nothing, how could anything have got started? Where could it all have come from? Time couldn't have just appeared out of nothing! Nothing was exactly that – nothing, not anything. So the idea of a beginning seemed impossible for me to grasp too. This puzzled me greatly. *A time that was forever was not graspable and a time that had a beginning was equally not understood.*

At the age of fifteen, there only seemed two possibilities to this problem. Either there was a beginning or there wasn't. They can't be both impossible. So I would attempt to concentrate on one and when it had exhausted itself, I would switch to the other, trying to work out where I had gone wrong; but I never discovered it. I became enslaved by the problem, and started to think about it during the day as well as at night. There were adults who I thought at first might be able to help, but I knew from my younger experiences that most adults were incapable of satisfying my questions beyond doubt. Nevertheless, I thought I would try. Either they admitted they could not solve it, and then went on to talk about other things, as if this particular question were not interesting enough even to discuss, or they actively dismissed it with a puff of arrogance. I couldn't understand their mentality. If they were unable as I was to answer the question of time and its beginning *(if there ever was one)*, how could they feel superior to it? Why weren't they disconcerted, and why didn't they even find it interesting? After several perplexing rebuffs I stopped talking about it with anyone and just quietly continued my thinking. My thinking led me to more questions and very few answers. As I thought about it more and more, I began to realise that if it is necessary for infinite time to have elapsed before the present moment were reached, it would be impossible for us to ever reach the end. Another was that for something to exist, it must have some sort of identity and that meant there must be something it wasn't, and that meant it must have limits, *so time couldn't be both endless or be beginning-less.* I became convinced that beginning-less time and endless time were both impossibilities. I had experienced the same bafflement with regards to space and the universe with Mr. Clutton.

After a lot of puzzling about time and space, I began to think that perhaps the mistake I was making was to suppose that *what I could think must exist*. Perhaps there was a difference between what I could think and what could actually be possible. It seemed to me that I could go on and on asking what next, what next and what next after that, forever and ever. But still it seemed to me self-evident that this was only something I could think but could not actually be. For example, I realised that maybe I could think *'infinity'* but infinity could never exist. Thinking deeper, I began to doubt myself again. Was I falling back into the mistake I was trying to climb out of? In any case, whatever the truth about this is – it wouldn't help me solve my real problem, because it didn't tell me what the truth was about; whether time did or didn't have a beginning.

Vikas goes into the Abyss

On the 18th of November 1995, two days after my fifteenth birthday, Vikas was in Leicester for the weekend. It was a Sunday. He had come back from Wiltshire where he was on a placement year with the MoD testing facility at Boscombe Down. He had come to see Neeta Fai. In the Indian family system the term 'Fai' is given to address dad's sisters. Neeta Fai lived in Tanzania, near Lake Victoria. She was deeply religious. She hadn't any children and devoted all of her time to the local Swaminarayan temple, teaching children Hinduism *(from a Swaminarayan perspective)*. Neeta Fai to this day stands out from all the people I have ever known. I often wondered why? She wasn't the brightest, richest or the most charismatic, yet she showed me something that no one up to that point had ever had. She had shown me *total dedication*. She was dedicated to her faith, her beliefs and her lifestyle. Everything else for her was irrelevant to the point where she would often sit with people who had come to see her and make them listen to her read the Swaminarayan scripture. People in those days politely listened, nodding every now and then to show that they were listening; of course they weren't. Neeta Fai often frightened her siblings and people became reluctant to spend anytime with her because she was indifferent to their presence. She would continue with her religious meditations regardless of who was there. Everyone else was repulsed by this. I loved her for it! Her commitment to one cause was admirable. Up to that point in my life everyone I had come to know were shallow, uncommitted, driven by sensual pleasures and very rarely thought beyond the *here and now*.

I felt refreshed, almost proud that here was someone in my family who I could spend the entire day talking about God, the universe and everything! And I did spend every hour after school with her. Neeta Fai has the most beautiful eyes I've ever seen. Everyone used to call her *(and I still do)* "Cheetah Fai" as her eyes were similar to that of the great cat. With her large *'cheetah-like' beautiful eyes* beaming down at me we would begin a discussion on the metaphysical. Of course she was trying to persuade me that God did exist and furthermore that the Swaminarayan order was the best route to achieve God realisation. I was deeply sceptical on both counts. I still am at least on the latter. She still hasn't stopped trying to persuade me in all these years, but she has realised that I am on my own path and journey. Her energy and dedication to her spiritual quest was formidable. Out of everyone in my family she was the most knowledgeable and philosophically clued up. Her arguments were often challenging and stimulated my young eager mind. I made it my mission to find holes in her understanding of God. I found many, but none of my arguments seemed to impact her dedication. I admired her even more for this. Back then she was on course to become a Hindu saint, now she's almost there! My family will never quite grasp her achievements, for they measure all things in life materially, and in these terms Neeta Fai is probably the biggest *under-achiever*. However, for those who genuinely bothered to spend time with her, mainly me, I saw irresistible strength and understanding. Neeta Fai had the character that I wanted to develop but not the intellectual reasoning I expected, and her often blind belief in things was shocking, yet understandable. For her the world consisted of one paradigm, she saw everything from a monocentric lens, through the eyes of a Swaminarayan.

Along with Neeta Fai, there was Kiran Fai, her younger sister and the youngest out of all of dad's siblings. Kiran Fai back in 1995 couldn't have been any more different to her sister. Kiran Fai was materialistic, *happy-go-lucky* kind of person, married with a gorgeous daughter and lived in Luton. Kiran Fai was a good looking aunt. She knew it too. When she was younger, in her teens, she was a nightmare to handle. She was part of a severely dysfunctional family, living at that time with Arvind uncle in London and *"the problem with Kiran"*, my grandfather would say, *"Is that she is naïve and men like her looks. Naivety with good looks is a dangerous mix"*.

Between the ages of five and about eleven she had shown me so much love and attention. For all the problems she might have given to my grandfather and Arvind uncle, to me she was the *'bestest'* aunt anyone could have. She bought me Easter eggs; she bought me presents on my birthday, Diwali and Christmas, what else could an adolescent boy want? I loved her. And I still do. She had a great influence in my early childhood. Her affection towards me was truly genuine. To this day, I am close to Kiran Fai who has become a life-hardened woman with two daughters and is a professional councillor.

Both of dad's younger sisters had a profound influence on me, Kiran Fai when I was very young. It was her love towards me and her bubbly character that had influenced me. Neeta Fai was much later, in my early teens, mainly through her total dedication to one cause. Influences from both of them were genuine, strong and life evolving. With Vikas, Kiran Fai and Neeta Fai all in Leicester *(along with my Grandfather, Mum and Dad)* on that quite insignificant November Sunday, all the most influential people in my life were present.

In 1992, Vikas went off to University and since then I had found an independence that I cherished. So whenever, he was back, I felt down, lacklustre and almost disappointed. I remember dad asking me on that day, *why it was that I was mulling around the house, wasting my time looking as if something sad had happened*. I remember replying "because he's back! And when he's back, he gets all the attention, he's the centre of this family and everyone compares me to him and I hate it", I said, feeling sorry for myself.

By fifteen my grades were quickly dropping below the expected target set by my brother who was studying Aerospace Engineering. He was smart, charming and sociable. People identified me as Vikas's little brother. I hated the tag and I longed to be parted from it. I wanted my own identity.

In hindsight, I think I felt the way I did because of a cocktail of negative emotions, starting with my poor attention span in school, resulting in less than expected, but higher than average grades. This was closely followed by the constant comparison between Vikas and me, in which I was doomed to come second every time. Thirdly, it was my challenging nature. I knew I was different; I knew I perceived a reality that others did not appreciate, yet I could appreciate theirs, and this caused huge levels of inner frustrations which were vented out on the football field every Sunday. I had received seven red cards that season. This cocktail of part jealousy, part helplessness and part frustration at the world before me, had resulted in a self destructive attitude. I was a contradiction of emotions and characteristics. I was aggressive, I could win a fight with most, and yet I was naturally sensitive to people's emotions, I could understand them. I was fairly intelligent and a quick learner, yet I suffered in school *(my grades were only just above average)*. I was a determined young man and yet couldn't resist skipping the afternoon French lessons for a game of football. I was inquisitive about all matters political and philosophical. I read books like the Bhagavad-Gita and Lord of the Rings by JR Tolkien, while simultaneously not bothering to read my history texts, French books or any English literature which was compulsory reading. I spent long hours into the lonely night thinking about metaphysics and the problems I saw with reality and yet I often walked into examinations totally unprepared. I would genuinely feel disturbed when I saw pictures of famine on the news which triggered long mental investigations into morality, yet I cared little for the people immediately around me. The inner calmness, sensitivity, care and honesty were reflected outwardly as anger, insensitivity, carelessness and dishonesty. The contradiction that I carried and didn't even realise was about to grow exponentially.

I fell asleep on that insignificant cold Sunday night not knowing that I had reached my first major crossroads of life. The contradictions were about to rocket.

At roughly 3.30am, in the middle of the night I heard my father swear for the first, and last time. I woke up in a fright and heard the word *"bastard"* shouted twice. My first impulse was to jump out of bed and make my way downstairs as fast as I could. The word 'bastard' had translated in my mind as violence but violence with whom? Vikas had left earlier that evening to go back to Wiltshire, there was no one else. Then suddenly I felt a chill down my spine, was it violence towards my mum? I ran downstairs, missing steps out along the way. As I turned to go in the kitchen, I saw a police officer leaning against the kitchen worktop. Another officer stood near a man on the floor. My mum was crying sitting on one of the dining room chairs with her hands comforting the other on her lap. As I looked for a second time, I realised that the man on the floor was my father. He was broken. Tears ran down his proud cheeks. His eyes were red with pain, pain that was too strong to comprehend. I looked at the officer leaning against the worktop and asked him what had happened. I can't remember his face, but I remember his words. He said as plainly as possible "your brother has had a car accident and we need your parents to come and identify a body".

The words didn't register in my mind. I was still dealing with the shock of seeing my father in such pain and despair. I went over and helped him to a chair. The police left soon after leaving behind an address where we were meant to go to identify the body.

Despair. There is nothing more real. When all hope is gone from a human being, all that is left is death.

Two
धर्म
"Not all who wander are lost"

All that is gold does not glitter,
Not all those who wander are lost;
The old that is strong does not wither,
Deep roots are not reached by the frost.
From the ashes a fire shall be woken,
A light from the shadows shall spring;
Renewed shall be the blade that was broken,
The crownless again shall be king.
— Lord of the Rings

THIS poem in the Lord of the Rings by JRR Tolkien helped me through those early days following the death of my brother. The poem became a symbolic icon in my mind of what life is all about; it gave me strength, wisdom and even a little companionship in dark lonely nights and bitter cold mornings. It is still my favourite poem to this day and it never fails to re-ignite the feelings of courage. During those early days after the death of my brother the entire family gathered in Leicester at my grandfather's house. People were deeply shocked and saddened. My mother during the first couple of days was hysteric, the only time she would stop crying was when she was sleeping. My father's strength seemed to abandon him. He fell inwards; the flame in his heart had gone out. The world was cold; it had lost its charm, its warmth. The good in the world that my father had always seen and his notion that everything occurred for a reason seemed like a foolish illusion. My father had lost his faith; faith in himself and faith in God. I don't think that he has ever fully recovered from Vikas's death. My father, the chief legislator of the house had just lost his entire army and police force in a single night, there was chaos in his kingdom; I, the citizen was about to go out of control and without an army to protect us, the future looked bleak.

To this very moment, as I type these words, I can clearly remember the coffin in which my brother lay in that mortuary. They had put a wooden box around his chest; his face was clean and looked to be sleeping a sleepless night. His chin had been stitched up and blood swelled around the deep cut. There were grazes on his right cheek but apart from that he seemed fine. I remember thinking as I first laid eyes on him, *'is he really dead?'*

This scene triggered a cataclysmic reaction in the depths of my mind. Death became a reality for me. I had experienced in full, the exact opposite of life – death! My rational mind went into a hyper-vivid and preternaturally powerful state. It wasn't fear or anxiety that I felt. It was a realisation. *I was living death.* It hit me that no matter what I did, death, for me and for everyone else was unavoidable. It was going to happen. Nothing that I could do, now, or at any other time would make the slightest difference to this reality. Not only would being brave, confident, ambitious or any other pride filled action not going to make any difference but I could easily be a "quibbering" coward, a liar, or immoral for the rest of my life and still it would make no difference. No matter what I did it was potentially insignificant. Death was coming for us all; it was just a matter of when and how.

The experience of being soaked in this realisation for four years changed my life and there was no going back. It raised several questions in my mind. The first was about meaning. *If death is going to happen, what does it matter what I do in life.* Everything I do is insignificant to death. And eventually everyone will die and everything will end, it will perish if not in my lifetime in some other future in which I will not exist. I initially began to think that life might mean nothing at all, at least in the long distant future. Most people I believe when they come across this question for the meaning of life assume that there must be one. I on the other hand made no such assumption. My mind would not allow it. It seemed like a very real, yet scary proposition that life might mean nothing at all for any of us. For a fifteen year old surrounded by despair and sadness, a certain type of contempt began to grow in my heart. It was contempt for life. Its mocking nature, it's delusion of pleasure, belonging and love were all just untrue, in fact I felt that I had been betrayed. *Why hadn't anyone around me mentioned this? Did they not know that death was coming and that it would come to all of us? If not, then why not?* These people were elders in the community, in life these people were meant to set me an example. Yet they were ignorant, absorbed in self pity and delusions. Within a couple of days after Vikas's death, my contempt for life spilt over on everyone dearest to me.

To anyone in this frame of mind nearly all human activities seem vain. In the eye of forever, a human lifespan is only a slight flicker. What can anything I do, mean or matter to me when I have passed into total *nothingness* for the rest of time? What can it matter to anyone else, either, when they too are eternally nothing? The void was the final destination for all of us, all value and all significance attributed to human activities was merely a great pretend. It was a game we humans enjoyed playing, making ourselves believe that we were important and that our lives meant something. It was like when little children play dress up – it was all an imagination on a grand scale.

Watching everyone around me soon after Vikas's death, I noticed that apart from my mother & father who were too devastated to do or think anything, everyone else busied themselves preparing for the funeral, cooking for the many hundreds of mourners that arrived in the course of the first week and engaged in petite banter. It is, it was, I believe, a willing pretence. It occurred to me at that time, that people could not bring themselves to face eternal nothingness, so they busy themselves with their little lives and all their small grandiose pursuits, surrounded by institutions that we ourselves have created yet we pretend are important, and which help us to shut the dark and endless night that surrounds each of us. I distinctly remember on the day of the funeral thinking that I am biologically programmed to desire to live, so I do. I eat, I drink, I sleep, I work, I went to school and try and ward off danger and so on and on. But I concluded sitting in that crematorium that it means that everything I will do and anyone else does is a pathetic little piece of self-delusion.

This conclusion was my second epiphanal *re-forging* experience. This conclusion was going to lead me deep into the realm of rebellion, self destruction, and metaphysical quest, into the realms of delusion and a world of make believe.

Falling through the Rabbit Hole

"Everything I did, will do and everything that anyone else will do is self-delusion".

This was the doorway to the rabbit hole. I had opened it and flung myself into it – all totally unconsciously. I didn't know this then, but the rabbit hole; just as in Alice in Wonderland was going to be an adventure, long, deep and lonely with a tinge of darkness. Like Alice, I too was going to experience things that only occurred in the realm of fantasy, in the world of make believe and hyped up Hollywood films. I would meet characters in my journey that would become my companions, my supporters and those that opposed my development and some that even opposed my existence. These came and went. Each one left his or her imprint in my conscious and subconscious psyche. Other characters merely existed from the subconscious; they were ghosts in the physical world and my guardian angels in the metaphysical. The rabbit hole is something I believe most of us experience at some stage of our lives – we may just never call it that or be aware of it. I eventually came out of the rabbit hole when I found the meaning to my life. Just as suddenly as I had plunged into the depths of the hole, it was as suddenly that I ascended to bright and clear daylight after spending four years searching.

Rabbit Hole is a journey, a crazy, wonderful, frightening journey, one that flirts between reality and delusion, between morality and immorality and a journey that re-forges the mind. It is an intellectual journey rather than a physical one. One can be deep in the Rabbit Hole frightened out of his wits while he is making polite conversation smiling at a friend's reunion party. A man can be in the midst of everyday life: waking up everyday at 6am; get ready; wake the kids; get them ready for school; quickly make breakfast and run out of the door at quarter to nine; drop the kids off to school; dodge through the morning rush hour travelling down the same monotonous roads; get to the office; make a coffee; run into the morning start up meeting just in the nick of time, and so on and on for twenty years. Even man in this god forsaking situation could be in the midst of this radical journey through the rabbit hole.

It is important that I spend sometime making clear what the characteristics of this journey are. This rabbit hole is not bound by space and time. What could be split seconds in reality could equate to hours, days or even months in the hole. In the time taken to leave the office and arrive safely at home, someone in the rabbit hole could have travelled through and covered vast amounts of intellectual space. The rabbit hole is an infinite series of interconnected intellectual tunnels that take you through the depths of life and beyond. *That which lies beyond life cannot be spoken about for it would be contradictory to do so.* That which lies just beyond life is also just beyond the boundaries of our language and so to talk about it would be inaccurate at best, and outright misleading at worst. I have decided to keep my silence. Words however are not totally useless when discussing that which is beyond life. They can be a powerful map finder, a navigation system if you will, that can show us to the edge of time and space but not beyond. We may be able to discover much about the boundaries of life by reaching them and may also be able to accurately predict what the hereafter might be like. By understanding the boundaries of things we naturally understand the beginnings of what is on the other side.

These intellectual tunnels can be confusing; they can become an intellectual maze, one that I am sure, some people never escape. They can be perilous if we are not careful. These tunnels run underneath our very existence, they run to the foundations of our physical and mental lives and beyond. They are dark by their very nature and incredibly lonely. They are the underlying tunnels of your life; no one else can accompany you, at best others can act us guides from beyond the rabbit hole, but how effective would a guide be if he or she has never travelled your journey. Rather than guides, I believe, that people can act as datum points. It's like tying one end of a rope to a tree and the other end to our waist, just before we enter a maze, to make sure that we can find our way out the same way that we have come in.

In the Indian Hindu traditions, a student, before entering a philosophical enquiry must have a *'Guru'*[1], one that understands the rabbit hole, the intellectual journey and knows its potential perils. This way a student of Hindu philosophy can go through his or her personal intellectual journey knowing that one who knows potential pitfalls is easily at hand, the Guru acts as a GPS system rather than a guide. He can tell you about the pitfalls but the freedom to decide still lies with the student taking the journey.

Another aspect of the hole was that it travelled deep not just through my intellectual space but intellectual space on which I existed. This is a rather *wishy-washy* thing to grasp. In essence it means that the rabbit hole could potentially take me to places from which I could not only understand my life better but also other peoples around me. The deeper and further I travelled, the more I went into intellectual space. Space that my physical existence was not founded in. So in other words anyone in the rabbit hole exploring these tunnels could transcend the physical and grasp the metaphysical underlying it.

All great discoveries in the world of science, mathematics, engineering, medicine, in fact, in all walks of life, I believe are made while exploring these tunnels of intellectual space. The rabbit hole allows us to access the subtle reality underneath our cruder conscious reality of time & space.

The best way to conceptualise these tunnels is by comparing it to an underground rail network. Above these tunnels is a city. Millions of people are travelling from one end to the other, just think of London and how Londoners travel. The city is equivalent to our physical existence in time and space. There are many gateways to these tunnels beyond time & space, just like many underground stations in the city of London. Each one will take you to the tunnels beneath the city. However, each station is on a different geographical location, hence one would enter that part of the tunnel which runs directly underneath that

---

[1] The word Guru means, he who can take one out of darkness and into the light. It does not mean teacher, as most people believe.

particular part of the city. In the same way one can access these intellectual networks via rabbit holes that exist at the particular point in ones conscious life. Just as I cannot enter London's underground network in the city and instantly expect to be transported to the outskirts, one cannot enter through the rabbit hole and just *re-appear* where ever or whenever one chooses. There has to be a journey from the city to the outskirts and then at the appropriate station one can leave the tunnels and carry on with life outside. Something similar happens through the rabbit holes.

The problem with intellectual space and rabbit holes is that unlike underground train stations we cannot see them or experience them with our physical bodies. Our sight, touch, hearing, smell and taste exist in the physical reality of time & space hence; they are of no use to us in the intellectual tunnels of existence. Our basic senses become obsolete. At fifteen I had no idea about these things. I hadn't even a clue to the fact that I had embarked on a journey through intellectual space, one in which I would be alone, a journey which did not correspond to time & space as I knew it, a journey that would take me to the frightening depths of my psyche with catastrophic consequences in my physical life.

Having made up my mind sitting on a bench in that crematorium that life was meaningless and that in the end we were all heading for the eternal void, I spontaneously decided to go behind the scenes and watch the coffin burn through a tiny glass covered hole, watching the final physical remains of Vikas disintegrate. As the flames surrounded the coffin I stepped back and asked *"where is he now?"*

As we were leaving the crematorium I gazed at the hundreds of mourners who had gathered to pay their final respects to my brother and parents. *All these people would go on living their normal lives with everyday cheerfulness and I thought how could they just go on? And how could they suppose that any of what they're doing matters?* To me they all seemed like passengers on the Titanic; except these people in the back of their minds knew they were heading for a fatal collision with the iceberg. In a short time every one of them will be dead, either turned into ash in an urn or a corpse, rotting underground with worms crawling through their skin. That situation will be every bit real as their situation now except their death will last a lot longer. *Why didn't any of these people seem to mind? Why were these people not frightened out of their wits?* Then I thought about my grandfather. He must have been in his eighties when Vikas had died. He was almost face to face with death. I wondered what was going through his mind at the time. I was perplexed that all human beings knew what was coming eventually, yet they lived as if it didn't matter – or it was something that they were perfectly happy with. All these people around me instantly appeared different. I had known some of them all my life. My father, my mother, my cousins, my uncles and aunts, friends, friends of friends, and so on and on; all these people appeared like a bunch of lunatics chuckling away their lives dementedly while death crept ever closer.

I didn't know this then but my instant change in perception about life and people was due to a fall through the rabbit hole. While I sat still in the reality of time & space listening to the service in a quite crematorium, I was in fact travelling. I was travelling or should I say falling quickly down an intellectual tunnel. It was the result of this rapid movement in intellectual space that caused me instantly to perceive everything and everyone around me differently. I wasn't in the slightest bit emotional. I couldn't understand it then. *Why was everyone else in the midst of sadness while I was numb to the whole experience?*

I was later to discover Freud who would explain much to me. The rabbit hole gave me my first proper perception of life. Until that moment I hadn't even a clue about what life or living meant. It just was. Life was just plain life. It appeared to me that most of the people were as ignorant as I had been. Under the influence of these thoughts my values went through sea changes. Everything that was limited to this life and this world came to appear insignificant. Without realising it myself I no longer respected any of the elders that I knew. My father, my uncles, my mother, my aunts, my cousins, my friends and pretty much everyone else I had known were not worth respecting. *A lack of respect in authority breeds trouble.* It was a dangerous formula to be playing around with. But it was all totally out of my conscious awareness. I was feeling things that I couldn't verbalise. They were feelings that I had never had. I had no words for them and so couldn't make any sense of them. Yet, I instantly, as if a switch had been triggered in my brain, became rebellious. I was no longer inclined to follow rules just for the sake of respect or tradition. If people couldn't satisfy my questions then their rules were to be discarded, and replaced with mine, that to me at least, had some reasoning.

The problem was that I had flung myself into the rabbit hole rather stupidly, without a GPS system or any kind of datum point that would allow me to find my way out. Looking back, I realise that peculiar things can happen in our normal lives while we are in these tunnels. I remember vividly while I was in my maths lessons learning some formula, that's exactly what I remembered – only the formula, without any appreciation or realisation of what it meant; its significance remained beyond my reach. But when I came across the same formula in the tunnels, I was instantly able to grasp its significance, and a certain realisation occurred deep within my consciousness. I not only re-remembered the formula but I could physically see it in action in the world around me. The formula had meaning, it had a use, and furthermore, I realised how I could use it and where I could apply it where it hadn't been already applied. I could effectively cross-pollinate between subjects. I could apply mathematical formulae to some other theory in anthropology, or to philosophy, I could see a connection that often people had missed. This way, I began to understand the interconnectedness of the world. I could potentially understand history better by realising some mathematical or physics formulae. I could understand Shakespeare better by realising the significance of the syntax of a completely different language, like Spanish.

It occurred to me, much later in life that the prime difference between thinking or learning and travelling through the tunnels, was that when we learn or think, we merely postulate, we remember, we conceptualise without really grasping the *'soul'* of the topic, whereas, in the tunnels, whatever we come across, we instantly end up *realising it*. We end up grasping the 'soul' of the topic. And by grasping this illusive soul, we gain a deeper consciousness about the topic. This in turn allows us to physically see the theory in action in our everyday lives. The tunnels bring to life what once were only some random symbols or letters on a maths book that I was expected to remember. Poetry began to physically come alive with emotion, character and personality when I came across them in the tunnels. Anything experienced in the rabbit hole was a realisation. A realisation, to me at least, meant several things. A realisation gives us a far deeper understanding of experience. It satisfies our thirst for the question "why", and allows us to physically see and be one with the moment.

The rabbit hole leads us to un-chartered lands. Lands, which I later realised had already been extensively explored and mapped out by the great thinkers of the ages, thinkers such as Einstein, Krishnamurti, Schopenhauer, Wittgenstein, and Kant, the writers of the Upanishads, Aristotle, Nietzsche and many others. But at eighteen, I discovered one of the greatest of them all. I found Plato.

Plato, to me at least, spoke directly. He was there with me, in that room when I first began to read *The Republic*. The most famous passage in Philosophy, for me at least, was Plato's metaphor of the cave. In it, he points out that what we perceive in our everyday lives as independently existing objects are in fact, no such thing; they are merely passing shadows. It is due to our human limitations that we can't but help mistake shadows for real objects. This means that everything we see, hear, taste, feel, think about, our language and so on and on, in other words, everything that is in the world of phenomena, is shadow, which we mistakenly take to be reality. Behind the shadows is a greater reality. It is this reality that casts the shadows. What we seem to directly experience are illusions, in Hinduism, it is called *Maya*. Behind this Maya is a more subtle reality. Plato called it the world of forms. Ironically, it was Plato, a Greek philosopher and mathematician who helped me discover a form of thinking that was right under my nose. Through Plato, *I discovered the depths of Hinduism.*

Three

धर्म

Discovery of the Self

THE search for meaning, I believe, leads eventually to the discovery of the *Self*. My journey of discovery was not a lonely one. In fact, I was accompanied through it by friends that I have never forgotten and ones that I miss everyday. These friends had no idea of the journey I was going through, nevertheless, their unknowing support was a life line, a rope if you will, to hold onto, in the dark rabbit hole. My friends all lived in, and around my neighbourhood, the best ones always do. I don't think I've ever managed to have friends like the ones I had when I was fifteen.

I grew up in Leicester, in an area called Belgrave. It was a grey jungle, filled with rows upon rows of terraced houses, full of families on benefits or on minimum wage. Mine was no different. But at the time, I didn't feel poor or working class, in fact at fifteen Belgrave was most of my world. I had no comparison to make, I had no upper-class friends, and I'd never been in a posh area. To me everyone lived in similar houses to mine, part from an extra room here or there. Real wealth was something that was confined to the television screen or in magazines. *Contentment it seems can also arise out of ignorance which saps the mind of its power to compare, and without comparison how can there be discontent?*

Jinesh Chandarana, a boy my age was my first proper friend in Leicester. I had met him in school. We were only six years old. Months after meeting him, I happened to move into the house directly opposite. I remember looking out of the old tattered blue wooden windows in the spring of '87, when Jinesh stuck his head out of the window and shouted across the street at the top of his voice without a care for the world. I still remember that voice. I was so pleased to hear it. Even though I was only six, I felt as if a huge weight had been lifted, my only real friend, one who I felt comfortable around and as luck would have it, one that I was going to grow up with. Often, in quite mornings, over a cup of hot spicy Indian chai, I have wondered how and why Jinesh and I were such close friends.

It has been a difficult question to answer, especially because I see so little of him now. Friends became increasingly important during adolescent years, especially when ones domestic life is under significant strain. In hindsight, I realise it was because I was searching for belonging and love, something that had dried up in my home. My parents had little, to no emotional energy to give. The loss of Vikas had caused an emotional drought in the depths of their soul and had dried up their emotional reserves. So, just like any person living in the desert whose water well had dried up, I began to look for another well from which I could quench my emotional thirst. And after a long time searching two things happened in sync.

First, just as any man wondering the desert, I began to hallucinate, I saw mirages. My mirage came in the form of a semi-delusional character, one that was part real and part delusion. This may sound strange. In fact it may even come across as little mad. To this I would ask, *what is madness?* The term mad is a relative one. I believe we are all a little mad, every one of us, to varying degrees. People who pray, and speak to God are mad, are they not? Who are they speaking to? Do they have any proof that it is even remotely acceptable that God exists, and furthermore that he can hear you? I ask these questions not to theologians or philosophers, but to people who do not live in the *ivory tower* that is the academic world. *The answer is no*. Yet they speak to this delusionary character that they have created in their minds with help from others who believe in a similar delusion. They speak, they even listen and then act accordingly, isn't this a form of accepted madness? Isn't this synonymous with those that believe UFO's can communicate with them or like psychopaths who believe that a devil sitting on their shoulder told them to burn the house with his victims still inside? The only difference that I can see is that one is morally uplifting *(most of the time)*, the other morally neutral and the final one morally degrading, but nevertheless, *all mad*.

I will come to my period of madness in just a little while. But before that I want to explain how I found the free flowing stream of emotional belonging and love outside my family home. It came in the form of friends, as it is with so many teenagers. *Why is this? Why do so many young people find belonging and love outside the family, at least in the west, what is happening within that leads them outwards?* Surely not everyone has parents that loose a child which they fail to overcome, resulting in a drought of love and understanding. I believe the answer is simple at its root and yet almost impossible to create a solution for.

Teenagers, and increasingly younger ages now a days are searching for love and belonging outside the home because they do not receive emotional energy and structure which they need from their parents. The root cause is the values that are being transmitted across society. The aggregate sum of values a society holds is called its *culture*. The root cause of this emotional drought which affects almost nine out of ten teenagers is a cultural one. It is a problem of values. It has nothing, or at best little to do with government. I do not really want to use the word culture, for it carries too much emotional baggage and preconceptions. Instead, I'll use the word values. But it is important that you understand what it is that I am eventually pointing the finger at.

So let me begin by pointing out some of the values which I believe encourage the exploration of emotional belonging and love outside the home. Everything that I write is based on my experiences and of the experiences of the hundreds of young people who I have coached in emotional intelligence.

I guess the first question we should ask is, what, if anything is wrong with teenagers searching for love and belonging outside the home? Without turning this into some academic essay, which a student of sociology or psychology would typically write, let me just say that it is a matter of *pragmatism*. Let me explain. The problem with finding love and belonging outside the family home is more difficult in the first place and infinitely harder to sustain over a lifetime, although not impossible. Family is our first source of values, it is the first institution that cared for us and raised us and it did so out of wanting to, and not having to. Furthermore, family will always be family, if not in terms of emotional attachment, at least in the sense of genetics. It is a lot easier to find sustainable emotions of love and belonging from family than it is from others.

Every human has needs. These needs are as follows. First, there is the need for food, water, shelter and other basic survival tools. Next comes, safety. Every human who has secured the basic necessities, needs the emotional energy which can only come from the feeling of safety. Once this is achieved every human has a need to feel belonging and love. This, if you haven't already noticed is nothing new, Maslow mentioned all of this in his hierarchy of needs. And only after one has achieved a sense of belonging and love, does one aspire for what Maslow called *esteem needs*. Esteem needs translate into ambition, motivation, vision, desire for academic success and other uplifting emotions. It is a question of focus. I found that most children who are academic successes and go onto fulfil a successful career are often those that have come from stable, two-parent families, where their need to belong was satisfied. These kids had no need to look outwards and hence could focus on esteem needs from the beginning. These kids have a distinct advantage. They already have a foundation upon which to build their ambitions. Without a strong sense of belonging and love, one cannot focus in on academics, creating ambition, focus and drive. These characteristics form, once we belong to someone, or to some group. We must feel accepted for who we are before we can set off on the road to success. This is why most people say that their happiest moments were when they got married, or when their first child was born, when they moved into their first home and so on and on. These are all events that are to do with belonging.

Emotional Thirst

Until the death of Vikas, I had felt secure. I had felt safe and most importantly loved. I belonged to someone. I belonged to my family. All that had now changed. I remember distinctly feeling as if I didn't belong in my house, the atmosphere was foul and often I had thought it was because of my existence. This is why I went from an excellent student to a poor one, from a calm, playful child to an overtly aggressive, competitive young man and from a secure personality to an insecure one, who would overcompensate in front of others.

I later came to realise that my new found confidence with the ladies, soon after Vikas's death, was due to my inner subconscious desire to find someone to belong to. Until Vikas's death, girls meant little to me. I had no interest in sweet talking them, taking them on dates or any other such trivial foreplay. I was too busy with sports, martial arts, laughing and joking with friends, studying and of course T*hinking*. The loss of belonging enhanced my other attributes to a hyper-sensitive state. I was always friendly and confident, this turned into arrogance and outright attention seeking. From being adventurous, I became dangerously daring. It was as if my libido was over-compensating for my lack of emotional energy and deep insecurity. Looking back now, I think its classic text book behaviour, yet I have always felt its paradoxical nature.

Essentially, I believe, those teenagers that bully others, who are extremely aggressive, rude and inconsiderate are often the most emotionally deprived. Their apparent misbehaviour is often due to a deeper insecurity caused by an unsatisfied thirst for love and belonging. I believe parents often get confused between the fact of belonging and its associated feeling. These are two different aspects. A child can belong to a family without ever realising or connecting with that feeling. Parents may love their child, but it is an all together different thing to their child *feeling that love.* It is a matter of transference, at least that's what I call it. Every parent should know, indeed every manager should know, that when a person does not feel belonging and love, their libidinal forces can often get the better of them. Furthermore, they will seek this feeling else where, away from the family or firm.

I was no different. My libidinal forces were released in an uncontrolled manner. Everyone around me was affected by it. Yet, to this day, it baffles me that no one had sat me down after my brother had passed away to tease out my emotions, thereby allowing them safe passage to dissipate. Instead, unintentionally, I joined a long line of other disgruntled members of society, mainly from the black, Afro-Caribbean community. These youths became my sanctuary. They were my well of emotional energy. I had found a new family, at least for the time being. I was fifteen, and at that age, we are all just a bag of channelled or un-channelled emotional energy. I was most definitely un-channelled.

Looking back, I can vividly remember the first time my libidinal forces of aggression kicked in. The best way to describe it is to compare it to when we slide a car into its most suitable gear, on a race track, rev the engine and feel the car kick into a life that we had no idea it could have. I guess to appreciate what I'm saying you'd have to have taken a normal 1.4 litre Peugeot 206, on a circuit to a speed of 135mph. I hope my father never gets this far into the book and finds out what his son was doing to his car!

The episode I am referring to is pivotal and exemplary of how emotions can vent themselves. It must have been around 8.20am before we left Nimesh's house to go school, on a crisp frosty winter morning, with clear sunshine. Nimesh was Jinesh's younger brother. One year younger to be exact. As usual, I would ring the doorbell at 8am sharp, Nimesh then would come thundering down his stairs shouting "am ready, just chill for a few minutes."

Fifteen minutes would pass. Sometimes I even had the prestige of watching him run around looking for his books. We would storm out of his house at around 8.15am and power walk to the school gates. As we passed these gates, we'd sprint to the main entrance, just to show the teachers who were waiting for late comers that we really cared and that we'd tried everything in our power to make it on time. Everything, that was, except waking up earlier. After a few weeks of this, the same teachers began to see us arriving late. We had received our final warning from the head the day before. This had been enough for Nimesh to be ready on time and we'd actually left his home at 8am. As we approached the school gates, we experienced a side to school life that neither of us had remembered. The morning hustle and bustle in front of the school gates is unique. As we stepped into the school compound, Nimesh was lead into the path of a teenage siren, whose name I'd rather not reveal. Nimesh, as usual, upon setting eyes on her would melt and fall into a trance of sophisticated obedience. He was prone to her every whim. As Nimesh floated away, I walked on still adjusting to the realisation that the time before school was an excellent social activity, one that I had been foolishly missing. Moments later, I felt a stiff jerk and a sharp pain, which nearly sent me flying onto the hard frosty ground. The push had taken the wind out of me just for a moment, which gave the culprit a split second to swing his iron fist on a collision, with my face. As luck would have it, he narrowly missed. Looking up was not an option, I took a step in towards his midsection, my right fist clenched and my left hand went firmly onto his chest. Then with a quick jab into his groin, I sent him to his knees. Now normally, I would have stopped here. I had won. I had conquered his brute force. But not this day! This day something quite primitive had been triggered in my brain. I felt a primal drive to kill, to punish and humiliate.

Any body who has been in street fights knows that everything moves in slow motion. It's a strange phenomenon, it is as if the world has slowed down, sound is muted, the background becomes blurred and the mind becomes thoughtless. Fights have a quality. *It is called silence.* This silence unleashes the human potential in ways that are otherwise incomprehensible. As he fell forward to grab his groin, I stood my ground. I grabbed his neck with my left hand, jerked him backwards only slightly and smacked him point blank right between his eyes. I felt his heavy body give way. I felt his strength, and courage leave him. He was venerable in the deepest way possible. His body had given in with my first blow to his crotch, but now with my second, much harder punch, I felt his spirit go. I hit him again and again, in quick repetition, supporting his head with my left palm. I felt his blood ooze and stick to my fist, as it made contact over and over again. His blood was warm. It felt thick and almost comforting, I remember the pleasure I got from his blood covering my fists. Eventually, a teacher grabbed me from behind, lifted my body of the ground and screamed to make me stop. It was this extreme reaction by an adult that had shocked my conscience back into life. It was as if I had been brought back from the dead. My personality had re-booted and I immediately realised what I had done.

I later heard, from a friend who had come to see me after school at my house that John was in hospital having his nose re-constructed. I had been suspended for three 'whole' days. Three days for disfiguring a person. My libidinal forces were not satisfied by this type of punishment. In fact, they were enhanced once I got back to school. My three days had passed fairly quickly. I spent most of it reading, running, boxing and watching Garfield. I had regretted what I had done. I felt deeply guilty and shocked at myself. While running every morning I was trying to artificially bring the demon inside me up to the surface once again. Nothing I thought of could bring it back. But I had certainly come to terms with one pertinent point. I could kill a man, if I had to. I have later come to realise that anyone is capable of killing. Let me put it another way. Anyone, given the emotional environment at a particular time, if uncontrolled, can conjure up the emotional energy that can result in homicidal violence. It seems to me that we all have varying capacities for channelling negative emotions. Those with a weak or insufficient drainage system for emotional energy are more likely to be violent, angry and aggressive.

When I was suspended, I was Sanvik. When I had returned after my three day suspension, I had become a kind of hero, a man not to be messed with or a guy that people should get on with, if they wanted credibility. People wanted to belong to me. They wanted to join my tribe. My tribe was suddenly very safe to be in because I was in it. This suited me fine. I was searching for belonging, and now belonging had come to me. As I had already learnt from my grandfather, strength breeds respect. This intense sense of respect became a drug for me. I liked it. I wanted it as much as possible and as frequently as possible. Girls began to see me as one of the tribal leaders. I was the Alpha-male in the pack. Girls, at that age want to belong. They want to belong to the group that is the safest and most pride worthy. Suddenly, if there were any doubts before about my popularity with the ladies, now there were certainly none. It's strange really, looking back at it. I often wander, how evolved are we as a species? Maybe Freud was right. Maybe we are all still as primitive as we once were when we lived in caves. Maybe, civilisation is just an extremely sophisticated way we humans have subconsciously developed, to dissipate our primitive selves safely.

I must make one thing clear before I go on. Please don't get confused with popularity through strength and those youths that are anti-social, in every sense of the word. I was never *anti-social*. I never spoke back to teachers, I was never a bully and I mostly liked everyone. My journey through the rabbit hole was keeping me firmly rooted to intellectualism. At times, it was as if there was two of me. One, attached to the body, driven by impulses and sense pleasure like everyone else. And then, there was the philosophical me. Philosophical me was seeing, merely observing and analysing the world from a parallel position through intellectual space, from the rabbit hole.

It was this spilt in personality between the contradictory urges of lust and aggression and my deeply philosophical journey that I had entered. I was experiencing one reality from two different paradigms. The first paradigm was created and experienced through the senses and interpreted by my mind. While the second paradigm was abstract and experienced through intellectualism and the journey of self realisation. It was like a layered effect. Two things were happening at once. I was seeing the world from two differing viewpoints simultaneously. What's more is that I was aware of this. It was this awareness that I believe caused my subtle form of madness. While reading this, if you *feel* what I am writing, but cannot verbalise it, then you've just caught the *wave of what am getting at*.

Healthy Delusions

My subtle experience of *madness* came in the form of a semi-delusional character. He existed but my mind gave him a delusional personality and worth. I was now sixteen. Leicester City Football Club had written a short twelve line letter to explain that my dreams of having a football career were over. They would not be offering me a contract at the end of the season. The letter had shocked me. I had had a good season. My goal tally was almost in double figures, I was happy, competitive and well respected at the club. My coach had assured me a contract in private. It was due to his assurance that I had turned down a contract from Bradford City football club, on the basis that I would rather play for Leicester. Back then in 1997, Bradford was in the old division two and Leicester in division one seeking promotion into the Premiership. I was deeply angered by the letter. I felt let down. In fact, I remember feeling devastated. It was as if my world travelling smoothly on a dual carriageway at 50mph suddenly crashed into a solid lead wall. I was flung through the windscreen and had been badly hurt. I wasn't in the slightest bit prepared to hear a "no" for an answer. I was supremely confident, to the point of subtle arrogance. I couldn't understand it, why had this happened? Football was a major part of my life. To some extents it still is. I was dedicated to it, I was loyal to it and in return football and I had complimented each other well. But now it had occurred to me that football no longer needed me as much as I needed it. The next day I walked to college in the freezing rain. It was a good five mile walk. I went over to the sports office and asked to speak with the college football coach. As I walked in to the reception area to see him, he was chirpy as ever.

"Sir, I don't want to play for the team anymore", I said.

He didn't reply for a few minutes and then said rather smugly, "Ok, you go and have a break for a while."

The tone of his voice *smelt* of smugness. I hated it. In hindsight, I think if he hadn't said what he had in that tone, I probably would have gone back after a few weeks and rejoined the team. But I couldn't get his smugness out of my mind every time I caved into my 'laddish' urge to play competitive football. I never rejoined the team.

The letter had brought with it a feeling of emptiness. I wanted football. In fact I had needed football. It was *my space* where I could loose myself and not think about Vikas, my studies or even my increasingly pessimistic view of life. I think our mind has a fantastic safety mechanism. In the same way as the body, to some extent, can heal itself, so can our minds heal our mental traumas. It was essentially a healthy delusion that I had experienced, looking at it with the power of hindsight. It gave me something the *'real'* couldn't have supplied at that time. At sixteen, I had become an evangelical atheist and an incredibly angry young man. I was obsessed with the angry lyrics of Tupac Shakur, and his words sprang out of my bedroom window, and into the quiet sober street, every weekday, between the hours of four and five in the afternoon. At five, the music had to abruptly stop, just before mum stumbled through the front door, after another day of slaving. Tupac's angry music helped me, to channel my anger, sometimes at myself, but often towards others. The loss of Vikas had triggered my emotional demise, and then the loss of football had amplified my thirst, for emotional belonging, which resulted in the birth of *big brother Dillip*.

Dillip was four years my senior. He was a drug dealer. He was the first 'proper' drug dealer who I had come across from the Indian 'Hindu' community. Of course, he had no real concept of what it meant to be Hindu, he just so happened to have been born into a Hindu family. But this had been enough for me to build a psychological closeness with him, at least in my mind. He was out of the same community as me. He was one of the tribe. I had felt proud that a Hindu could reach such *greatness through strength.* Of course, bear in mind that my definition of greatness has changed greatly since those days. Nevertheless, traditionally my Hindu peers were weak, physically and mentally. Dillip was an exception. His parents had passed away when he was just entering his teens. He had been living with his grandparents, before moving out to live on his own, aged eighteen.

    The first time I had met him was at my kickboxing club. He was regarded as a Don at the club. He was a champion kick boxer, the pride of the club, and the protector of all. To mention Dillip's name was to mention the holy name of the messiah. Everybody respected him. We were completely loyal and would never say a cross word against him, nor would we allow anyone else to slander his 'good' name. It was a form of devotional worship, the kind that often goes on in offices, where the lowly graduates will emulate their superiors in the hope of one day *'de-throwning'* them. He was very much like my grandfather. He had an abundance of strength. So much so, that when he entered the room, everyone fell silent for a split second, just enough time to catch a glimpse of the great man before carrying on with our activities. Dillip was only a little taller than me. But he was walking muscle. No matter what he wore, his muscular figure would show through. The veins on his arms were always visible. His shoulders were broad, his body lean and his skin dark. He had a bushy box beard and locks hanging down to his shoulders. He was the only Indian man I had known, who had grown locks as a conscious effort to look tough. From afar, he looked black. He dressed immaculately and his persona was like that of a sophisticated gangster.

    I had heard many a story about Dillip. One which immediately comes to mind is a legend that I first heard when I was fifteen. Apparently Dillip had got himself into a fight with an out of uniform police officer. He had beaten him so badly. By the time he realised that this was a police constable off duty, he beat him even more, taking this man to the brink of death. He then stopped and wrote a little note for the bludgeoned police officer, vividly reminding him of what had happened, and if he ever told anyone or took any further action, he would find himself thrown into the River Soar. Needless to say, nothing came of it. I doubt that this actually occurred and even if it had, I doubt Dillip was in such control. Dillip, after an intense training session once told us, "that people only fear legends, nothing else. So if you want to be feared, create your legend."

    After I had got to know Dillip, I had seen him in action. I remember waiting for him outside his apartment on a wet Friday evening. He was casually strolling up the mute street without a care for the world. He liked the rain. I was only later to find out, but Dillip had run into some trouble, with a group of real tough nuts from Manchester. This group called themselves Code 10. Dillip and his worshippers labelled themselves as the Firm, which derived out of some hip hop track or another. Dillip, by himself, was walking up towards where I stood, when suddenly he felt a heavy thump on the back of his neck. He instantly lost his bearings and I saw him collapse onto the soaked pavement. I panicked and was just about to set off in the direction where Dillip had fallen. But it was all over before I could even come to grips with what was happening. Moments later Dillip had felt hands exploring his body as if people were looking for something. Without warning he grabbed a wondering arm and snapped the stranger's wrist, with a quick but firm jerk. Before the dark shadow could cry out in agony, Dillip grabbed his shirt collar, pulled him closer and rammed his open palm through the tip of his nose. The dark shadow suffered a broken wrist and nose in fractions of a second. Other prying hands quickly retreated, allowing Dillip to get to his feet. From where I stood everything was happening too quickly and all I could make out was Dillip squaring up to two other shadows. Moments later a fist went flying into Dillip's chest. The heavy impact forced Dillip to fall back a few steps, but he reacted, as if the punch had been a puff of wind. By now Dillip had grown into a monstrous rage. He charged into the two shadows that were still standing, catching the one on his left with his elbow, and almost simultaneously, as if in one motion, punching the other to his right, flat on the nose. Both fell like mannequins being pushed over. These were no small mannequins, you understand. Far from it, they were both bigger shadows than he was and he didn't stop the beating there, oh no, he continued. He carried on kicking the fallen mannequin to his right. I heard quiet whimpers from the fallen soul. A few more minutes passed and Dillip walked over to the front door where I stood 'gob smacked' at what I'd just seen. He turned the keys and walked into the bright hallway where I remember him saying "am soaked and I think my jeans have got dirty".

    This was the man whom I'd given a delusional personality. At my first return to the kick boxing club, after Vikas's passing into the eternal void, it was Dillip who triggered my delusion in a fleeting comment. He came up to me and said, "We're your bothers, every one of us."

    Now, what I had so distinctly heard was, "I'm your brother". It has taken me years to accept this fact. I have always known the truth of that comment and yet, for years I deluded myself and others, not out of malice, but out of inner suffering caused by emotional bankruptcy. I had convinced myself that Dillip was my brother. That night I remember walking home in the bitter cold, feeling so alive due to the self-professed belief that I now had a brother. Someone who would look out for me, encourage me, guide me and even occasionally tell me off but most importantly someone who I could look up to. Looking back after all these years, it seems that my psyche needed a guardian. An all encompassing force that would look after me, and allow me to flourish, a force that was impenetrable to the extent that I would be an untouchable. I think we all need role models, and consciously or not, we are always searching for such types. I think this applies to us in greater portions when we are going through the turbulence of 'teenagehood'.

Whether Dillip had wanted to or not, I now emotionally was connected to him. He was Vikas reincarnate. As I got older, I began to spend more time with him and very quickly realised that the man behind the legend was far more vulnerable than I could have imagined. I remember the first time he invited me to spar with him in the ring. The pride I felt back then when he asked me, can still be felt as I type these words. It was a pivotal moment in our developing friendship and all the more so because my reality was slowly creeping closer to my delusion. As my emotional connection with him grew, at least in my mind, so did his responses, to my unspoken requests to spend greater time with him. Just as I had discovered through my friendship with Mr. Clutton that people in authority, seek meaning, and their meaning is often sourced from the eager student. So it was with Dillip. The stronger and more entrenched my delusion became that he was my *'actual'* brother, the more he seemed to respond in a likewise fashion. Just as with my grandfather, Dillip was the second person from whom I learnt leadership skills, albeit in a completely different environment.

Dillip was a leader because he carried influence. And his influence didn't come from academics or any dry qualification. His influence stemmed from the hard knocks of life. He was orphaned at the most vulnerable age. He was severely dyslectic, to the point that he struggled to read a short article without missing out lines and sometimes entire paragraphs. He hated reading and his maths was non existent, and yet at the age of twenty he was earning £20,000, tax free. His business existed, underneath the officialdom where most of us earn our bread. And yet no one should make the mistake of "snubbing" Dillip's business credibility. I have since met many hundreds of 'smart' people, many in business, and yet I know Dillip to be smarter and more successful, than most. Observing him in those early days has boosted the growth of my own businesses. I should spend some time explaining what kind of business animal Dillip was.

He was above all else meticulous and disciplined. He never took marijuana himself, and he openly mocked any drug dealer that smoked his own gear, often saying, "Do you like burning your own profits?"

He ran eight miles everyday. He boxed at least three times a week and obsessively recorded each deal he made. He would hold sessions at his flat twice a week. He used to often invite me. I said little, but observed everything. I got the nickname 'Saint' because I wouldn't drink or smoke with them. These 'sessions' were not sleazy drinking pits, where everyone came to get high. Far from it!

Dillip would never allow his employees to behave so unprofessionally. These sessions were meetings. At these meetings each runner had to report to Dillip on all sales he had made that week. A runner was anyone who took a block of gear, normally around five hundred grams and then sold it. Dillip never sold anything to anyone directly. He had over fifty runners working for him throughout the week. I noticed that he ran reward schemes for the best runners and he always, gave motivating mini speeches at the end of most sessions, to boost the under achievers. He spent time with each runner, building up a relationship, he would hold appraisals and he even held teambuilding sessions, once every two months.

The only difference, between his business and any other, was the terminology. The teambuilding activities were called *'roping areas'* and his appraisals were called *'respect hours'*. Looking back, it was brilliant the way he managed so many disgruntled, immoral individuals through reputation and meticulous control, accompanied by a fair distribution of rewards for all. He once told me, "Saint, remember one thing, business is about trust. If you haven't got trust, you aren't in business. And another thing, no one ever works for you, remember that, people only work for themselves. They aren't with you to make you money. They're there so they can make money for themselves. When it comes down to it, they'll leave you in a flash."

I've never forgotten these words. Today, I see more clearly than ever that in business, one needs people working *with you* and never *for you*. As soon as a manager begins to think that people are working for him, he's already sat on the slippery slide down.

Another lesson I learnt from observing him was how he managed to motivate people. I realised early on that he used one of two incentives – fear and greed. He would use fear in two ways. The first, what I call negative fear, would be his menacing reputation to physically hurt those that stood in his way, but to be fair he only used negative fear rarely. Instead, he used to show people, what I call positive fear, that by working with him, and doing things his way their fears would be alleviated. They would essentially feel safer if they followed his instructions. Negative fear creates compliance not commitment, but positive fear develops longer term commitment and in business this is far more vital.

He also used people's innate greed to motivate them. But not greed only in terms of money, which of course he often used, but he would boost their ego by recognising their achievements and worth to the Firm. People are also greedy for recognition, prestige and respect. Dillip gave all three to those who he felt needed it. Between the ages of sixteen and seventeen I had learnt two clear ways in which people can be motivated by simple observation. I believe my delusional closeness with Dillip indirectly taught me the foundations of good leadership.

I believe, we have all had opportunities to learn good, and all too often poor leadership, through observation, but these can only truly be grasped, when we co-exist in the rabbit hole – the intellectual tunnels on which our physical existence is based. I was slowly becoming aware of the subtle fact that I was experiencing the world in a different light in comparison to others. My awareness was growing and yet I had much to discover about the self.

The Abyss takes Dillip

"What we sow is what we reap – Karma spares no one."

15th January 1999, Dillip was driving back from Nottingham. He had just entered Leicester, coming down the A46. He stopped at the lights, it was midnight. A car pulled up next to his. A man fired a single shot, from the car and killed him instantly. Dillip was twenty-three years old. He died, with no one in front of him and no one behind. Soon, when everyone who knew him and loved him is gone, he will cease to exist. It will be as if he never was. His parents were already waiting for him in the long hereafter. He had no siblings, no partner and no children. I hope that I can capture his spirit in the next few paragraphs, if for no other reason, than to remember those whom society neglected, who in turn harmed it.

Dillip was no saint, nor was he a hero. He accomplished nothing great, and lived a life full of knocks and hardships. Yet, he has forged my thinking. As I write these words, sitting in a quite flat on the third floor of an apartment block, at The Hague, in Netherlands, my eyes swell and I'm sure tears will soon shed. He was my guardian when I was at my weakest. He was my inspiration when life had become meaningless. Vikas and Dillip were the first two, to recognise my true inner potential. Vikas protected me intellectually, Dillip emotionally. Whether he loved me as much as I did him is beside the point. Vikas in death showed me the eternal void, whereas, Dillip's death showed me the beauty of life.

I found out the day after that he had been killed. I remember curling up on my bedroom floor and wishing that Vikas would come and take me too. I cried, quietly, throughout the night. Tears ran until there were none left. That night the dam of sorrow locked deep within my mind gave way. My mental space was flooded with emotional sorrow. This night, I cried not only for the loss of Dillip, but also for the loss of Vikas. I was eighteen. At his funeral, which I had arranged, as there was no one else, only forty odd people came to pay their respects. Dillip was cremated at Gilrose cemetery, in Leicester, at the same place where I had fallen through the rabbit hole when Vikas had died almost four and half years earlier. This time sitting on that cold wooden bench, I had my third *re-forging* experience.

Whereas, Vikas had intentionally set about protecting, nurturing and toughening me, Dillip had done all these things by accident. At this time, he was my brother. People had actually believed that he had been my sibling because the way our friendship had developed. My father had once said to him that if ever wanted a real family that he should move in with us and start a fresh. Dillip never took his offer seriously, at the cost of his own demise. I had begun to tell people when they asked, if I had any siblings, "Yes, I have an older brother." I was convinced that we were related, it was a most powerful delusion.

The few months before Dillip's death, had been difficult for the entire Firm. I had begun 6th form. I got through my GCSE's with average grades without revising for a single subject. I was doing poorly at college and most likely to fail all my subjects. I had nothing to do with Dillip's business, but due to our close relationship, rival gangs would naturally draw me in. On one occasion, on my way from college, when I was alone, someone in a hooded top ran past, slashing me on my side with a knife. He'd luckily not made proper contact and the only damage he'd done was worth fifteen stitches, just above my bum. I have a thick scar to remember him by.

On another occasion, three guys came up from behind, and began to harass two girls that I was walking with. I was never one to hold back. I reacted, and the next thing I knew a bottle was smashed over the back of my head. I fell instantly onto the pavement, and the beating started. I squeezed my eyes shut and curled up as tightly as I could. The kicks and stomps flew in. I saw nothing; I heard nothing. When I came back to reality, I was numb and my clothes were covered in blood. It was another trip to the local A & E. I was beginning to make some real friendships with the nurses on duty there. After ten straight years of kick boxing and street fighting, a physical beating of this kind was something that my body could quite easily take and recover from, in a short space of time. Some people actually began to think that I was one of the boys at the top of the Firm. Nothing could be further from the truth. People spread rumours that it took three guys, with weapons, to take me down and that the only way to beat me was to use such techniques. I had built myself a reputation as a bit of a fighter. I was no softy, but to compare me to the likes of Dillip was a little far fetched. People love talk, and with talk, legends are born. Dillip had said, *'If you want to be feared, create your legends.'* Well, I had mine.

While all this was happening, I never spoke to anyone about it. I kept everything to myself. People at college, including teachers assumed that I was purposely missing lessons. In fact, I was often lying in bed, nursing my wounds, which I would expertly conceal from my parents.

Dillip was the way he was; he did what he did, because essentially society created and moulded him in that way. After the death of his parents, his grandparents were not really capable of raising him, and his severe dyslexia meant that he was doing extremely poorly at school. This knocked his confidence. He grew up a lonely child. He knew only one way to retrieve some sense of dignity and self worth, and that was to become tough. *And my word had he become tough.*

I think his immense toughness came directly and proportionally to his own internal suffering and feeling of hopelessness. He survived and learnt to live well from doing what he had taught himself to do. He was completely imbalanced and had extreme ends to his personality. Towards me he was firmly gentle, and fairly protective, yet I knew he could and had killed people. He reaped the seeds he had sown, but we also reaped the seeds we too had sown, when we failed to recognise his needs, when he was at his most vulnerable. By no means am I blaming any one particular person or group. What I am saying is that monsters who inflict harm on society have a human tragedy lurking deep within their past. And monsters don't create themselves. If Dillip and people like him are monsters, which we should fear, or lock up and throw away the key, then society and more specifically its values *(or culture)* is Dr. Frankenstein. *Without the good doctor there can be no monster.*

Discovering Me

While all this was going on, my mind was often floating somewhere quite different. Instead of reading my physics text book, I would be reading Plato's Republic. Instead of completing my Maths homework, I was too engrossed in the works of Gödel, the Austrian mathematician, who came up with the idea of the incompleteness theorem. In it he said that foundationally, all mathematical equations are based on unproven assumptions. Hence, he proposed that mathematics could never accurately decipher reality. To me this was far more thrilling than any dry case study on differentiation. When I should have been drawing circuit diagrams for electronics, I was too busy musing and gazing long into the night and asking the questions that matter. Questions such as *what is mathematics?* If all science boils down to mathematics and if mathematics is inherently limited, then, what does this tell us? The only subject, in which I excelled, was Philosophy. I was an A-grade student. It came naturally to me. It was the one subject which corresponded with my journey through the rabbit hole.

Until Dillip's death, I was quite unable to connect my experiences through the rabbit hole with the actual world. In the actual world I was a dithering idiot, who knew little to nothing about his subjects. I came across as lazy and care free. My relationship with my mother had degenerated to the point where the only time we spoke, was when we argued. She couldn't understand her only son. He had gone off the rails and she worried constantly. My father, as always, tried to be supportive where he could, but he still hadn't recovered from Vikas's passing. I had few, what I call *'proper'* friends left. I was spending increasingly large periods of time by myself, pondering, thinking, and running.

I remember on one occasion, I spontaneously decided that I was going to walk from Leicester to Luton, where Kiran Fai had lived. So I rang and told her my plan. I can't remember what she had said, or what she had thought. Nevertheless, she agreed to pick me up from Milton Keynes bus station, the following morning after dropping the kids off to school. I forced my father to drop me off at the nearest M1 junction. He reluctantly did so. And that was it. I walked the sixty odd miles from Leicester to Milton Keynes. It took the best part of 24-hours. I initially began to walk on the hard shoulder before police stopped me and asked what I was doing. So I told him. I clearly remember him looking bemused. He didn't quite know what to say. The awkward silence went on, for what seemed like ages. Eventually, he said, "right, you don't want to be walking on the motorway, you need to cut across these fields in that direction and keep going until you get to the A5. Then walk straight down it and it'll take you to where you want to go."

"Right officer", I replied. Just as he was ready to get back in his car, I asked, "Aren't they private fields? Weren't I get into trouble if I cut across them?"

He looked at me, scratched the side of his face and replied, "Not from me you won't."

This mini trek was the first time that I had experienced the English countryside. It was beautiful. The fields, the tiny rural villages, the peace and tranquillity were something I had never experienced up until then. Crossing the fields was no walk in the park. The length of the wild grass concealed the wet, damp muddy ground. Within these fields were wild nettles and thick branches, covered with one inch thorns. It took me four hours to cross three fields and to jump five barbed wire fences. By the end of it, I had ripped my sleeping bag, which I had tied to the bottom end of my backpack, my boots were covered in sludge and I felt my socks getting wet. As I jumped the final barbed wire fence, and landed on the A5, I had felt like going home. But how would I get back. These were the days when mobile phones were still at their infancy, everyone was using pagers back then. Two things stopped me from turning back, firstly, it was self pride, and second, I had forged a never quit attitude. The rest of that day went by without incident. I walked along the edge of the A5, alone with my thoughts.

While on this walk, I had been still trying to answer the question what is mathematics? I was now deep in my thoughts. I was not only walking a great distance but I was pushing my mind a great deal too. I can't exactly remember how I came with the answer, but I did. It was this answer that re-ignited my passion for studies; it gave me the reason to know mathematics. My answer, when it came was *simple*.

Mathematics I realised was a language. It's a language just like any other. It has rules, it has syntax and it is used to communicate. It occurred to me as cars were speeding by only centimetres away, that without numbers I couldn't really say much about the world outside me. I couldn't say how old I was without numbers; I could verify my weight or height without numbers; and I couldn't say how far things were or what things were worth. Just as words communicated and made sense of the inner world, numbers made sense of the outer physical world. It dawned on me that mathematics is learning the grammar of the physical world.

Even though Gödel had said that mathematics could not accurately show reality, at least, it gave us a way to communicate that which we could know. From this simple realisation, it doesn't take a rocket scientist to figure out that if you want to be the master of your own life, then one must come to grips with the logical language of mathematics. Without learning mathematics, one would always be dazzled by the outside world, as little would make sense. It would be as if we were confined permanently in a magic show. The world would be the magician, and our lives would be the audience. We would always be awestruck by the world and when things didn't work out the way we wanted it, we would feel helpless. Just as magicians in a magic show entertain us, baffle us and often beguile us, so the world would appear as such, if we were illiterate in numbers and its logical rules. Mathematics was a philosophy of numbers. It was the tool, to which we could build solutions for the physical problems we faced. Once I had been soaked in this realisation, I felt the urge creep up inside me to go back home. This urge came not from physical discomfort, but intellectual disharmony. I wanted to get back to my room and start doing maths. This urge to master mathematics remained with me until I completed my Masters in Aerospace Engineering almost five years later.

Shortly after coming back from this *'spiritual retreat'*, Dillip had gone into the shadow. His death, after all the tears had been shed was a re-birth, for my life. Vikas's death was slowing killing me; Dillip's death had re-ignited my passion to live. I had been in the rabbit hole, travelling intellectual space for long enough to know, I had something deep within my spirit that was unique. I had something to offer others. I had something to contribute to the dialogue of history. I was experiencing a unique view of the world and I knew I had the inner capacity to make things happen. I knew I could change the environment around me. It was just a matter of will.

Weeks went by, and I became consumed in my Physics textbooks. I had little time for anything else. I did however; spend a lot of time with my grandfather. He too took note of this sudden frequency of visits. As usual he would do all the talking, or we would sit their in silence both pondering about life, the universe and stuff. With my grandfather lived Kishor kaka, he was my fathers youngest brother and had severe learning disabilities. Since a young age I had a great deal of empathy towards him and his children – Kamal and Hemal, Bhavika was yet to be born.

Kamal was ten years old and Hemal three. Hemal was born with the same learning disabilities as his father. I remember Kamal would quietly sit next to my grandfather, as he and I rambled on about religion, politics and his youthful days, living in Africa. Kamal would listen intently. There was a slight tinge of irony in all this. Just as I used to sit and listen to my father and Vikas rant on and on, at the dinner table, so too did Kamal listen to my grandfather and I do the same. These were the seeds, I believe, that have resulted in Kamal becoming the self assured young man that he is. From a very young age I introduced Kamal to the rabbit hole. I would entice him into philosophical and moral problems, to which he responded surprisingly well. Most children become fascinated for a short stretch of time before moving onto watch Neighbours. Not Kamal. He stayed the course. In actual fact, he soon learnt the art of harassment to get his regular philosophical doses. I knew he was in the rabbit hole, because his daily actions were being deeply effected by our philosophical explorations. I would only introduce him to areas of thinking that I had already explored well enough to guide him safely through. Kamal was my first step in my new direction.

My new direction was change. Change those things that you have strong feelings for and do not like its current state or direction. I knew Kamal was born in a paradox. He had a father. And yet he was fatherless. Kishor kaka was there in person and yet emotionally he was non-existent. I had recognised from a time when Kamal was very young that he would need a brother that could meet his emotional needs, which should traditionally have come from his biological father. So it became, that I was his emotional father and physical brother. The relationship has since evolved, and as he has matured so to proportionally have we become brothers, physically, and increasingly emotionally. Due to Kishor kaka's condition, I knew that Kamal would suffer from a deep insecurity that would stem from his inability to feel safe. And without safety he would find it increasingly difficult to find belonging and feel loved, and thereby extrapolating his insecurities. So I made it my task that Kamal should feel safe. I put word out to boys at his school that no one is to bully Kamal, and if it occurs then they should go and support him. In essence I had short-circuited the system of bullying. I had told all the potential bullies and other social *cool cats* that Kamal was to be supported. And because Kamal was now indirectly friends with the social hierarchy of the school playground, naturally everyone fell into line.

To ensure that his need for belonging and love was satisfied, I effectively outsourced this to Kiran Fai. She was much better equipped than I was for this task. Kiran Fai with all her energy and enthusiasm would take Kamal for the holidays. He would spend a week or so with her. She would take him to zoos, theme parks and to watch films. They would go out to eat – something that would never have occurred with his biological parents, as they could neither drive nor speak English. Kiran Fai has always been a warm glow to those that will appreciate her. To this day, just as I had received a lot of love and devotion from her, so too did Kamal. A lot of Kamal's outgoing personality, I believe, has stemmed directly from Kiran Fai. We both owe much to her. It was due to this that Kamal at a very young age became interested in chess, moral discussions, art and above all else dinosaurs. These were all esteem needs that he was now aspiring for. He was pursuing, what J.S. Mill called the higher pleasures, and in turn this developed his ability to intellectualise.

Kamal was born into a classic text book family that was most vulnerable to social upheavals. In other words, he was born in a dysfunctional family. He was born into a situation that had all the tell tale signs, of a person who was most likely to suffer from gross insecurities, underachieve academically and socially. He was prone to being bullied and in turn would victimise others. All of this was avoided simply because his basic foundational needs of safety and belonging were met from an early age. His extended family was compensating for what his biological parents couldn't give. That's not to say Kamal faced no problems, he did, but the major upheavals have been avoided due to the support network that was provided by key individuals around him.

It was on that long sixty mile walk that I had decided to change myself, my outlook and those that were dearest to me. It was that walk and this realisation, which has influenced Kamal's life so greatly. It's something that he would have never have known if it wasn't for me deciding to write this book.

Channelling my energies on my younger cousins wasn't the only thing that I had decided to change. I had decided consciously that I would begin to break all my ties, with anyone who was affiliated to Dillip and the kick boxing club. Needless to say but I decided to quit boxing too, so that I could now seriously concentrate on what I wanted above all else – grasp of academics.

Between the months of January and June, 1999, I was putting in fifteen hours a day studying Physics and Electronics. Everything else was unimportant. My learning was rapid for two reasons. Firstly, because I had always been a smart cookie, but now, I was putting in the hours that mattered, and secondly, due to the fact that I had realised *what mathematics and science, in actual fact was*.

I was living the physics I was learning. This was no dry text book, parrot fashion learning. Far from it, for I had captured the soul of the topic. I was learning all the while, I never stopped, not because I had to, but because I wanted to. Let me share a vivid memory of such an experience. I was waiting for the local bus, number twenty-one, which would take me into the city centre. As I waited, I saw a boy, who couldn't have been a day older than seven crossing the road at a set of traffic lights. As the traffic signals turned red, and the green man signalled for him to cross the road, a car that must have been travelling at some speed suddenly had to brake. I saw the drivers face tense up as he braked, no doubt worried that he would hit the boy. He didn't, he managed to stop the car just in time. In my mind, I re-enacted the scene, this time however, the car didn't stop, and in fact it didn't even brake, and just smashed into the boy. I pretended that the boy weighed 1kg and was crossing the road at a speed of one kilometre per hour. I equally pretended that the car weighed 100kg, and was travelling at ten kilometres per hour. The car hit the boy at right angles. What force would the boy be hit at and if he was to be thrown, how far back would he fall?

In my mind, I used simple mechanics to work out the impact force, and using momentum equations I roughly calculated how far the boy would have fallen if this were to happen. This is how I lived, whatever it was that I was learning. I now recommend all my students to muse in a similar way. I encourage them to actively simulate their theory on the world around them. That is not to say that we should all think of little seven year old boys been smashed to bits by psychopathic drivers, who drive far to slowly, and never brake when it matters, but the more interesting the scenario one comes up with, the better the chances of you actually getting to grips with the problem.

I had been disengaged from education for so long that my new found enthusiasm for it came as a bit of a shock for my parents. They never really mentioned much, but I noticed that they had noticed, me working much harder than I had ever previously done. My dad many years later said to me, "In those days, I saw you spend as much time on numbers as I saw you looking up at the stars."

It had, and still is a favourite hobby of mine to stare up at the night sky and get lost in its magical beauty. I still haven't lost my enthusiasm for education. I am still a compulsive learner. If I could afford to, I would prefer nothing better than to wander the corridors of universities and keep taking on new courses to learn. Knowledge, to me at least, is the simplest path to finding satisfaction from this life. Nothing would pleasure me more.

Another change that stemmed out of my spiritual retreat down the A5, was that I should go onto university and study Aerospace Engineering. Vikas was in his final year of an Aerospace degree when he died. I had heard many times how close he was to becoming a *'somebody'*, how hard it was to study his course and everyone always assumed Aerospace must equate to *'super brain power'*. I liked that naïve assumption people made. I thought that I could take on two birds with one stone.

First, my parents would feel that I was accomplishing something that was very dear to them, and which they thought was way out of my academic reach. It would be nice to prove them wrong. And second that I could go on studying essentially mathematics, something which I had only recently fallen in love with. I didn't really feel like divorcing with mathematics just yet. When I told my parents for the first time, about my ambitions, I think they were genuinely baffled. In hindsight, I can imagine how it must have come across. Here in front of them was someone who hung around with a drug dealer, hadn't done every well academically to date, didn't ever show an interest in aircraft and in their eyes at least, was a serial day dreamer. My father didn't say much, and if he did, then I'm sorry to say, I can't remember any of it. I do, however, remember my mother's reaction. "Do you know how hard it is to get a place on this course? It's not something that you can just walk into. Your brother struggled through it, so how do you think you will fare?" she quizzed.

I realised then that when I had suggested studying Aerospace, I not only belittled it, but also Vikas's legacy. The subconscious point must have been something like, *if this lay about can do it, anyone can.*

In June 1999, I took my A-level finals. I had worked relentlessly. It was the first time in my life I had done so. The night before the finals I had decided to call it a day with studying. To this day, I never study the night before an exam. My mid-teens were dark. I wasn't a happy child. Physically and mentally I was a forty year old, in an eighteen year olds body. It was fitting that the night before my finals, I became myself.

I went across the street to see Jinesh, who I knew would be in his usual panic ridden state. You see, Jinesh, while I had been putting in fifteen hours a day for the last six months, he had been gallivanting around the college as the student president, a job which he took very seriously. In fact, he once said, "It's all about popularity, nothing else." In his spell as president, he managed to do nothing apart from organise a leaver's ball, for which, ironically he won an award. Jinesh was great. He still is. He never fails to make me laugh at some of his shenanigans. At college Jinesh had found a new level of popularity, and along with another two friends, whom I also got to know fairly well, called Anand and Shillon. It was socialising to a point where even lessons were only meaningful to catch up with friends. I thought that it'd be entertaining to see him panic, while I spoke to Nimesh. An additional benefit, I thought would be to sit in front of his dad, looking relaxed, while he saw his own son in considerable stress. I knew he would take this to its logical end – I had worked hard and so was relaxed, while his son had wasted his year with girls and other time wasters. He would then call Jinesh down and have a go at him, while Nimesh and I would enjoy the night's entertainment, with a bowl of popcorn. Getting another in trouble with their respective parents while you were there was always held in high esteem.

I went over at around eight in the evening. As I walked through the front door, I was greeted by the normal polite pleasantries that Jinesh bestowed onto all his guests. "Oi, I'm fucked you know. I'm stressing", he said.

I had to laugh.

He went on, "And don't think you can come here and get my dad started. If you try anything, you watch, I'm gonna tell him about you and all your fucking girls, you've been having this year."

I must have looked surprised because he went on, "yeah, don't think I don't know Bacchu. I've seen you bring in a different girl every week, back to yours when your folks are at work."

This was a slight exaggeration. It was at least once every other week. Bacchu was his nickname for me when he wanted to get a pertinent point across. Sure enough at that moment, his dad came downstairs to watch his usual dose of news.

"Alright Sanvik", he said as he walked into the front room. "Why aren't you studying? Don't you have exams now?"

I looked at Jinesh, who had his back to him and carried an 'I won't, if you won't' smirk on his face. "Um, actually my exams start a day later", I lied.

As fate would have it, Jinesh was landed right in it, not by me, but by Anand. The front door must have been left open, Anand walked in and didn't realise Jinesh's dad was sitting in the corner. He bent over slightly to shake my hand, as I was getting comfortable for the nights entertainment on the sofa. He turned to Jinesh and blurted out, "I had to come here man, my dads on a mission to shout at me. He reckons me, you and Shillion have been wasting our time this year. Plus I need you help with tomorrow's paper."

That had been enough encouragement for Jinesh's dad to get started. "I knew it", he said, surprising Anand.

"Alright", greeted Anand, with a little wave of the hand.

"I've been telling Jinesh for months that if he doesn't get into a university, I'm going to get him a job at my factory". He went on, "I know you, Shillion and Jinesh have been wasting your time. I keep telling you people that you should study. This is the time to study. Girls can come later, when you get married. But you people don't listen."

Jinesh looked at me, and then turned to Anand and mumbled, "You're a dickhead."

I had to grin. This was going to be a fun night. Perfect exam prep I thought. Relaxation with gentle laughter, followed by a relaxing sleep and then onto the examination hall. To my disappointment, Jinesh as quickly as possible, walked out of the room, Anand swiftly followed. Now, I knew as long as I sat there, Jinesh's dad would keep on going. So I did what any other loyal friend would do. I sat there, positively nodding as if in agreement with Jinesh's dad. Seconds later, Jinesh walked back in, to my surprise.

"Dad", he said, "let me tell you something about Sanvik".

I knew what was to follow. It would be Jinesh's subtlety at its crudest. I jumped to my feet and dragged him out of the room. I quickly said bye to Jinesh's dad, before leaving. We spent that entire evening outside, on Jinesh's front porch. We were later joined by Shillion, the tobacco chewing Radia, Rakesh Kanani and Nimesh. We laughed; we joked, picked on one another and treated the night, as if it were our last. For me at least, it really was. I've never spent a night like that since. We were there, talking and laughing, outside until the early hours of the morning. Every time anyone ran out of things to say, we'd all pick on Radia, who had unusual sweat glands. He had a tendency to sweat while he stood perfectly still. Now, when I mean sweat, I don't mean a little hot under the collar, I mean dripping with sweat. *It was hilarious.*

Four

धर्म

Angels Come In All Sizes

I still remember the day. It was 12th of March, 1999. I was having lunch by myself in the busy college canteen. It was packed as usual. By this time far fewer seniors could be seen socialising. The exams were approaching and seniors had migrated out to the library. As I had gotten up to leave, Aarti tapped me on the shoulder. Now Aarti was Jinesh's friend. He had introduced me to her some months back. Most guys, including Jinesh found her to be stunningly beautiful. I however, was lured by her best friend, a girl named Asheeta. I had first come across Asheeta, on the first day of enrolment, eighteen months earlier. I'd found her instantly eye catching. She carried an aura that pulled my spirit towards her. She was a tiny girl, no taller than 5"2; she had straight, lightly coloured brown, short shoulder length hair. She was always well dressed. The one word which best describes her, back then, is sensual. She was alluring. When I first laid my eyes on her, I knew she was poison ivy. She had stunning looks and a body that would melt you away. And every time I saw her walking by, I knew that she knew she had it – that special something those sirens in the myths of old possessed. As luck would have it, back then, she didn't even know I existed. I found this to be baffling.

Back in 1998 to 1999, I was at the peak of my physical stature. I knew that girls found something about me attractive. Some found my looks appealing, others my friendly open personality and a few my mysteriousness. In 1999, I had received twelve Valentines Day cards. Not that this is a particularly robust way of evaluating ones popularity with the opposite sex, but it gets my point across adequately enough. When this little flattering bit of news got round, all those girls who had sent me a card were churlishly embarrassed. For me it was a nice massage to my already well placed ego. I'm sure there were a few girls, like Asheeta who didn't know I existed or for whom I did nothing, in terms of physical attraction. Not withstanding those few, I was having a whale of a time with girls.

I learnt a lot in those years about human nature. Freud and Karl Jung, both of whom I had been reading deeply, acted as great guides, when I was travelling the labyrinths of the female psyche. There were times that year where I had several different girls on the go at the same time. I even knew why I was doing it. I now deplore, and did so back then, people who behaved in such ways. Throughout those years I was deeply unhappy. Life meant little. My search for meaning led me down a hole from which I couldn't escape. These girls were my welcomed lapse from reality. When I was in their company, nothing mattered. The degenerative relationship with my parents, the un-dealt sorrow of Vikas's death, the fear of being stabbed, or worse shot, and my falling grades at college could all be forgotten. I was, as bad for them, as they were for me. What I gave them was an abundance of strength and confidence. They could belong and feel safe when they were in my company. It was a mutual emotional trade off.

It was in this backdrop that I had found it depressing that the one girl who I had this deep yearning for, didn't even know I existed. Aarti, back then, as she still does, has a habit of hugging anybody she knows. It must be comforting for her to hug people, or why else would she do it? So I gave a reluctant hug, as I felt really uncomfortable giving anybody such contact. To my surprise, as I looked over her shoulder stood Asheeta. We made direct eye contact. She was wearing a coy smile. And with it she fired the first words that would remain in the forefront of my mind for time immemorial. "Where's my hug?" she asked.

The cheeky devil, I remember thinking. She had ignored me for the best part of eighteen months and here she was asking for a hug! These were the words that are the bedrock of my life thus far. If she had never said those simple three words, I wonder what would have come of me. If my intellectual yearnings led me to fall through the intellectual tunnels, then Asheeta and I instantly fell into an altogether different well.

We hit it off instantly. We talked hours on end. I knew instantly, after our first conversation that she found me to be mysterious. She had never met anybody like me. Years later, she told me what her first impressions were. She found me to be patently honest, to the point where I didn't appear to care what negative effects my honesty would have, this appealed to her. She rightly translated my crude honesty with self assuredness. She liked the subtle truth that I was communicating through my eyes that none of what we were talking about really mattered and that there was a deeper side to me. She took penetrating my depth as a personal challenge. She wanted to know what was lurking behind the over whelming physical and mental toughness, which was accompanied by healthy doses of confidence. During these early days of foreplay and emotional sparing, I was a little concerned that she would begin to put me in the dreaded 'just good friends' category.

Every man's most frustrating nightmare, is when a woman that they physically fancy, end up boxing them in the *'nice to talk too, but would never kiss'* section. I saw back then, and continue to see today, plenty of men who are put in this section by the girls they would like something more with. Back then this box was called, *'he's like my brother'*, and it'll be no surprise that it was the women who would label the box as such. The guys that thought, this was the best they were going to get, would accept the categorisation. I would do no such thing. But something told me that it would never come to that.

Asheeta's eyes were as deep as the rabbit hole. Furthermore, they were as revealing to those who knew how to interpret the signs, as Mandarin is to someone in Western China. Her eyes told me she found me attractive. Not just sweet attraction, but the lustful type. There was something primitive in her eyes that told me a powerful passion was building up deep within her heart. Our conversations were lucid. We would sit on the red, partly ripped sofas that lined the college canteen walls. We sat with our shoulders rubbing against one another. We would constantly make subtle contact, through light touches. It was here that Nimesh bounced onto the scene.

I had told Nimesh about Asheeta. I'd already told him that I felt differently about this one. My precise words were, "she's bad. She's got something, something that I can't understand, but whatever it is, I want it."

He understood exactly. Nimesh was and still is extremely sensitive to people. He is emotionally very fluent and has the ability to connect with others instantly. Which is why, he too was a charmer. He was quite the opposite of Jinesh. It was Nimesh that was always honest with me when it came to girls. It was him that said, "Sach, let me find out a few things about her."

A few days later, we bumped into one another in one of the many narrow college corridors. He grabbed my arm and said, "Oi, I gotta talk to you. You've got a real live one here."

Before we could say anymore, the flow of human traffic carried us in opposite directions. His comments had got me thinking. I pondered on the idea that Asheeta might be toying with me. She might be using me, for some quick short term gain. I thought to myself, why else would she decide to notice me now? My wonderings had got the better of me. I began to believe that I had already been used. That evening, I crossed the narrow road where Nimesh and I lived, and knocked on his front door. Nimesh came strolling down the stairs and guided me outside into his front drive.

"Watch out for her", he warned. "Do you know who she was seeing before you?" he asked in the way people do when they already know the answer.

I nodded.

"She might be playing two heavy weights off against one another, so be careful" he said.

Now, I was well aware of this annoying little detail. It was a well known truth that Asheeta had been seeing Jay, another senior, who I had known from my Soar Valley days. Jay and I were similar in some respects, but irreconcilable. We were adversaries. There was a cold war between him and I which was purely on the egoistic plane. It was a shallow war of superiority. Who was the better man? I have never been interested in such trivial matters, but Jay was the kind of man who would belittle people if they didn't put him in his rightful place. He had tried once with me. Let it be known that he was put in his place swiftly and without any great deal of fuss. This had left him bitter. So he took his proxy war to the imaginary level. In short, Asheeta had dated him for several months before, and then they had fallen out and still had seen each other on and off for a while. Jay was also seeing some other girl at this time on and off. Nimesh had been worried by two possibilities. The first possibility was that Asheeta had realised that she could get one up on Jay by dating me, or at least appearing to be doing so. And second, was that Nimesh had heard through Jay's friends that she was a wild one. She was, in Nimesh's words, "a man-eater". So I did what any self-assured mature young man would do – I hid from her for a few days.

I knew that Asheeta would be found in the canteen or in the library. I avoided both places for several days. Eventually, I had to stroll into the library to return a few books. As luck would have it, Asheeta was sitting on the front isle. She happened to look up at the exact point when I had noticed her. Our eyes met. She smiled and invited me over. Like an obedient puppy, I strolled over and sat next to her. She didn't say anything. She carried on studying. A little surprised by this, I sat next to her, took my books out and began to read. A few minutes passed, and surprisingly I got into my reading. My hands were resting on my lap, underneath the desk, when suddenly I felt a soft, smaller hand touch me. I remember exactly, as it was, even after all these years. There was something extraordinary in that simple act of human affection. It was warm, comforting and gentle, to the point of innocence. I didn't react and neither did she. I carried on reading and she went about scribbling her notes. Half an hour or so later, we went for lunch at the canteen.

This is where and how Nimesh bounced in to our intimate scene. He stood there grinning. After a pause he said, "So you two going to kiss or what? The whole college has been waiting to see you guys, together, can you please just get on with it."

I was bemused to the point of shock. Here was Nimesh, who I had mentored for years on the art of relationships and girls, putting me in an environment which couldn't have been imagined as being more awkward. Asheeta turned to face me. I was far too hot, and an instant sweat broke out on my forehead. I was embarrassed, and I was going to physically kill Nimesh after this. In the corner of my eye, I knew Asheeta was smiling. She gave me a quick peck on the cheek. I remember thinking, what the hell is going on; I looked up to give Nimesh a stare, which would powerfully, but subtly communicate his upcoming death. Instead, my face turned to mush, my facial muscles relaxed and her quick affectionate, but cheeky peck had been enough to show Nimesh, that he was right. I can't remember how that awkward scene passed.

That night, I received a call from Asheeta. She was in the library. Her voice was a tiny soft whisper. She wanted to know whether I was going to the college leaver's ball at the Grand Hotel. I remember the conversation well.

"You know I hate those kinds of do's, I'm not going. Why are you asking".

"Oh, nothing just wondering if you were coming, it'll be fun", she concluded.

"Nah, I don't think it's my scene, to many people suffering from delusions of grandeur", I replied. "Besides", I carried on, "what do you care, you're going with Jay."

There was a short but what appeared like a long silence. "Umm, I don't think I'm going with him anymore."

"Oh really", I quizzed, trying my best to sound surprised with a tinge of regret.

"Yeah, I don't think I want to go with him, besides were only going as friends", she clarified, encase there was any doubt.

I paused for a few seconds; we both knew where this was going. But I wasn't going to say and she wasn't going to readily ask. "So who will you be going with" I asked, leading her to the place where she'd rather not go.

There was another long pause, before she replied, "Don't know, but I do know who I'd rather go with."

I couldn't help but smile. She wasn't only teasing, but she knew it would put me one up if she came right up and asked me to accompany her.

I did what any emotionally competent man would do, I asked, "Really, who?"

This went on to and fro for a few more minutes, before she reached a cunning emotional middle ground. She manoeuvred herself perfectly and suggested, "Why don't you ask me, I'll say yes, and then you'll know that it was me that really asked you. Others can think that you asked me. But what do you care what others think, right?"

I couldn't refuse her after coming up with such a delicate solution. She had read my concerns correctly. She knew I had doubts about her personal intentions, and I was well aware that she wanted to keep her head high in the social arena by always having the boy ask her out. We were both winners. We knew personally that Asheeta had come onto me, but socially it was I who came onto her. I cared for the personal, she for the social. And so this is how Angels can appear, at least this is how it happened to me.

In hindsight as I write these words, it's uncanny that it was my longing for personal development and her longing for social development that eventually separated us after nine years of growing together. I guess some things cannot be reconciled.

We started dating on the 11th of May 1999. It's been almost nine years, as I write these words. I found her more attractive and enjoyed her company to a greater degree in our latter years, than I did in the early days. I can confidently say that I loved her. Furthermore, I also know what love is. How else could I make the statement "I loved her", if I didn't know what love was? I do find, however, that most people don't have the foggiest about what love actually is, and use the term, as if it's some magical force that they simply *'feel'*. And there lies the problem with love. Most of us merely feel it. We don't know why we feel it, where it comes from and most importantly don't know how to sustain it. I will come, shortly, to my journey through the rabbit hole in discovering love, what it is, how it comes and what we can do to sustain this illusive feeling. But before that, I should start somewhere more appropriate.

Asheeta had depth. She still does. Her depth wasn't visible outwardly. In fact it still isn't. Outwardly, she comes across rather average, typical and if I were to be daring, even a little shallow. She makes appoint of coming across this way to the world outside. She is multilayered, as are most of us. The challenge we face is de-layering people so that we can see where their emotive energies originate from and how they travel up to the surface. The first time our eyes met, as I hugged Aarti, I felt her depth. I saw it. Her eyes reveal things that often even she isn't aware of. I often teach on my courses, body language, and I make a point of emphasising on the eyes of the other person. I believe, as Ernst Hemingway did, that *our eyes are the gateway to our soul*. Our eyes are like elevator shafts that run right the way across a huge skyscraper. Through the eyes we can go to any number of layers of anyone's personality. We can effectively see how high the skyscraper is by looking down it. As I explored the depths of her eyes, in the summer of '99, I realised that right at the bottom of the shaft there had been a fire. It had wreaked havoc inside her. The fire had burnt itself out, but the damage had been done, at least in the deeper layers of her personality. I could make out the damage, but could not know much else until she allowed me to journey deep within her psyche. This was enough for me to connect. I felt an instant affinity towards her, because I knew that deep within me, there was a fire that was still raging, and it was causing huge damage to my towering personality. I found a metaphysical commonality with her. It would be this simple, yet powerful, observation that would form the bedrock of our early relationship.

We spent almost everyday of that unusually long summer vacation, together, which always lies between college and university. Back then, as I have begun to do again, would run between five and eight miles every morning. I would be out of bed by six, brush my teeth, put on a pair of running shorts, have a quick glass of water, feel the cool liquid trickle down my body and walk out the front door to begin my run. It was the same every morning.

Asheeta, had wanted to come running with me, and I'd always said no, because running is my time. I would often use the phrase *me, myself and I*, to describe when I wanted to do anything by myself. But now that the exams were over and the long summer lay ahead, I thought it might provide an excellent opportunity to get to know this seductress. I remember running the four miles or so, the distance between her house and mine. I ran up the quite London road, until I climbed the hill to the top and turned left onto Evington Road. This road had always brought a sense of vulnerability to my heart, as Dillip's rivals all controlled the streets here. Evington was pretty much like Belgrave. Rows upon rows of terraced housing, people living on low incomes or on benefits. There was however, a distinct feel about Evington. It housed an altogether different community than my own. Belgrave was predominately working class Hindu and white, whereas; Evington was Muslim and Afro-Caribbean. This created, even at six in the morning, a distinct atmosphere around the neighbourhood where Asheeta had been brought up.

As I ran down Evington road for a mile or so, I came across Kedlestone Road on my left. I ran until I reached a great big pub. Asheeta had told me that she lived opposite it. It was 6.20am, I was ten minutes early. I sat myself down on the steps leading up to the entrance of the pub, and helped myself to a few gulps of much needed water. As I felt the water cool my insides, I saw someone walk out of Asheeta's front door. It was her mother. That was the first time I had seen her. I was a distance away; she hadn't noticed me sitting opposite. She came out of the front door and got into the car parked in front. As she reversed out, I remember my observations. She appeared much taller than Asheeta, which surprised me a little. Her general outwardly appearance came across exactly as I would have expected to have been, totally based on what Asheeta was like. Moments passed on by. I waited for a full fifteen minutes before Asheeta yelled from her upstairs window,

"Hello Sanvik. Sorry I can't come with you because my mum said no."

I replied with a casual "ok", put the lid of my water bottle back on and started running in the direction of home. It didn't annoy me in the slightest bit that Asheeta had made me run four needless miles. This was so, not because I enjoyed the agony long distance running can cause, but because my intension was to get to know Asheeta a little better. And I had done exactly that. I got to know something about her world that I had no knowledge of previously. Throughout that summer, I learnt a great deal about her, and as an exchange, I undid the curtain hiding my mind, giving her clear sight into my consciousness.

From the rabbit hole, I saw the world differently. I was not only sensitive to the physical, as most are, but I perceived the physical from the filter of the metaphysical. Just as I had come to understand death, through living it, I had come to realise life by reflecting upon the abyss.

When Asheeta and I first began our ongoing journey together, I was in the process of realising love. Love as experienced in the physical world is *feelings orientated*; in the intellectual tunnels through which love is delivered, we can actually understand its nature. We can come to grips with the soul of love. And when we come face to face with the soul of something we instantly live it, and by living it, we realise it, and through the process of realisation, we become one with it. In the intellectual tunnels, we become love, just as I had become death, during Vikas's funeral service. Even though realisation can be instantaneous in terms of time, to practice and live by it is an altogether different proposition. It is a layered process, something that I will explain presently, and I believe it goes something like this: deep *ignorance is the lowest forms of all existence, followed by Hedonistic tendencies, where most of us dwell, a little further up the consciousness ladder is the awareness that there is a 'greater reality' in which we exist, but nevertheless, are still driven by our senses, and from this point, there is a great leap to the next plane, where, we actually learn to live in the greater reality rather than the lesser one. In other words, we learn to view, feel and live through the rabbit hole, rather than seeing the rabbit hole, through merely the physical life.* This may have come across a little "sketchy", but I hope to explain myself through using my relationship with Asheeta as a reflective device, something that will practically show you what I mean. It is worth pointing out at this point that it would be prudent to hold back any judgement of what it is that I am about to say, until you have read the whole exposition.

Firstly, we must come to grips with what love in essence is. Love is manufactured by us. It is not a magical feeling or something that exists outside of us that we just come across. So, I'd hate to break the hearts of any idealists reading this book, but the notion that *it was love at first sight*, is a crap one! It simply cannot be true in practical terms, and love is a practical reality. If love was a dish, it's a dish best served cold.

This dish is made from certain ingredients, and if cooked in the correct way, love is the outcome. Just as one can make hundreds of different forms of pasta by subtly altering the cooking process, so too, every love, will be cooked according to the different personalities involved. Nevertheless pasta can only be labelled as such if pasta plays the central role. In the same sense then, I will only be highlighting the core, or soul of the dish, that we are discussing, that is love. Furthermore, it is worth noting that the examples I give of the love, created and experienced by me, in our relationship is just one form of such a process. Everyone will have their subtle differences and so the appearance of the dish may seem different, but in essence the heart of it is the same. So what is love?

Love is the feeling generated when we feel 100% content with ourselves. This is a rare feeling indeed, and when we do experience it, it quickly escapes our clutches. The question then manifests itself to how do I become 100% content within my relationship. At this point, one should note that I have used the word relationship. This means that love is something that can be created in any form. It can be between any number of people, objects or even ideas. Contentment arises out of the satisfaction of our needs. Needs by definition are short term. They are often daily or at maximum weekly or monthly. These needs can be physical, emotional or intellectual.

For example, I had a need to be hugged by Asheeta who genuinely cares to understand me. This is a physical need, to satisfy an emotional thirst. My reason to be hugged comes from the fact that I am very stand off-ish with people. I don't like to show much in the way of feelings to people who I don't know or particularly care for. Additionally, I perceive a hug as a moment where one can rest on the other, both physically and emotionally, and I don't like to do either with anyone apart from the people closet to me and those who I know can support me. I may be very close with someone, but if I feel that they are incapable of supporting me, then a hug is not a viable option.

Another example of a short term need is to be made to smile. Asheeta makes me laugh. She was definitely the funny one. Her humour was stupidly funny, and often crude – I loved it. I do so because again, I don't really find too much to laugh at in this world, with the exception of Red Dwarf and Rory Bremner. Furthermore, she made fun of me. I was her victim most of the time. It was never offensive or hurtful, it was mainly about my mannerisms and then taken out of all context to make it funny. I could quite literally sit here all day and list the hundreds of needs Asheeta satisfied, by being herself. And that is where the penny should drop. Asheeta does what she does, not by thinking about it, or by creating a *to-do lists* writing 'make Sanvik laugh', she does it naturally. She satisfied my needs by being herself.

So far I have only illustrated my needs which Asheeta satisfied. But it should be reciprocal in any healthy relationship. Asheeta too, had needs. They were completely different to mine, and yet they were mutual in worth. Take her need to *'off load'* verbally, her daily toils, as an example. Asheeta needed some space or time where she can just talk about what she did that day, and get all those things that upset her off her chest. This was a need that gets satisfied within the confines of our relationship *(at least it used too – remember dear reader the relationship is no more)*. Of course, this need to offload onto others isn't exclusive. She will often have her need satisfied by her younger sister or Aarti. The commonality between all three of Asheeta's 'off-loaders' is that there is a time tested trust, which she shared with all three.

Another need that she had, one which remains strictly in the confines of our relationship was her need for a strong, mentally resilient partner; someone who could take her emotional weight; someone that could satisfy her need to feel pride in her partner. Asheeta craved strength, and furthermore, she needed to feel this strength everyday. I satisfied this quite naturally. I didn't have to do anything, I could be myself and it got taken care of.

Now, let us suppose that I began to soften up, or for whatever reason I could no longer provide the feeling of 'pride' Asheeta needed; what would happen then? Well, potentially one of two things. Either, quite consciously or subconsciously she would find someone else who could give her the sense of pride through strength or she would remain dissatisfied in our relationship, which would naturally result in a build up of emotional frustration. This swell of emotional energy would vent itself sooner or later, often in an uncontrolled manner. The bottom-line we need to remember, is that the feeling of love, would seem like a million miles away!

The next core ingredient to creating love is a shared purpose. The term purpose can sometimes be a little vague. Whereas, needs are short term and are mostly different, yet mutual in worth, purpose is longer term. Furthermore, purpose must not only be mutual but shared. For any relationship to flourish there must be a common end goal in mind, an aim or future that all parties aspire to achieve together. All relationships exist in time, at least until they transcend into the metaphysical plane where transcendental love exists. Transcendental love however, is a topic for another book. We are talking about normal human relationships.

My example would be that Asheeta and I both claim to be academic. But of course in time we did *fall out of love*, and amicably decided to go off on our own way exactly because we didn't share a common purpose. But for the sake of the example, a good few years ago, we enjoyed learning. We encouraged one another to aspire for higher academic achievements. It was due to this shared purpose that we could allow one another as much space as was needed to study. She had just graduated from medical school, for which she needed a great amount of time, and likewise, she had given me days upon days of needed isolation so that I could have written this book.

(The sharpest of you readers would have gathered that Asheeta and I fell out of love while I was writing this book; but don't confuse that with this book being the reason for us separating.)

Another shared purpose we both felt strongly about was our ideal life style. We both intensely desired to be mobile throughout our lives. We never wanted to be bogged down to a mortgage or a job. We both desired to do our bit for developing the third world. Asheeta had strong sentiments about one day developing a hospice for children in India. I too, shared this dream with her. It's a shared purpose that bridges the gap in short term needs between people, and often is nothing more than a shared idea, albeit a powerful and intense one.

The final ingredient in love making *(excuse the two-edged sword)*, is structure. Structure is the mechanism that is geared towards delivering the total satisfaction of mutual needs and a shared purpose. Structure is made out of the invisible *'bits'* that goes on in relationships. It is an internal culture of habits, tastes and routines that all add up to what I call structure. To continue using my ex-relationship with Asheeta as an example, let me share a simple 'bit' of our otherwise complex structure.

No matter how busy we may have been during the day, as long as we were in the same country, we would always either speak to one another on the phone or text each other. The phone call didn't have to be long and often only lasted thirty seconds. Nevertheless, some sort of communication was made. We had this bit of structure from the beginning. This system of texting and ringing grew organically. Whenever, any of us broke this structure, instantly one of our mutual but different needs was left unsatisfied. In my case to hear her voice; and in hers it was her inability that day to off-load.

Whenever, a structure was broken, we'd feel its effects, larger the breakdown of structure, bigger the consequences. I have also found that a large number of relationships breakdown or fail to experience love because of conflicting or irreconcilable sex drives. Often one of the partners is highly sexed while the other is not. The partner that is highly sexed normally ends up repressing his or her feelings for the sake of the relationship. Sexual frustrations develop, and in time are let loose, often uncontrollably and at the cost of the relationship. This is a matter of satisfying needs, in a structured but organic manner. I am not advocating that couples should set aside an hour of day for sex – far from it, what I am saying is that we need to raise our awareness of what is going on within our relationship.

So far I have merely pointed out the three ingredients for producing the elevated feelings of love. Let me go one step further. These are the ingredients, if managed correctly, for sustaining levels of love. Any relationship involving at least one human being, exist in this format. Love is simply when our daily and long term needs are satisfied effortlessly. When this occurs over a period of time, we use the phrase, "I'm falling in love". The challenge is can we stay in love? Just as easily as we have a tendency to fall in love, so, we can equally fall out of it, as I have recently discovered with Asheeta.

Of course, so far, I have been focusing this theory based around the kind of relationship that occurs between lovers. Let me expand our horizon. Let's take the relationship that people have with their mother. People, and especially mothers say, *"I love my child unconditionally and all the time."* To this I would ask something of the order, *"what do you mean love all the time?"* When you are shouting at your teenage daughter because you might have caught her in bed with a forty-five year old man, I seriously doubt that you love her in that instance. We often get confused between our natural programming to care for our offspring, and the attached notion of love.

We are biologically conditioned to care for our children. We can care for them, without ever loving them. This may be a bitter pill for many, but if we look closely, and honestly at what is happening in a great many households, we will find families that are completely out of love, and yet care for one another. What I believe mothers mean when they say, *"I love my children all the time"*, is that they feel a strong biological urge to care and protect them, even at the cost of their own wellbeing. I briefly mentioned earlier, on the issue as to why so many children look for their emotional belonging and love outside the home. The answer is right here – they live in homes which care and provide for them but offer little love, as they have poor relationships with other family members. The relationships are so poor because their needs and shared purpose is not being satisfied. This is patently due to the structural difficulties – in other words, the system of the household; the culture within the home is not effective. The reason why child psychologists often recommend the idea of rules and boundaries for young children is essentially to develop structures, in which their needs can be satisfied, and a shared purpose can be created between the child and parents.

We live with the lineage of time. This inevitably adds complications to managing relationships. The problem with time is that our needs, whether they are physical, emotional or intellectual, are always changing. This is why; people can *grow in love* and also *grow out of it*. At the early stages of any relationship, and it was no different with mine that we want to spend every minute of the day with our new found love.

Essentially, most relationships begin with the physical. We are sexually attracted to our partners, with this sexual attraction comes the need for sex. The early stages of a relationship are often filled with romance *(which is essentially the foreplay leading to sex)* and passion. Emotional attachment is the outcome from the first stage. We become emotionally dependent on the other, due to the deep levels of intimacy developed during the early stages of sexual exploration. This is where problems can arise. Men, generally travel at a much slower pace than women, and so often end up desiring the elongation of the sexual stage, while women would have moved to the emotionally dependent stage. When this tension occurs, both individuals have distinctly different needs. One wants sex as much as before, while the other isn't sex averse, but wants something more, something emotional. If we are sensitive to this fact, then we can use Aristotle's third way; *compromise*.

The one, who is still desiring the elongation of the sex stage, needs to be gradually satisfied, while at the same time he or she, recognise that there must be more than just dry romanticism and sex in the relationship, if it is to last. From the emotional stage, we begin to develop the shared purpose behind the relationship, which is beyond the daily satisfaction of needs. Essentially, this is the intellectual stage of any relationship. This is where people become serious about one another and show signs of long term commitment. When both partners are having their daily needs satisfied on all levels and show signs of a progressing towards a shared purpose, feelings of love will naturally develop.

Hopefully, you have stayed the course through this maze of love. But let's leave the idea of love aside for a moment or two. What about relationships in general? Ninety percent of all the relationships we will have in our lives will dissolve into *nothingness – why is this*? Also, why do we connect with some and build relationships that last a lifetime, and others we just label as friends, often short term, or as work colleagues? Most relationships are only brought into effect to satisfy the basic short term needs of the parties concerned. Once these needs are satisfied or can no longer be provided for, by the people forming the relationship, it will naturally dissolve. As Baz Luhrmann said, in his track, Sunscreen, *"friends will come and go, only a few you should hold onto"*, rather sums up the situation well, I think. Let me share a few examples of what I mean from my own life.

I am no longer in regular touch with anyone that I was friends with at university. The occasional text saying 'happy new year' is far as it goes. Yet, at university we used to spend great amounts of time in one another's company. We even lived together for two or three years and got on really well. Yet as soon as university came to its eventual conclusion, and we all got jobs, the relationships with all of them gradually dissolved. People often say to me, it's due to the lack of time that relationships dissolve, or the gap in geography – both would be true in some respects, but the underlying truth is that these people no longer offered you satisfaction of your needs and in all probability vice versa.

Several things happened when we left university. First, each of our needs, in a short space of time, radically changed. Second, we went onto different things. I went onto continue my education, while others moved back home to look for jobs. This naturally created a new set of needs within each of us. As soon as our needs changed, and subconsciously realised that we could no longer offer each other what we needed, we gradually drifted apart. There is an exception to this however. And that is when one has developed an emotional bond, beyond the merely physical, in other words a shared purpose. The only person, with whom I had developed this, was with a guy called Dain.

He and I shared a great amount of synergy. We both were travelling through the rabbit hole. We each saw life from a uniquely different perspective from the others with whom we had lived. This shared purpose is something that we both still have. Yet, we have no need to maintain a regular relationship, as we do not need one another on a daily or even monthly basis. One would occasionally ring the other; we would spend hours talking about the spiritual and metaphysical, once a year we may even meet up and share a coffee together. This is the extent of our *close* relationship. We no longer have mutual needs that the other can satisfy, but we do have a shared purpose, and this keeps us in touch infrequently. The reason why, this relationship has maintained its closeness, even though we hardly see, or speak to one another is due to our mutual acknowledgement, of exactly what it is that we are both striving for, and how the other can assist the one, and vice versa.

I have heard people often make comments like, "I don't know why we didn't stay in touch, I would have liked to", or "I made so much effort with them at the beginning and they just couldn't be bothered to meet up, so we just drifted."

I hear these sorts of comments over and over again from people who, for whatever reason didn't manage to keep in touch with someone that they would have liked too. The truth of the matter is that whereas, these people had identified a regular need, whether it was physical or emotional; the other party who didn't stay in contact had no such need. And hence we have a mismatch in needs, and when needs are not mutual, there cannot be a sustainable relationship. Resentment is often the product, when a relationship breaks down, due to a mismatch of needs and an uncommon purpose at the heart of it. The one, who is having their needs satisfied often, but not always, becomes resentful towards the other who had no longer valued the relationship in the same light. The question you're probably thinking of right about now, is this may be all very true, but how on earth can I identify what the needs are, whether we have a shared mutual purpose and in what kind of structure does our relationship exist? Sadly, there is no black and white answer to this, and to develop this awareness of human relationships takes a great deal of time.

There are however, several signposts that I would like to highlight, ones that I think will act as prerequisites to mastering human relationships. These consist of basic skills in human communication. We must become sensitive to ourselves and others. We must learn to primarily observe the bare reality that presents itself to us everyday without judgement and without the veil of emotions that stems from a premature judgement. When we learn to see the bare facts for what they really are, only then can we begin to highlight our needs and the needs of others. I would say it is much easier to highlight ones own needs and purpose in any given relationship, if we are sensitive to ourselves. To understand the needs of others however, takes a little greater awareness.

Firstly, we need to develop the art of pure simple observation. Second, we need to learn to listen and try and understand where the other person's words are originating from. In other words, listen to what they say, but also be sensitive to why they are saying it. The highlighting, of the "why" will take you to the source of their words. Third, we need to become more sensitive to the daily routines, habits, greetings, language used, and traditions and so on and on, which we share with other people. Only when we actively begin to develop these other aspects, what are commonly labelled as people skills or interpersonal intelligence, will we be in a position to acquire enough information, to identify the skeletal framework of our relationships.

Asheeta and I rarely had a cross word to say to one another. I nearly always experienced the feelings of love with her because my daily physical, emotional and intellectual needs were being satisfied, effortlessly. There were occasional lapses and we stopped loving one another for a short time; one of our structural pillars to our relationship was that we would not rest until our disagreement had been resolved, so that both of us by end of the day felt happier. We never left an argument or left the other feeling upset, we would take as long as it took to resolve any issues, even if that meant giving up things, in order to spend sufficient time in resolving our problems. In short we never walked away from a problem, no matter how little or large. What this meant, was that we always *repaired* the structure of our relationship as soon as possible to ensure that we were still satisfying one another's daily needs, which in the long term should surmount to moving towards a greater shared purpose. *Of course that shared common purpose never materialised.*

Nevertheless, for the sake of the book, I think there is much that can be said about relationships when using my experiences with Asheeta as a reflective tool. What usually occurs is that if she had upset me, I would feel it first and foremost. I would then analyse and clarify what it was that I felt? I became sensitive to myself. Then once I had clearly identified what it was that I felt, I would highlight its cause. This is where I would often, quite literally, get pen and paper, and jot down which needs had been unsatisfied.

I always attempt to highlight two aspects. Firstly, which needs had remained dissatisfied, and on which plane do they exist; for example, was I suffering from a dissatisfaction of physical needs, had Asheeta not given the attention she usually gave, was it an emotional dissatisfaction, in that I hadn't been made to relax and be humoured by Asheeta in a long while; or was it intellectual, in that we hadn't had one of our semi moral, semi philosophical debates in a while. Once I had highlighted potential problem areas, I began to immediately understand which parts of the structure had been breached or inefficient in delivering these needs. Note that I focused on the shared structure that our relationship existed in; *I'm not focusing on Asheeta*. The failure of the structure usually meant that we needed to spend some time together focusing on the issues at hand. Experience had taught me that the loss of love was usually down to both of us straying quite innocently from the bounds of the structure, or that an inter-connected relationship had influenced our *love space*. This leads me onto the next and final issue with managing relationships.

We are all interconnected. Every relationship we have is somehow overlapping on another. There is never a case where a relationship can exist in isolation. At least, I haven't come across one yet. A little logic, tells me that I am never likely to come across one either. It is worth while to understand how it is that other relationships can play a significant role in the one that is the most important to you. This can get rather complicated and a little tedious, so I will try and share this with you, through a few examples.

Asheeta and I had a relationship that is expansive. Many hundreds of people were affected by our relationship, to varying degrees on a daily basis; most probably they didn't even know it. In turn, our relationship had affected by hundreds of different people, on a daily basis, in tiny little ways that were often insignificant, but sometimes could be devastatingly important. Take a very simple situation; I run my own business. I have many clients who require my attention as soon as possible; it's the nature of a Consultancy firm specialising in understanding people. If they rang at a time when I'd be in the middle of my one minute daily conversation with Asheeta, then sorry to say, they'd have to wait. If I was to cut Asheeta off, in our sacred time, then I would have broken the structure, and both would be adversely affected. If this happened as a one off, the damage would be inconsequential. But, if I regularly began to put my clients before Asheeta, during our one minute calls, then *a well* of frustration and dejection would be building up inside her, which in all honesty, she would probably repress, until one day, suddenly she flipped out and vented her stored negative emotions, disproportionately. In short then, my business relationships are directly influenced by the structure Asheeta and I lived in, and vice versa, we were affected by my business relations.

A deeper, rather more complex and significant example is that of the influence, our relationship had, on my relationship with my own mother. At the time when I met Asheeta, my mum and I barely spoke. She did what any mother would do for her child, she cooked, did my laundry and generally made sure that I wasn't starving or in any particular physical discomfort. Beyond that, however there was very little of anything else. There definitely was not any love involved. Soon after Vikas's death, all our previous efficient structures had gone into meltdown. She had little idea of what I was going through, and the same could be said of me, in that I didn't or wouldn't grasp her mental state. The deepest forms of insecurity had overwhelmed her. Her eldest son, who was her great hope for another wise normal future, had died. Her much younger son, had completely gone off the rails, at least from her perception, and to some extent, she still thinks I'm a little off the mark, in comparison to where she'd like me to go. I think she would have preferred if I had actually become an Aerospace Engineer, instead of gallivanting off to study 'wishy washy' philosophy. But that is another story.

My point is that the sudden end of a relationship between Vikas and I, Vikas and mum, and Vikas and dad, had resulted in this catastrophic demise. Our loving warm family had become a cold, barren landscape, where once love grew in abundance. It was an unintended side effect of the relationship I had with Asheeta that planted the seeds of love once again in my home.

Healing Scars

Asheeta had a wonderful relationship with her mum. It may be surprising now, but back then in the summer of '99, she had been the first person I had ever come across that genuinely always got on with at least one of their parents. I observed for months, how Asheeta and her mum connected so well. I had become quite an expert on people watching by then; I was picking up all the tiny movements that were going on between them. I noticed that most of it was completely sub-conscious. Neither of them was aware of what they were doing. What made it easier was that Asheeta's younger sister, on whom I will come onto later, had a rather contrasting relationship. One always felt a divide, a gap between them. This gap has somewhat closed in recent years, but back then it was quite apparent to anyone who was sensitive enough. I noticed the subtlety of Asheeta's actions. In order to make sense of what it is that I'm exploring, it is worth making a quick comparison between my mother and Asheeta's.

I found there to be striking similarities and some odd differences. Asheeta's mum, Mina, is a few years younger than my mother, but they both come from similar childhoods. Both came from an orthodox Hindu family with strict, often claustrophobic structures and traditions. Whereas, my mother had escaped the orthodoxy *(and created her own new orthodoxy)* by marrying my father who was a liberal in the very sense of the word, Mina had no such opportunity. She married into another strict narrow family, in which her early marital life was deeply unhappy. My mother's life had been free, but challenging, due to the dysfunctional nature of her new family. Both suffered hardships. Both had been toughened by the processes of life. I found both women to be resilient and mentally deep. Both believed in mindless superstitions or as I often like to call it; treat it with the respect that it deserves – *mumbo jumbo*. Both were stubborn and could be extremely judgemental, and often what can be best described as "snappy". Both were pessimists, they always saw the danger first. Both had a similar approach to bringing up their children, in that they each allowed plenty of space for their children to aspire, in any direction that they felt was suitable.

There were also some odd differences. I think they originate from the fact that my mother found whatever positive energy and security she needed, from my father, whereas, Mina got it all from her children. Asheeta's dad had quite an unusual personality, in that he was nice enough, but he kept quite a visible distance with his wife. He also lacked, and still does, simple communication skills; he is an introvert to a rare extent. Mina by nature is an extrovert, albeit a repressed one. What this meant was that until recently, Mina felt extremely lonely in her life. She couldn't live the way she wanted, and there was a growing urge deep within her to begin living. Mina suffered from a deep sense of insecurity that only loneliness can bring. This insecurity has meant that she lacks confidence, which results in her being a *repressed pessimistic extrovert*.

My mother on the other hand had my father. They loved one another deeply and lived for, and through each others existence. My mother was an introvert who my father had made, quite by accident, a semi extrovert. She had lived the life she wanted when my father and she were young. She wasn't deeply demanding in that sense, and was quite content with her lot. All she wanted was dad. Her insecurities crashed inside her mind on the day Vikas had died, and had grown ever since, because of *me, myself and I*. There lay the difference that created all other differences between what are now my two mothers.

Asheeta managed her relationship with her mother through playfulness. She never took anything too seriously with what her mum said when she was "snappy". Asheeta laughed, at, and with her mum all day long. It was a playful relationship full of hugs and caresses. Another aspect of their relationship, was that when Asheeta had done anything to upset her mum, her mum would just come out and say it, whereas, with other members of the family it was not always so. I wondered for months as to why this was? Eventually, I realised it was due to Asheeta always being completely open with her, which was reciprocated in turn. With the other family members, there was always a communicatory gap, which created unnecessary distance, and so her mum would just keep things in until they got the better of her. Asheeta, on the other hand, when her mum was about to explode with anger, would simply find a way of allowing her to vent life's frustrations out in a constructive way. By constructive, Asheeta usually meant, going shopping, or for a facial with her mum. And it worked; her mum would come back feeling refreshed, or at worst a little less angry. But above all else I noticed the power of human touch, to make someone feel secure. All I did was to transfer what I had learnt, through observations and try to apply it on my own mother.

Asheeta had noticed within the first few months that my mother and I were a world apart. This affected her. To this day, I'm a little unsure as to why this was so. Nevertheless, it did. We spent many an afternoon, strolling Watermead and Evington Parks talking about our mums. I knew I was going to find it difficult to develop a 'touching' relationship with her. At the back of my mind, I also knew that I was going to university in a few months, and so the gap I would get from mum, would be useful. It could mean that I would have more of a reason, to hug her and rest my head on her shoulders as she watched TV, rather than to randomly go and hug there and then. In all probability, if I had done that, she'd accuse me of being drugged up.

Instead, it was a gradual, conscious effort to hug her, to hold her hand, to rest my head on her lap, to laugh off most of her hugely inaccurate judgements about my life, to play fight with her and occasionally, as Asheeta had taught me, to imitate her; there by showing her how she appeared to others. It took the best part of four years to slowly develop a loving relationship with mum. It took a while, but it was worth it. She is still insecure, not about my values and education, but about my desire to become self employed. It is an insecurity that is coated in mutual respect and care, rather than worry and despair. This is how emotions and its resulting actions can influence other relationships we may be in. On my courses, I often spend considerable time on mapping out, how, and which relationships impinge productively on our most important ones.

A significant number of people have now been on my human dynamics courses, where we cover managing relationships. It has been pleasing to know that many of the people who took up the course in a mood of scepticism have become ardent supporters of this theory. It has radically, for the better, changed their lives. Many of them have excelled professionally; others personally; and a few even with their children. I am often touched by some of the emails I receive from students; the before and after state of some of their relationships is quite amazing. There is nothing really to it. The problem isn't external. The challenge of managing our relationships isn't outside. It is within. When we raise our inner sensibilities; when we raise our own consciousness and live in a field of greater awareness, then the world will fall into its place. As Mahatma Gandhi once said, a phrase that has been far too often used, *"be the change that you want to see in the world."*

Love isn't a rational emotion. Love is transcendental, something which cannot be verbalised. It is something that makes life worth holding onto when the darkness surrounds us. It is this irrational force that I have tried to conceptualise through the rabbit hole, and have reflected upon it by using my own life experiences. When we follow these loose cooking instructions; are brave enough to experiment, fail and try again, you will find the balance that is right for you, and love is what will ooze out from you onto others. A final point on the force of love is that it's not an end in itself. Far from it!

When we achieve the elevated feelings of love consistently, we will begin to pour this excessive love into the environment around us. We will smile at strangers, who will often be compelled to smile back; we will help the less fortunate; we will give without expecting any sort of return. Love, I believe is one of a few gateways to the transcendental, the greater reality that underlies this one. It is where I believe rabbit holes lead too; it is where the intellectual tunnels end.

Where we leave intellectualism, we have to leave behind out language too, and where there is no language, how can there be thinking? Without thinking, there will be emptiness; we will feel clear, our minds will experience a silence that is unparalleled, and through this silence, finally, we will arrive at bliss. It is this bliss that I seek, and ultimately what we all quietly want; as Thomas Aquinas said, *"only angels can bless us with bliss."* I have been lucky; lucky enough to have been blessed.

On Meditation

I began practicing daily meditations when I was seventeen. As I have grown in spiritual and philosophical truths, my meditations have become more consistent and clear. It was at seventeen that I began to realise the absurdity of believing or not believing in God. This was my *fourth re-forging* experience. The tunnels showed something that is right there, in front of us all, and yet we do not see it. It took a long while, to realise why we couldn't see it, and finally, as it is with all the important discoveries of our lives, it just came to me. I realised it. I felt it, the transcendental fact of the idea of God.

I have already said that the transcendental cannot be spoken of, as it lies beyond our rational thinking faculties, and our language is quite incapable of doing justice to the subtlety of the highest plane. The clues of the absurdity lie in our own language. To say *"I believe in God"*, or that *"I do not believe in God"* is *equally foolish*. Do we say that "I believe in air?" Do we say that "I believe I am writing these words?" We do not because it is fact. It is fact that there is air; I breathe it; I know it to be there physically; I know it intellectually and I feel the consequences of it at every moment. Similarly it would be absurd to say that "I believe I am writing these words", for it is a fact. Where there is fact, there is no need for belief. It is when our minds run out of facts that we create beliefs, and beliefs by definition are not fact. It is obvious that truth is that which is fact, and that which is fact is truth. So where is the room for beliefs? I *believe* there is none, at least when it comes to the matter of God.

The challenge, as I realised when I was seventeen, was to change the question. Without asking the right question, we will never discover the correct answer. If God is fact, then it would have to be experiential. To go on mere beliefs would be futile. For me to *'know'* the truth, I have to be able to *feel* that truth. The intellectual tunnels have the ability to take us beyond the limitations of the body; they even have the abilities, if we become conscious enough, to take us to the realm of the transcendental. The thing we must know is that when we experience the transcendental, we can never talk about our experiences on the physical plane, simply because our language isn't capable. So I have no intention of talking about God. I merely wish to talk about the journey that took me to the edge of the physical, and onto the gateway of the subtle reality. Beyond that as Wittgenstein has already told us, in his concluding statement in the Logico Tractatus, *"Whereof one cannot speak, thereof one must remain silent."*

I have already spoken about the nature of the intellectual tunnels. When I was fifteen, I had fallen in the hole, unintentionally. By seventeen, I was beginning to figure out where these invisible holes lay. I found that the easiest way to enter the tunnels was to spend some time meditating. To give myself some space everyday; to think, until thinking ends, this is the safe passage into the tunnels.

At seventeen I realised that something was not quite right about the position of theists or atheists, both of which I had already taken. It often works as dialectic; like a pendulum swing. We have so much potential energy at the beginning that we swing from one extreme to another, only to realise that there is a limitation to this extreme as well, so with less energy than before we swing back and forth. Finally, we end at Aristotle's middle way. We end at rest. Something similar can be said about my inner quest to discover God. I began as a believer, and then swung to become a non believer, and then at seventeen I began my swing back the other way. For several years I went from one side to the other, and with each swing I felt myself to be getting closer to reality. The journey I am about to superficially map out is something that took place over four years. I say superficially because if I wrote about in any great detail this would become a two volume epic. Furthermore, I do not intend to discuss the viability of God as that would be a futile point to write on. Instead I just want to share my experiences of mediation and what it is; why I did it; and what did I get out of it. The question of God will only be secondary and a reflective device rather than a core area of discussion.

Meditation is a practise. It's something that we actually *do*. There are also different forms and depths to mediations. Meditations are the rabbit holes I described in chapter two of this book. They lead to the greater reality which lies beneath our physical universe; beyond space and time. Meditations are thoughtless. There is no thinking involved. This is not some theoretical, abstract philosophical concept; it is a fact; it is experiential. There is no belief at work here, it is truth. The first time I came across meditation, I must have been very young.

Within Hinduism meditation has always been the greatest path to the discovery of truth. I had heard my grandfather talk about great Rishis or holy men he had seen in the mountains of India, who meditated and had developed magical powers, something which, I had always been sceptical about, at least the latter part. I remember the first time I sat down to mediate, it was quite a waste of time, but necessary, I think in hindsight. I sat down exactly as I had seen people do it in books and on TV. I closed my eyes, waited for a few minutes and expected something to happen. Something did happen, but to my frustration it wasn't what I had wanted.

I had imagined that I would be taken up to some magical state of awareness where I would begin to see things for what they really were. No such thing happened. I sat there thinking. My mind raced. It went from here to there, thinking about everything that I was consciously trying not to think about. After a few minutes, I begin to feel itchy. So I scratched here, and then there. I became restless. Next my back began to hurt, and next my knees and ankles were getting sore sitting on my bedroom floor with crossed legs. I became ultra sensitive to time. I began to believe that I had been sitting in one place for ages, and that I had been thinking so much that my brain was physically getting tired. When I couldn't bare the restlessness anymore, I uncrossed my legs and stretched them out before me, with a huge sigh of relief, as if I'd just done hundred press-ups. I looked up to see the time. My eyes took a few minutes to adjust to the light. I felt a little light-headed and to my utter shock and devastation, I had sat there for all of ten minutes.

The truth of that first experience of meditation was that I had spent ten minutes waiting for something to happen. I thought about the most trivial things during that time, and I felt anything but enlightened. I realised that when I closed my eyes and it wasn't to fall asleep, my mind became hyperactive. My mind was a young child high on Caffeine. At the same time as becoming hyperactive, it also became 'scatty', to the point that it would leap from one thought to the next in, what appeared as random leaps; the frequency at which it did this as soon as my eyes closed was duly noted. I wasn't one for quitting, and I persisted with daily attempts for the next few months. I hankered with different sitting positions, in different places and at different times of the day. Nothing seemed to really help. My mind remained hyperactive and scatty as before. I took out books from the library on meditation. I found most to be really abstract and full of useful passages to use for poetry, but very little to use practically.

Eventually, it hit me, while I was watching a game of amateur football. I had gone to watch a friend play. The game had already started by the time I had arrived. He was playing on the right wing, and so was close to the touchline where I stood. I tried several times to grab his attention. He just ran past me as if I wasn't there. Initially I was rather annoyed at his impoliteness, and then it occurred to me by watching him on and off the ball, that he was totally fused into the game. *He was the game.* He wasn't any longer playing the game, he was it. I pondered on this notion for a while and then it occurred that there was no gap between him and the game, in fact he had become the game. He was so fused with it that nothing else mattered; the world beyond the game had melted away. I was quite literally not on the same wavelength as *he* was. I wondered. I stood there watching him, and only him. His every movement, his every breadth and the drop of every eye lid had a sense of oneness with the game. Watching him took me back to when I played football competitively. I realised then that I too had been in that frame of mind where nothing else mattered, nothing else even existed. There was only football. There wasn't even an '*I*'; there was only football. The 'I' had melted into football. Those were the best kind of games, and one always left feeling elevated spiritually. *Was this meditation? Was my friend on the right wing meditating? If so, what type of meditation was this? Was it the same as when people in books sat still for hours?*

    As the final whistle blew, and all the players went around shacking hands grudgingly, I walked over in the direction of my meditating friend.

    "Hey, Sanvik, how are you mate, how's it going?" he asked, in his usual chirpiness.

    "Well", I replied.

    After the game we went for a coffee at a small dingy rundown café. I spoke to him for hours about the game. To my surprise he was rather forthcoming with my abstract, *airy fairy* questions. I soon noticed that he was struggling to communicate some of the subtle points that I could see he had experienced during the game. He would start explaining himself, then stop suddenly, think, and then say, "Well you get my point".

    To this I would reply, "No, I don't; carry on", forcing him to keep trying.

    During our conversation I could see a visual change taking place within his eyes. My questioning him, about the game was raising his own self awareness, and this in turn was rekindling his inner spirit. I had begun to realise that he was never going to accurately depict his experiences during that game, not due to any lack of ability, but rather due to the fact that the transcendental cannot be clearly communicated, at least through language. This had been the realisation that I had needed to further my explorations on meditations.

I began to experiment. The next morning, instead of trying to sit in silence on my bedroom floor, I decided to go running. I ran to my college and back. It must have been around seven miles in total. The first few were a struggle, intellectually speaking. As I got into my usual rhythm, I was tentatively searching for the rabbit hole; the moment where one becomes thoughtless; the moment where one leaves time and space. I ran and ran, yet my mind continued to think. I was focusing on my physical hardship, and then I began to daydream. I began to think about my friends, and a soft guilt began to rise up within, due to the fact that I was missing my lectures for this experiment, which was badly letting me down. One should bear in mind that I was still only seventeen, and in the midst of my *'Dillip'* experiences. I hadn't as yet met any Angels and hadn't begun my academic quest. That came a few months later, after the death of *Frankenstein's creation*.

Months went by, and by now I had ran plenty; still with little to show for it, at least transcendentally. *The good doctor's monster had gone into the abyss.* I had suffered mentally as well as physically. I had been on my long walk to Milton Keynes and had just met Asheeta. I was still trying to capture the moment when I fell through the rabbit holes; it was happening frequently enough, but I was never in control of it. I would be in the middle of some daily trivial act, and suddenly *'BANG',* I had realised something beyond. I was growing philosophically at an exponential rate, but couldn't understand the forces behind the growth. I was convinced that meditation would be my path to controlling my realisations. As it was with most things in my life, it just happened.

Asheeta and I had been walking hand in hand at Watermead Park, on the outskirts of the city, near a village called Syston. It was the autumn of '99. The park had quietened down; the summer crowds were safely back in their caves, preparing for the winter. There was a serene lake with a gravel path running all the way around it. As we walked, I remember the touch of her soft palm as it rested in my hands. She was talking about her childhood and recalling some of her pivotal episodes, or as I have called it, the prologue to her life; I starred in front, listening intently. I absorbed her every word, I heard her every pause, and felt her anguish, as well as her joy. Her memories had become mine. I felt her spirit let loose. It fused with mine. At that moment there was no Asheeta and I, there was only us. The separation between us had dissolved. I felt what she felt, and she knew it. Our bodies mirrored what our spirits did. We were close; we were emotionally one, intellectually still; and spiritually connected. It was then that I had finally saw the depth of her spirit. Her eyes had shown me the depth of the elevator shaft, but now I was actually travelling up it. Her words were transcendental. I was being shown each level of her personality and its corresponding forging moment. Soon, her words were not heard. She was still talking but I was no longer on the plane of language and emotions. I had surpassed it; I needed no words; I didn't have to listen anymore; I knew; I knew transcendentally. *I was not listening to Asheeta, because I was living Asheeta.* I was beginning for the first time ever to realise another person. I had fallen yet again through the rabbit hole and into the tunnels without having expecting it.

It was here that I sussed out where I had been going astray in my exploration of meditation. For months now, I was looking for the doorway; I was expecting to find it, and that had been the blindfold which had restricted me. I noticed that every time I fell into the rabbit hole, I had no expectation; it just happened. With the football game, which had been months earlier, it had been the same; I unexpectedly realised what meditation was. And now, just as then, I realised why I hadn't been able to consciously do so. The problem, I realised was that I was expecting, I had desire, and where there is a rational, intellectual will, no rabbit holes could emerge. The meditations that I "desired" would remain unreachable as long as I "wanted" them.

This is quite a strange notion. It is slightly paradoxical. On the one hand we meditate for a reason, and on the other, if you have a reason you cannot meditate. So the challenge that we face when we meditate is not to have any conscious reason for doing so. As soon as you develop a reason, the meditative experience will escape you. But then why would anyone want to meditate for no reason? This has been an unanswered question, due to the fact that it is nonsensical. Once we understand what meditation is, the question as to the why, will naturally disappear.

Meditations are the medium to experience the subtle greater reality that exists. Meditation is the way to the transcendental. The experience of the transcendental is always the same. I had experienced it with death, with life, mathematics, football and Asheeta, amongst many other things. In all these realisations, there was a similarity. At the level of the transcendental, there is no *'I'*, and there is definitely no *'it'*. The gap between me and the other disappears. I become it, and *it is me*. Through *it* becoming me, I realise the fullness of *it*. For that moment, while we are in the tunnels, we no longer experience a fragmented reality, we feel a unified whole between the subject and object, or in other words, between I and it. The *'it'* can be anything. When there is no physical or psychological gap between things, we experience the interconnectedness of the world. We realise that we are but a fragment of the whole and at the transcendental level all things are one.

The challenge that lay before me was how could I meditate? I knew that as soon as I would make the conscious decision to sit down and meditate or go for a run, I would fail in my endeavour. I was unable to answer this question for quite literally years. During my second year at university I had stopped attempting to meditate altogether. I just allowed it to happen. It was by discovering and understanding the writings of others, the likes of Plato, Freud, Jung and Krishnamurti that I eventually came to answering the question: *how can I do something without desiring the fruits of that activity beforehand?* In other words, how could I bring myself to meditate when the very conscious decision to do it would block my progress? The depth of meditations eluded me for many years, but it finally did 'click'; it was an unforgettable realisation and shall share later on.

People had often said that girls would distract me from all the things I should have been concentrating on; mainly academics. And these people were right; girls had indeed distracted me. Asheeta however, had a completely opposite effect. When I had met her I had already realised what mathematics was, and had quickly fallen in love with it. I was studying for vast amounts of time every day. I was spending hours musing about physics and the equations of mechanics. People feared that Asheeta would once again distract and pull me away from this newly found love of numbers. No such thing occurred. Asheeta's presence in my life actually motivated me. The extra motivation came from the fact that she was driven and ambitious. She was smart, and not just pretty. She worked hard. She was focused to the point that she knew she wanted top grades in her A-Levels. I was further inspired by the fact that my presence didn't seem to bother her in the slightest bit, as far as studying was concerned. I was surprised by this. I had found that the early stages of a relationship are always most absorbing. Not with Asheeta. We automatically knew when it was appropriate to spend time together and how much. There was a maturity in her that wasn't usually present in people when they are that age. It was great. She was self-regulating for both of us. I liked it. It gave me the sensation of freedom and empowerment.

Another aspect that Asheeta deeply influenced was my sense of living. In the early months, I had noticed a new *sense of living* growing deep within me. Prior to Asheeta, I hadn't liked life very much, and especially disliked people; I had thought of them to be deeply ignorant and immensely simplistic. Asheeta was beginning to give me a brighter view of life. She did this not by talking, but by showing. She was joy. She was someone who was completely unaware of the rabbit hole and the intellectual tunnels, yet had suffered greatly, at least emotionally, and still had exuberance. Her positive view of the world was beginning to influence me, and this mixed with my already growing vision of change would create a drive in me that to this day burns strong, and I foresee it doing so, for the rest of my life. The drive of change and the idea of a positive world would soon fuse to create, a Leadership Academy, take me to the presidency of the youth wing of a major political party and would help me create a new business model that I would one day fulfil. But above all else Asheeta was the *'Angel of Luck'*.

Luck comes in Gangs

Without ever saying so, but instead showing it, Asheeta had shown me glimpses of the man I could become. I no longer had to run away from life, but I could confront it, change it and above all live it. I believe anybody who prospers in any activity has to have had some luck. But what is luck? Luck, *I believe*, is that which we so desperately need without knowing as such. It's something that was completely out of our hands and yet had huge influence in the direction of our lives. Luck can be good or bad. We all experience it. I know I have. And all my luck seemed to come in gangs, one after another, in the summer of '99.

My first bit of luck came in the form of a modelling contract. *Yves Saint Lauren*, or YSL for short, was looking for a young 'ethnic' man to model their range of sun glasses that were targeted at people aged eighteen to twenty nine. YSL used a modelling agency which happened to have an office in Leicester. Apparently YSL wanted a 'non model looking model', someone that would represent their customer's aspirations to look rugged, yet smart. Even though YSL are a huge name in the superficial industries, this particular contract was relatively small.

The lady in charge of sourcing this model happened to have a son at the college which I attended. She must have come to a parents evening and saw a picture of the college football team. It was in this picture, that she saw me. She asked the receptionist, if she could get my details, to which, one can only assume that she was refused. The next day, this lady came back to college to see the principal. She must have said the right thing and shown the appropriate amount of cleavage, because she got my details. Effectively, she had got the principal to break the data protection act. While she had been seducing the principal, an act which I cannot prove, I was busy trying to come to grips with integration, in mathematics. It must have been around lunch time when the phone rang. I wasn't going to pick it up; whoever it was could wait and leave a message at the bleep. By late afternoon, I had decided to call it quits with integration. I walked over to the phone expecting to hear a message for dad. It was brief but direct. I remember my first reaction was that one of the lads had convinced a girl to leave that message for me, in the hope that I'd believe it, gallivant over to the agency, where they would meet me at the front door, and laugh themselves to death! I had no intention of killing anybody, so I ignored it.

Luck, when you choose to ignore it, can be persistent. Moment's later mum stumbled in through the front door, after her daily toils. As usual she made her way to the phone and heard all the messages. As I came down from my bedroom, mum didn't say anything apart from "Jai Shree Krishna".

I had come down to have my afternoon tea. It's a ritual that mum and I still have. Our afternoon teas are crucial in our relationship. It allows me to spend at least fifteen minutes with her everyday. As I loudly crunched my way through the first Bourbon, mum highlighted that there was a message for me. I immediately dismissed it and said that it was probably a few friends playing a prank. She thought about it for a moment and then asked if I'd even bothered to ring the number that was left. Again I dismissed it with a wave of a hand. I think this annoyed her, and her annoyance took me by surprise. "You could have at least rung back, the woman on the phone sounds mature", she pointed out.

I'd never noticed that subtle point, she was right; the woman's voice was mature. I was also surprised that mum wanted me to bother with something as fickle as modelling. I saw a whole new side to her. She became proud that her son had been asked to model. You must remember that mum feeling pride in me was a rare commodity indeed. I wasn't going to let this go without cashing in on the emotional payback. So I rang the number that was left in the message. It was quarter to five. A firm sounding woman answered the phone, even her hello was tough. I introduced myself, to which she softened. She asked me to come and see her as soon as possible. I went the next morning.

She quickly briefed me on what they did as a business and why they had contacted me. She got her photographer to take a few pictures of me and then said that she'd be in touch. A few days later I received a letter from the Look Agency. Apparently *I had the look*. These are their words, not mine I assure you! So that's how I went from a teenager who worked part time at Barrett Shoes for £2.10 an hour, to one that modelled for YSL, Gucci and House of Frasier, needless to say that I no longer worked as a shoe sales assistant on weekends.

I was a little embarrassed about telling anyone but thought that it may be worthwhile sharing this piece of news with Nimesh. Within a few days of going back to college, I had counted no fewer than twelve people who had asked if it was true that I had got a modelling contract with YSL. Reluctantly, with an awkward nod, I would confirm the hot piece of news. Nimesh was openly advertising it and adding his own bits of spice. What I had found awkward was dealing with people's reaction to the news. Now bear in mind that I could read most teenagers in the same way as I read books; I knew what they thought of the news. Kids at that age, most of my students now, are transparent. There was a stark difference to see the reaction between boys and girls. Boys who were friends, would shake my hand and make some smart ass comment about how I could 'pull' more girls, or how the modelling agent must have been my mum, so on and on. Boys that felt threatened by the news reacted with a tinge of malice in their comments. I can't say that I blame them. Here was me, who was already fairly popular with girls and now I had some sort of official endorsement. Girls on the other hand, reacted in all sorts of interesting ways. Some girls were forthcoming and really complimentary, others who I already hung around with, I sensed had a subtle swagger about them, a few girls would naturally like to have shot me down, encase I was letting it get to my head. The most common phenomenon that I found to be happening was that most girls became interested in just talking to me, finding out what modelling was like, and whether I liked it. It was most definitely an interesting experience, something that I hated at the time due to its superficiality and crudeness. Nevertheless it financed mine and Asheeta's trip to Torquay & Switzerland, and if for nothing else, it was worth doing it just for that.

  The next bit of luck came in an altogether different way. Even though I had quit the college team, I was still playing in the Sunday leagues. I was captain that season of a local team called Humberstone Rangers. It was May 1999. We were two goals down by half time against a bunch of minnows. I was not happy. As we came off for our half time talk, the coach asked me "what was going on out there?"

  At first I didn't say anything. The coach went on about tactics and how if we just kept playing the way we did, we'd hammer them – it was all complete and utter nonsense. We were underachieving because the team had been complacent; had been physically muscled off the ball, and been out run and out passed. This had little to do with tactics; it was to do with human spirit. Just as the coach had finished and completely re-arranged the team, I was boiling up inside. I stood up just as the opposition team had finished their talk and had confidently run out onto the field, no doubt charged for the upcoming battle. I pulled all our lads back. I got them to sit down, only I stood. The coach looked puzzled.

"What the fuck are you all playing at", I yelled. "Look at what shirt you've got on, we're Rangers, not bunch of pussy footing minnows", I went on. "Now we have two choices in front of us. One is this; we go on that field half hearted, embarrassed and weaker than the opposition. If we go out like this we'll get beat. Fuck it, we'll get hammered. We've been played off the park by these, and I'm sorry to say that I think coach is wrong, it's not about tactics; it's about fucking spirit; the spirit to fight and to do what it takes to win."

Now while I was in the middle of this war cry, the opposition coach was carefully listening to what I was saying, I was completely unaware.

"The second choice" I carried on, "is that we play like Rangers, we play to win, we fucking fight till we bleed and we don't stop running till our legs fall off. If we do this for forty-five minutes, we'll walk away with pride. So what do you want? In forty-five minutes you can become men or we can leave here as a bunch of pussies." At the top of my voice, I yelled "What are we?"

"Rangers" came the proud call back.

The lads were awake and fired up for the fight.

"Who are we?" I yelled again.

The name "Rangers", echoed across the field.

The team played like champions; we won the game by four to their two. It was an incredible performance. After the game, we went to shake hands with the opposition. Their coach came directly over to me. He shook my hand, firmly but with respect. His eyes told me that he was proud, of his team but also, of me. "Amazing come back", he said.

"Thanks", I acknowledged looking down.

"Don't know if I like being called a bunch of pussy footing minnows", he came back.

I immediately looked to gauge his facial expressions. He was smiling and relaxed. "Sorry I didn't mean for you to hear that", I said rather meekly.

"You have quite a character, I've never seen a coloured boy like you" he blurted out.

His face showed no sign that he acknowledged what he had said was racist and deeply offensive. He said it innocently; there was no malice in his voice or on his facial expression. As we walked in the direction of the changing rooms, he spoke again, "have you thought about what you want to do with your life", he asked.

"No, not really", I replied.

"Well, from what I've seen today, I think you'd make a great officer in her Majesty's Royal Air Force. Why don't you come to the recruitment offices on Rutland Street in town, and I'll personally take you through what the RAF can offer someone like you."

It took a while for it to sink in. The sound of *Her Majesty's Royal Air Force* echoed in my head all day. Excitedly, I ran home, dropped my dirty kit in the washing basket and told dad what had happened. He could see I was excited, and so supported the idea.

"Make sure you go" he said.

Monday morning at nine, I stood waiting for the offices on Rutland Street to open. Lt. Sanders greeted me at the front door. I read his name tag.

"What does the Lt. stand for" I asked.

This was the depth of my knowledge about a career in the armed forces. Later that morning I learnt that it was short for Lieutenant. Lt. Sanders took me through a vast array of careers and pay scales; he showed me what a wonderful, fun packed life I would lead. He told me some of his own experiences; they were thrilling. He had sold the RAF so well that I had left their offices knowing it would be an ideal career choice. In fact by that morning I had even booked my first interview with their recruitment officer. Four weeks passed, and it was the day of my interview. I went dressed in shiny black shoes, trousers of the same colour but not shiny, and a navy blazer. I'd felt like an officer before I'd even got into the interview room. The interview lasted half an hour; I breezed through it. That was the first formal interview of my life. Looking back, I wish all of them had been as easy as that one.

My A-Level exams were over, and a long summer full of hope lay ahead of me.

First I met Asheeta, then I had become a model, and now I could be on my way to becoming an Officer in the RAF. All three things had occurred in a short space of time, and none of them I had intended. Within two days, I received a pack welcoming me to RAF Cranwell and an invitation to attend the three day selection process. Cranwell was essentially a training station, located in rural Lincolnshire, near Sleaford. That week, I spent my time reading cover to cover all the information they had sent. It was all a great game at the time. I had no idea of what it was that I was committing too. The three day selection process is something that everyone wishing to join the RAF has to go through. I had signed myself up as wanting to become either Intelligence or a Piloting Officer. Both had come across as being ideally suited to my personality. With the pack arrived my rail travel pass. It was my free ticket to Cranwell and back. On the front of it, in great big letters with the insignia of the crown, it read *In Her Majesty's Service*. I was James Bond. It was thrilling to get the pass, I showed it to Asheeta on our next meeting, and she found it as exciting as I did, albeit in a different sort of way. Let's just say that I got more than a hug that afternoon.

I was well aware that if I could get through the three day selection process, my university application worries would be over. Due to the fact that I had done so badly in my previous year of A-Levels, all the major universities had rejected me. I hadn't a single offer. But the second year, I had known to be different. I had worked hard, and my finals went extraordinarily well. I was confident that I would get decent grades, yet I had no university to go to in September. I knew the air force would be my solution to this little problem, if I could get through what seemed like a daunting three days. I also thought that my desire to study Aerospace had great synergy with the RAF.

I began preparing for the selection weekend by running five miles everyday, followed by fifty press ups, fifty leg raises, and forty chin ups. I did this routine every morning until the day of departure. Occasionally, when Asheeta could be bothered to get up, she would count me through my exercise. On these rare mornings, I seemed to perform better as Asheeta was watching, and her judging eyes made me get through everything quicker. The additional benefit of having Asheeta there was that I knew it was a great turn on for her to see me work out so intensively. After my morning shower, our afternoons together were always rather passionate.

I was suited and booted. That morning I had to leave Leicester train station, to go "On Her Majesty's Service". I was a little tentative and unsure of what to expect at Cranwell. The train journey passed over smoothly. Due to Cranwell's remoteness, we had to catch a hopper bus from the last train stop. The bus was full of RAF hopefuls. I was the only "coloured boy" on the bus and the youngest. I was in the company of men, and I felt instantly out of my depths. The sudden change in environment had sapped all my confidence. As I climbed onto the coach everybody, including me, knew that I was in well over my head. Some people nodded, others smiled as I walked by, looking for an empty seat. I settled in to a seat near the back of the coach. I starred out of the window for the entire duration of the trip, all the while thinking "what on Earth am I doing here?"

There was no real selection orientated activities that day, it was instead for acclimatisation. We were debriefed by some commander or another. He welcomed us, and gave us an upbeat talk about how some of us would become great military leaders, and how invaluable those of us, who got through these three days, would be to *Her Majesty*. He then waffled on about the greats that had been here before us and how privileged we were. I was completely over roared by the whole occasion. This was *'real' England*. I was surrounded by the 'real' English, in fact, this was Her Majesty's England, and suddenly for the first time in my life, the question of identity flared up deep within. I will come to the question of identity later on, but for now it is worth noting how the question arose.

I chatted with a few other guys and one girl. We had formed a little click and so had everyone else. I realised early on that this was the second or even third time some of these people were here, having failed previously. They knew exactly what to expect and their confidence fuelled my insecurity. Chris Chamberlain was the other guy who was roughly my age. I noticed too that everyone was from private, or at worst Grammar schools, and from rural England, predominantly from the Home Counties. They were well spoken, very bright and totally dedicated to the cause. I duly noted that many of them had other relatives already in the armed forces and some even in the air force. I had felt back then that I was at a huge disadvantage in every possible way. Culturally I was backdated, in the sense that I had never experienced anything like this before, educationally unproven, and socio-economically poorer, having no idea of what the RAF was. The first evening dragged. I'd wanted to crawl into my room and wake in my own bed, but somehow I knew this wasn't a possibility.

That night I thought. I thought about everything that had happened so far. I starred into the moonlight for hours. *Why was I here? How did I get here? And now that I'm here what do I do?* I drifted from one thought to another, trying to decipher a meaning to my predicament. Hours passed, and the moon was soon covered by dark clouds. It was dark outside, but darker in my heart. I hadn't felt scared in years. I was tough; life had made me that way. I was beaten by the forces that be, until I was solid. I was frustrated as to why this sudden weakness had come over me. What was it that I feared?

Time passed by and it was late into the night, the moon was back and shone onto the airfields directly opposite. I knew I was out of my comfort zone. I was surrounded by people like of whom I had never met. I remember shutting the curtains as a sign of indignant surrender to the world. I got into bed. I closed my eyes, and I began to feel warmth of the kind that I missed. Vikas came and went from my consciousness. What would life have been like were he alive today? It was from here that I remember finding my courage.

Life was the way it was, it was simple and primitive. It was about competition, the best would succeed and the rest would recede. I got back out of bed, pulled out a notepad and pen, and began to write. I listed everything that I had, which made me an untouchable – no body else could have these attributes. I had to show off my strengths, bring the competition to my level and compete. The first day I was on their level and I felt overwhelmed. Well, let's see how grand they are when they come to my level. I must have been really young, maybe six or seven, but I remembered my grandfather once told me, "your ancestors were warriors, your heritage is a proud one, and in everything that you do, you represent all of us."

These words came swirling back from the depths of my memory to re-ignite a passion for competition.

The morning came and I hadn't slept a wink. But it didn't matter. I looked fresher this morning than I had done the entire previous night. I knew my game plan. I knew what I had to do in the interviews, in the leadership challenges, and in the individual problem solving scenarios. I had to be tough, mentally and physically. I had to show that I was intelligent; I was mature but above all else; I was a born leader. And in this spirit, I left our quarters. I walked across to the officer's mess, and realised that I was the first to arrive. As luck would have it, and I was having plenty of it, the commanding officer of the station was pouring himself some tea. He was a little surprised to see me, probably for two reasons. Firstly my youthful looks which gave away my tender age, and the colour of my skin, would have, I am sure raised just a tiny eyebrow. Not out of any prejudice of course, on the contrary, I found most senior officers to be extremely cordial towards me, and actually admired people from my background "who gave it a right old go" – these were their words, not mine.

"Would you like some tea?" he asked.

"Yes, please", I politely replied.

I knew from all the insignias that here was an officer, who in all probability will be my interviewer's CO *(Commanding Officer)*.

"You're early", he said, "Excited at the prospect of the next two days are we?" he questioned.

We sat down at the table, and spoke to one another for twenty minutes before the next group of candidates arrived. As we saw the others cross the air field which cut across our path, he quietly said to me "Sanvik, I think you better go and sit at those tables over there", he pointed to them with his gentle eyes, "these tables are for wing commanders only, even full time officers never sit here on these tables."

My face reddened. I looked at him and was about to apologise when he said, "its ok", he tapped the back of my hand to reassure me, "you weren't to know, and besides I enjoyed your company so much that I didn't want to tell you to move. Good luck."

He smiled, and I got up to leave his table. I never spoke to him again, but I have always felt that he influenced the direction of my life quite significantly.

Other members of the mini click arrived in a pact, and along with them entered the Officers who would be spending the next two days with us, and probably judging our every move. We spoke gently; we made light conversation of how daunting all of this was, and I noticed that each of the Officers had seated themselves on different tables, apart from ours. I found this to be a little strange, had they consciously decided to leave our little table out? A few minutes passed and our morning drivel had become a heated discussion, on which aircraft had historically been the most significant in war time. I hadn't a clue. I sat there observing and acclimatising myself with the environment. I became sensitive, to all that was around me. It was then that I noticed an officer had ploughed himself behind us, and in a position where he could eavesdrop on several tables at once. No doubt he'd already tapped into our historically futile conversation, where egos of men were flexing their muscles for the upcoming battle. And that's what it was. Men around me were growling and flexing their intellectual muscles to one another, to show that they were the perfect candidate. I noted that on every table there was some debate or discussion going on. It occurred to me, that here we were, all strangers, who were meant to display their leadership capabilities, instead everyone seemed to be intellectually threatening one another. There were some clear winners and losers. I saw people get out muscled, out fought and out gunned, metaphorically speaking. The omens didn't look good for the losers, but the winners left breakfast feeling supremely confident. I however, had kept my cards close to my chest.

The morning passed by, we waited in long cues to have our bodies checked out. There were all kinds of tests; hearing, sight, colour coordination, psychometrics, hand to eye coordination in which I did extremely well, and other physical checks, including the dreaded cupping. I ended my rounds of physical examinations with the body mass index, mine was 21.1. We waited in the foyer for our results to be processed. Even though we all knew we would pass, there was an invisible taste of apprehension in the air. The results came, and to my surprise two people were called into the Medical Officers room. I saw one guy who had been here before, signalling to his comrades with a finger running across his neck, to indicate they were axed. We were handed a clear sealed envelope, with no markings and told to give this to staff that requested it. I suspected it had the results of our physicals.

We walked into the Officers mess to eat. Next we were going to be put through our paces, mentally and physically. For me lunch consisted of roast potatoes, gravy, peas and salad. I remember it because, after I had cleaned my plate of all its contents, I was actually hungrier. The banter throughout lunch had been similar to that of the morning except this time the male testosterone was even more visible. It was all very high brows and polite you understand, but if you just saw beyond the façade, it was there to be smelt. The walls at the officers mess was decorated with the photo frames of 'famous' commanders of the station and in the centre of the front wall, was the picture of the Queen, in whose service we had all come.

There were fifty-five candidates left, with two already having been told to go home, at least that's what I assume, as we never saw them again. We were split into two groups. Group A, of which I was a member would do the physicals first and then move onto the interviews, Group B would do it the other way round. We quietly walked across the disused airfield, and back to our quarters to get changed. We all had to line up in two rows. The CO, meaning Commanding Officer, came forth. The armed forces abbreviate everything; it gets rather confusing after a while, especially when I heard some people talk in abbreviations only.

My stomach felt empty, my heart was beating slowly but heavy, and I was tense. It was the quite before the big plunge. I had been here before. Every time I entered a semi contact kick boxing tournament I had felt like this. I loved the thrill, the anticipation of the big fight, the adrenaline kicks in and the ultimate silence surrounds you. Then to my utter shock we were told that the afternoons physical test would consist of a two mile run, followed by fifty press ups, sit ups of the same number, and as many chin ups as we could muster. The anxiety of the unknown storm had become euphoria in my mind at the news of this proxy little test. The CO was going to be timing each of us to see how quickly we finished the exercise.

My heart was still pumping, but now with the expectation of winning rather than competing. The whistle blew and I immediately took on a swift pace down the airfield. I was breathing well, and I quickly found my rhythm, my legs moved in soft motion and my ankles were landing well onto the tarmac. The first mile had passed swiftly and the group of twenty-five had spilt into three. I was in the middle of the leading pack. I glimpsed at the competition as we passed the mile and half marker. I was waiting for my time. I saw some people around me struggle, to keep this pace and soon, a few more dropped off the ever quickening pace. Sweat was now running down my brow and into the direction of my lips. I loved it. As the final quarter of a mile approached, I burst into a speed that took the others by surprise. I quite literally accelerated away from them. As I passed the leader of the group, I saw his face strain incredibly hard to keep me from doing so. From jogging quickly I had begun a gradual increment to the point of a sprint, I knew I was in the lead by quite a few yards, but I didn't let up. I loved every second of it. I had taken everyone by surprise, including the CO whom I could see waiting at the finish line. I crossed the two mile marker in eight minutes and twenty seconds. I felt the congratulatory tap of the CO as I went by him. Next I got down to do my fifty press ups. One, two, three…and before I knew it I had got to fifty. My mind was blank, sweat poured off my body, I was in a trance. The time was nine minutes and eleven seconds. Next were the sit ups. I crunched my way to fifty in no time. We had to get up and run to the make shift finish line, where there were hanging bars for each person to jump onto and begin their chin-ups. I had completed my two mile run, fifty press ups and fifty sit ups in ten minutes and eighteen seconds.

    I had the quickest time so far and as I jumped onto the bar, I realised how far ahead I was, of some people. This realisation actually slowed me; my concentration lapsed just for a moment. I took a couple of deep breaths hanging off the bar. I then started my chin-ups. I knew I could do forty quite easily, but I had run a quick race and I knew it would be tough. As I had got to nine, another lad, jumped onto the bar next to mine. He was doing then much quicker than I. Before I knew it he had done more chin-ups than me. My arms ached, my stomach stretched and my thighs raged. I had got to forty. I was breathing heavy, my arms were beginning to tremble out of fatigue, but I was in no mood to come second. We were both struggling; I more than him. It became strange; I would do one and hang still, then he would do one to show me that he could do it; I would then do another and wait for him to follow suit. Eventually, I had got to sixty one, and I collapsed off the bar. Quite literally seconds later, he fell off and we crunched down together, admiring each others resilience.

    The CO was looking at the both of us intently. Another officer came and tapped us both at the same time. "That was quick chaps. Well done. Saashin, I think that was the fastest I've seen anybody ever do press ups", he complimented.

"Thank you sir", I acknowledged, still squatting in the recovery position.

No body could ever pronounce my name properly in the air force. It was something that I got used to. As we strolled back to our quarters, to go and shower and re-suit ourselves, Debbie, the only girl in our group came and congratulated me on my impressive time. "That was so amazing. You and that other guy were really going at it. When I was doing my sit-ups I was too distracted by you guys, and I think my counting officer was too, because he wasn't watching me. You must do sports, right?" she asked.

"Umm, a little", I said.

I didn't really want to tell anyone that I was a keen footballer, a semi-professional kick boxer and could quite easily beat the crap out of most of the guys here. We walked in silence, until the girls quarter arrived. We said our semi goodbyes and separated. I never saw her again either, she wasn't there at the interview stage. At the time I didn't notice it but we were being watched in everything that we did. For whatever reason, Debbie must have been axed based on her physical.

As I began my walk across the airfield, I was tapped on my shoulder from behind. It was him, the resilient guy. "That was great", he said, putting out his hand, offering the age old sign of mutual respect, it was an honest handshake.

For the rest of the day and the next, we stuck closely to one another. It's strange how human beings behave. We are more animal, than we often like to believe. Tom had been here before, he was twenty, studied Mechanical Engineering at Kingston University, the same place where my brother had gone, and was on a Scholarship programme from BAe Systems. He had no intensions of staying with BAe; instead he wanted to be a pilot. His mannerism, in all likelihood was probably modelled on Maverick from Top Gun, a film that he'd clearly watched one too many times. He was tough and intelligent. I liked him. His grandfather had been a pilot in World War Two. He had been killed. His village had two memorials for his grandfather, who had clearly inspired Tom, to the extent that one got the impression, Tom too, wanted a memorial for himself someday.

As we entered the foyer again, we were each handed another unmarked envelope, this time to give to the interviewer. I waited for what seemed like hours. I starred at all the grand looking pictures on the walls, all the insignias that captured so much of what it meant to be British. There was so much history, there was so much Englishness there, and it was quite awesome. Time ticked along slowly. My body was nicely tired. The kind of feeling one gets when they are pride struck. I had done well today, and I began to feel a lot more comfortable in my surroundings. I noticed that everyone took me as a serious contender, and I felt their approval every time I happened to make eye contact. I had no idea what they would ask. We had been told nothing so far, and all the little booklets they had sent in the pack, revealed little as to the upcoming challenge. I was naively thinking that it would be a polite chat, about my ambitions and why I had wanted to join the RAF, to which I would give all the standard answers.

An aged, but powerful, tall black officer came into the foyer. "Mr Nanandha", he ordered.

To my annoyance, they could never pronounce my family name either. I stood; he glazed over me and walked down a corridor. I swiftly followed suit. We entered a small interviewing room which was no bigger than five metres in either direction. In the middle was a desk and two chairs, one on either side. There was a notepad and pen on the desk along with a tape recorder. He sat at the side nearest the door, which somewhat surprised me. He made me circumnavigate round the desk and onto the other side. As I sat down, I instantly knew why he made me sit here. I could feel it. It was threatening. I had no where to escape. There was no window, and he blocked the only way out. He looked stern. I handed my envelope over to him; he took it and put it aside. He looked at me silently for what seemed like forever. I was nervous. Should I smile, should I gaze back or should I look away? I didn't do any of those things, and instead showed openly that he had frightened me. My confident demeanour was gone. He had sapped it away by doing nothing.

"Tell me young man", he started, "are you violent, or have you faced violence of any kind?"

This was not what I had expected at all. He looked squarely into my soul. I was naked in front of him, I was vulnerable.

"No sir, I haven't", I said spontaneously.

He took a small lick of his lips and pulled out a piece of paper.

"On here it says that you have some severe scars, deep cuts on and top of your behind. You have further smaller cuts on your arm, shins, knees and thighs. In total you have sixteen cuts and seven are severe. What do you think? Is this the wrong report?"

I sensed sarcasm in his voice.

"Oh them", I smiled, making it sound as if it was nothing, "you see sir", I began, "I play a great deal of competitive sports, mainly football and its in the nature of the game to get a little cut here and there."

He absorbed what I had said. "Do you play football with knives", I remember him asking.

From here my interview became an interrogation. It went from bad to worse, and from worse to disastrous, and finally, from disastrous to unbearable. He quizzed me about my life, what I had studied, why my grades were so poor and what made me believe that Aerospace was the right course for me. I vividly remember his final question. "Tell me, why are we based in the Falklands. The RAF spends three million pounds a day, in keeping islands that has an entire population, which can be housed and given a million pounds each to resettle back in the UK. This would be cheaper. Why are we there?"

I hadn't a clue. I sat there looking blank. "I don't know sir", I spoke in surrender.

He took a deep breadth and said "for oil, that's why we are there, for oil."

The interview lasted forty five minutes, but it felt much longer. I had failed and I knew it.

I was asked to wait in the foyer. An hour or so later, names were read out loud to the group. Mine wasn't said. I knew what was coming; I was going to be asked to leave. How my day and been turned upside down in forty five minutes. Those whose name hadn't been called were handed another unmarked sealed envelope. As I was given my, I was tapped on the shoulder. It was warm and comforting. Did the Staff Sergeant feel sorry for me, had she believed that I had been hard done by, or was it that I had made it? I looked into her eyes for a fleeting second. Her eyes said everything. It was good news. I knew I was in. I was on my way to becoming an Intelligence Officer in *Her Majesty's Service.*

By that evening only twelve people were left, from a total of fifty seven. All twelve sat on a large table, and we ate together. It was a merry evening. Everyone, still suited and booted, was beginning to feel the light at the end of the tunnel. I was the youngest one left, and only four out of the final twelve had been there for the very first time; the rests were on their second or even third attempt. They spoke about what the following day would have in store for us, and what the CO looked for in potential candidates. There were going to be two leadership exercises, and one individual problem solving challenge. We would have been finished by lunch time the next day. After dinner, I didn't stay behind like the others for a few drinks. I went straight to my room, after a long detour around the base. I saw Hawks lined up one after another. There were a few Harriers and a single Tornado GR1A. I saw a model Spitfire, and plaques which remembered the dead. One plaque read, *"The Tip of Sword was sharpened here."*

These words have been imprinted on my psyche. We were being sharpened not to cut a cake! We were the tip, which would enter first into the body that politicians wanted killed. It was Napoleon who I believe said, "God is on the side of the army that has the biggest cannons."

Mankind I realised hasn't evolved much at all. We are still as primitive as we've always been. Here was a training centre where talented young men and women, were being selected, and then trained essentially for warfare. It was here, and thousands of places like these that Napoleons 'biggest cannons' were being manufactured; here at Cranwell in the form of people. It was at eighteen that I realised an aspect of the global human condition. The words on the plaque had sent me down the rabbit hole.

As I walked the short distance from the plaque, back to my quarters, I was moving at a rapid speed through intellectual space. I was about to experience massive changes in my values and consequently actions were going to change. What I realised on the small walk was that the human condition could be summarised by a single word – *FEAR*.

We were all little creatures inhabiting a tiny planet and consequently, frightened of everything. We were frightened by our own selves, we were frightened of other people, other communities, other religions, races, nations and most of all we feared nature. We feared our lives in its entirety, and we feared it due to a paradoxical irrationality. We want life, we want to live, and keep on living so desperately that we fear everything that construes it. We see, smell, hear and feel death everywhere, it's a hidden obsession, we run from it, we conceal its existence, and we choose to ignore the darkness and the eternal void that surrounds each of us. We fear death so much that we spend our entire lives in fear, looking for security from it. Evolution has taught us that death can come from anywhere, and so we spend our entire lives finding out new wonderful ways to protect ourselves from the one thing we cannot avoid – DEATH.

I pondered on the ideas of Nuclear weapons. *Americans had invented it, Russians followed close behind, why? Probably, because they were frightened, ok, so why did America develop it in the first place?* It too, was frightened by others, and so wanted to have something that would keep the night away. The problem was that because Russia acquired WMD (and we all should be familiar with this term, in our fear stricken society) it meant that all of Europe became frightened, and so they developed such weapons. And once Europeans got hold of them, well this frightened everybody else; lets face it Europeans didn't have a great record on Human Rights or colonialism. Soon, China would create Nuclear weapons, because of its desire to not be frightened by anyone, including America and Russia. In turn China frightened India, and India frightened Pakistan, they in turn made Iran feel a little shaky. Iran has made the United States a little uneasy and so the cyclical effects of Fear continue. I realised at eighteen that one day Iran would acquire Nuclear weapons; it didn't take a qualified diplomat, to figure that out. I also realised that the idea of some countries being *"allowed"* to have Nuclear weapons, and others not, was the ultimate sign of insecurity. I realised back then, in the hot summer night, at RAF Cranwell that people feared that which was the inevitable. We were being selected for a profession that would alleviate some of the insecurities of our nation.

I slept well that night. The morning sunshine crept into my room and fell onto my face. It blessed me with its presence because it woke me. I had forgotten to put the alarm on my clock that I had brought with me, it was 6.30am. I knew I had been lucky. This truly was becoming the summer of luck. I had a quick shower, got my shirt and trousers on, and nipped across the airfield into the Officers mess for a hurried breakfast. The leadership challenges consisted of a group exercise, as well as an individual one. There were twelve left.

We were split into two groups. The group activity consisted of figuring out how to construct a bridge that would safely transport our team of six across the gymnasium. I had never been in a situation such as this, but I thrived off it. I got stuck right in. By no means was I the most vocal or the coordinator, but I did do a good job analysing potential solutions the team arrived at. Our group failed the exercise. Tom and another guy quickly turned on each other, not verbally or directly, but subtly, and everybody including the CO noted it. I had been so fused into the challenge that I didn't even care that we'd lost. This was a first time experience of this sort of thing and I had thoroughly enjoyed it. In fact as we walked back into the main foyer, the CO asked what I thought about the activity, I remember my answer well – "I loved it", I replied.

The individual leadership challenges were surreal. We were each given, in turn; an opportunity to lead five members of the officer training team through a maze, constructed out of bean bags and six inch cones. I was selected to go first. While I entered the restructured gym, all the other eleven waited outside, in the foyer. To my surprise my team was blindfolded, they were also not allowed to speak. My task was to get all of them safely across the maze by giving them clear instructions, as quickly as possible.

While the CO was explaining the rules of the activity, I was drifting off. I remembered a time when Dillip gave instruction to his runners. Now his runners were not very bright, and commonsense was something which sadly evaded them, this day, I was in a similar position to that which Dillip had been. I quickly labelled each of my "runners" as a number from one to five. When I called out their number, they were to raise their left hand, to acknowledge that they knew I was instructing them. I created two pairs and one 'dummy' runner. I would use the dummy runner to find out the correct way across the maze and then have the two pairs follow in his footsteps. When I'd got all of my team members across the maze, I thought I'd done it perfectly, it couldn't have gone smoother. When the results were released, I had come second from bottom. Clearly, it hadn't gone as well as I had envisaged.

We said our goodbyes after the de-briefing from the CO. We shook hands and wished each other well. As I went to gather my bags from our quarters, I realised that I still had the unmarked envelope in my bag. I hadn't passed it on to whomever it was that I was meant to give it to. I rushed back to the foyer to see the CO. When I showed him the envelope, he looked puzzled briefly and then told me to wait. I asked him upon his return "who did all the others give their envelopes too?"

His answer was a little strange, "they didn't have envelopes. Envelopes usually mean your cue to go home."

Moments later, before I had a chance to absorb what he had said our Staff Sergeant walked in to our little enquiry. She whispered something to him, after which, he turned to tell me that I should hold onto it. It'll make sense when you get home. I had no idea what he meant. I picked up my bags and caught the hopper bus back to train station at Sleaford. Asheeta met me at Leicester train station, that afternoon. We walked down Granby Street, she lovingly waffled on about *her* exciting few days, and I just listened.

A few days passed. I spent a lot of time thinking about all that had happened. My exams were over and this was the first significant time I had to myself, where I could think. I thought about Vikas, and wondered where or what; even when he was? I drifted onto Dillip and his recent demise. It had only been six months and he already seemed like a distant dream. I had met Asheeta and was quickly becoming infatuated by her. I had been sacked from my part time job at Barrett Shoes, earlier that May, soon after me acquiring the modelling contract. I had decided to watch the FA Cup final, instead of turning up to work, and had bumped into my manager's manager. The rest, as they say, is history. And now, I was about to start another adventure on her Majesty's behalf. I still hadn't secured a university placement, but I didn't care. I could feel my life taking on a new direction. It was about to change. Another week flew by. I remember spending my sunlight hours with Asheeta, and the moonlit sky with the stars.

Then I received an envelope with *"On her Majesty's Service"* plastered across it. I knew these were the results from the RAF. I excitedly opened the envelope. It was a short letter, no more than five lines in length. As my eyes glanced across the letter I realised immediately that I had been rejected. I quickly glanced over the words and through the letter onto the coffee table. I collapsed back onto the sofa and wondered where I had gone wrong. Then I noticed that there was another envelope addressed to me. I immediately remembered the blank sealed envelope that I had not opened on the final day at Cranwell. I quickly ran upstairs and rummaged through my junk, and found it curled up inside my folder. I opened it and found a letter addressing my parents. It didn't have the Royal Air Force insignia; instead there was some other logo. It was definitely armed forces or something to do with government. I read across the few lines that were written. It informed my parents that I had been approached by *Her Majesty's Ministry of Defence* and that they should know what the implications of this would be. They ended the letter by advising them to keep this piece of information to themselves. I was confused. I hadn't even known anything about the MoD. I went back downstairs and opened the other letter. It was from them. I read across the lines in eagerness. After reading it I was bemused, what was going on?

I rang the helpline number to speak to a man called Jeffery Richardson, he would be my enrolment officer; should I decide to join. The receptionist kept me waiting for five minutes before Jeff came on the line. We spoke briefly; he could tell quite obviously that I didn't know what was happening. He arranged it so that we met at Leicester train station the next day, at lunch time. I showed the letters to my parents later that evening. They were as clueless as I was. Mum had got worried that I might have been in some trouble with the law. Dad reassured her that I hadn't done anything wrong.

I remember the night I got those letters, I went out with friends. We had a great time partying and the questions of career seemed a long way away. The morning came. I wore my crisply ironed shirt, through on some aftershave for good measure and strolled over to the train station. I hadn't a clue as to who I was waiting for and where he would be standing. At first I wasn't sure as to what I could do? Should I go down to the platforms and wait there? I knew he was coming up from London and all trains from there stopped on a particular platform. But what if he was already here? It then occurred to me that if I stood under the main archway which led outside, blatantly showing that I was waiting for someone, he would at least come and ask. Furthermore, for him to leave the station he would have to go by me and thereby increasing our chances of meeting. A few minutes went by, and a man who had been waiting against the far wall, began his walk towards me. It was Mr. Richardson.

"Hello Sir", I greeted him with my hand out.

"Sanvik, great to meet you", his sweaty hands met with mine.

I was a little surprised at Mr. Richardson's appearance. He wasn't as smart as I had envisaged and he was over weight and sweaty. He had a residing hairline and a briefcase that looked worn. He was nothing like the people at the Air Force.

"Tell me, why you were waiting there underneath that archway?" he asked.

"So hopefully you would notice me as you came up from the platforms", I answered quickly.

We had spontaneously moved into a poorly lit café that stood adjacent to the main entrance of the station. We sat down at one of the tables at the back. I had brought the two letters that I had received from the MoD to show him. I had them at the ready. He took them, had a quick glance and handed them back. We spoke for two hours. He bought me lunch, something that he would do many more times over the next five years, in places all around Europe. He explained what the MoD did; what he did for them and why I had been approached. It was Mr. Richardson that had personally seen my psychometric test scores, and had heard my interview.

"Look, Sanvik, the RAF treated you harshly, and it's their loss, as far as I'm concerned. We want you to join us; it's a better life style, better pay and a lot more interesting", he said.

I was listening but not really in any position to ask questions, he was flattering me continuously, and soon I was too drunk on it to really care about the small technicalities.

"We're not going to put you on some recruitment process, we want you, period! Now we know that you've had problems with the law, all minor offences, and I know that you don't have a university place yet."

In hindsight, I should have been awestruck at how he knew all of this, but I wasn't. I was drunk on my own ego.

"We can help you secure a place at university; you know... just give you a few tips and write you a nice reference", he suggested with raised eyebrows.

He handed me over a piece of paper with around twenty universities on them.

"Tell me which one you applied to, and for which degree, we'll even do the application on the day your grades come out."

"Kingston", I said.

He paused and then spoke, "of course, its sentimental I know, but can I suggest Kings College, it'll be much better for you."

Again, I should have caught onto his comments. How did he know about Aerospace, I hadn't told him as yet? How did he know that Kingston was sentimental to me? I told him I'd think about it over the summer; speak it over with my parents. He told me at some length about what the MoD did, and which departments did what, he was using a lot of jargon, and technical terminology, most of that conversation went straight over my head. Time flew by, and we eventually got up, with Mr. Richardson leading the way. We shook hands and went in opposite directions.

"Oh Sanvik", he shouted, as he was walking away, "Keep it to yourself for a while."

And then he went down to the platforms.

As I walked down Granby Street that afternoon, I had felt elated. I was wanted. I was in demand. People valued me, and not even because I was smart or tough or good looking, but because I was me. A deep level of comfort, and what can only be described as, professional confidence grew within me. This was my doorway into the thrilling murky world of Government and Politics.

The MoD looked after me, it became my Guardian, they always knew what was best for me, and they nurtured me, taught me, showed me, all without any pressure or demands. It was as if they were looking after me, because *I was me*, for no other reason. I would later find out that the whole conversation with Mr. Richardson had been a fix. They had told the RAF to reject me, and then they would offer me another way. It was standard recruitment practice. I was enrolled onto the *'fast track management scheme'* at the MoD. It was at, and through the MoD that I realised what Politics was. The MoD is at the fore of global affairs and quite literally shapes certain aspects of the human condition. They are an organisation like no other; they are totally geared towards protecting us of everything that we fear. They are an organisation that not only protects us on the back foot, but has the capacity to thrust forward and instil fear into others. I was on a scheme that would nurture me, to one day stand at the forefront of this organisation.

During my time at university, I could enter the intellectual tunnels at a greater frequency, and intentionally now, through my growing capacity to meditate. I was realising how I could essentially become one with the subject matter. And so it was that I came to realise, as Plato had done, two thousand years before, the *form of Politics*.

What is politics? I believe very few people truly know. In fact, most people in Politics fail to realise the 'platonic form'. By the form, I mean Politics in its most simplistic nature. If we cut all the fleshy bits, the propaganda, the systems, the rules, the media, economics and elections, what would we be left with? What is Politics in its essence? Without knowing the source of all that we call Politics, how can one truly appreciate it? The answer is that we can't. Most diplomats and high flying PPE graduates from Oxford, and I have spoken to many, have little true understanding of the essential nature of what it is that they are so deeply, and often passionately involved in. I do not wish to come across as "a-know-it-all", because I do not. In fact there are huge gulfs of ignorance in my knowledge of politics. What I do know, and have realised, is the essence of the subject.

Politics according to academia is a social science. And a social science is a study of physical human movements – Psychology, Sociology, Economics and Politics all fit under this umbrella term. Politics is at its heart, the activities associated with gaining, or using power, within organisations or groups. All the other fleshy bits I mentioned earlier are its basic manifestations. Politics *is about power*. It is about gaining and then using power to benefit oneself and the wider society. Additionally, politics occurs at every level of human existence, and its essential nature is the same. Politics occurs at home, at the work place, among social and professional groups, between organisations and of course in and between other nations. Politics is all around us, at all times, furthermore, we all play the game whether we mean to or not; it is an intrinsic aspect of human life.

As I wondered around Westminster gardens in late November of '99, I asked myself how politics is created. If it's about power, where does the desire for power stem from?

As I wondered across the gardens, with the Palace of Westminster on one side, and Government buildings scattered all around, I slipped into intellectual space. In a short amount of time, I travelled vast amounts through the tunnels. It came to me while focusing on an orchard which stood before me. The world is limited. Everything is finite. All the resources that we so strongly yearn are limited. In addition, to this limitation, we are all so different. Each human being has different strengths and weaknesses. We have different skills, we have different pain thresholds, we have different emotional make-ups, and we have different tastes and ambitions and so on and on. When we combine the finiteness of the world, and our unequal physical and mental build, we produce a comparator; we attempt to equate the scarcity of the world with the differences of human beings. The ones, who have the physical and mental stature to do so, feel that they deserve a greater share of the resources, and so create hierarchy putting themselves at the top, or as high as they can possibly get away with, and thereby consuming greater resources. The further up the hierarchy one travels, the more resources one can consume, and it is through the consumption of resources that we produce and wield power.

    I sat myself on the park bench, besides the orchard. I sketched a diagram depicting what it was that I was realising through the intellectual space. I imagined five people. I supposed that three out of the five knew how to cut a tree down, and only one knew how to skin the bark. I don't know why, but I just imagined that they needed to skin the tree after they cut it, in order to use it as fire wood. I also supposed that there was a much older man out of the five who was considerably weaker than the others, but he knew how to make an axe. Every person needed heat to survive. So the old man made the axe. He could have gone to cut the tree himself, but the group realised that it would take him far too long by himself, so it was better that the three strongest go. The old man showed the other three how to use his tool. They cut the tree. Once the tree was cut, only one of the three knew how to skin the bark. So he carried on with what he knew. The others watched. Then feeling tired, he passed the skinned log to the fifth person, who had contributed nothing, and told him to cut it into small pieces. As night fell and the cold grew, they all sat round the camp fire.

    After sometime, the old man realised that he had a skill without which, everyone would have frozen to death. He wondered. He then realised that actually, he could have cut the tree, and skinned it, and cut it into little pieces all by himself, albeit, slowly. So he knew that he needed the others for convenience, not as a necessity. He then realised that there was one among them who had contributed something so small, that it had no worth – the cutting of the log into smaller pieces. And yet, he too, enjoyed the same comforts as the others. A certain superiority complex began to grow in the old man. He was invaluable to the group, so long as he knew the art of tool making. So one day he vocalised his analysis. Soon, the man who was physically strong and knew how to skin the bark realised that he too had something quite better than the other three. He knew that the old man was still crucial, and that he needed him for his own betterment. In his head, he began to realise the need for him to learn how to make tools from the old man, for two reasons.

First reason was because it was his tool making skills that made him an untouchable, and second, he was old, if he died, we would be without a tool maker. The other two men who were physically strong and had helped cut the tree but knew, or cared for little else, were beneath the old man and himself. They had some extra potential value, in that if any wild animal attacked us, they would be useful to have. Finally, he too realised, that there was one amongst them who was dispensable. He had nothing to contribute apart from his labour. He was not too strong or intelligent. What use was he? The old man, and the second one realised that he would make a good labourer, he could do all the tedious, unwanted jobs. And in return he would be allowed to enjoy the heat of the fire.

This was the creation of power. This was the birth of politics. But how could they wield their newly discovered political power? How would the hierarchy reward those at the top? The heat at night was given to all, so what would it matter if one was at the top, or the other at the bottom, the mere role within their society wasn't enough. Everyone had to be clear in their positions, and the ones at the top deserved extra wealth and opulence due to their untouchability *(in terms of skills)*. The two, at the top of their five man hierarchy decided that it was only fair that the old man sit higher than the others so that we can show our gratitude for his wisdom. The second one, *the tree skinner*, decided that only he had the right, to learn from the old man the art of making tools, as he was the most intelligent. He was also charismatic, and so successfully influenced the other two physically able men, who lacked care and intelligence. The old man and the second able man, rewarded the lesser two men through praises, compliments and little 'bits' of left over resource, but made out to appear as hugely generous rewards. This was how their loyalty was bought. The man at the bottom of the hierarchy was always made to work the longest and hardest. It was his job to care and look after the needs of the others. He was not to join the fire, until all his chores were complete, and then made to sit a few yards further back. This is how politics is created – through the finiteness of the world and the natural inequality of mankind all fused together by greed.

Adam Smith, the father of modern Capitalism, I believe explored these same tunnels that I had discovered. He realised that human beings were far too primitive to transcend their evolutionary conditioning; something which every religion has always claimed was possible. The only language human beings could understand is the language of resource. He wanted to make Politics less brutish and more 'civilised' by using that which Politics was designed for – Finite Resource. Adam Smith knew that trade, controlled by a system that could transcend human insecurities and yet was controlled by them, could bring about a more peaceful world. He showed us the effects of supply & demand. I will come to discuss Capitalism *(probably in a different book, if the publishers make a nice honest buck out of this one!)*, but the soul of Politics at least, had been caught.

Politics has become infinitely more sophisticated than the analogy, but yet its nature, its essence, or as one in the tunnel experiences it, as the soul of politics, has changed little. I got up from the park bench thinking that the old man was the government, the clever second man, was the business community, the two brutes as the armed forces, police, civil servants, and finally the bottom of the hierarchy was the majority. My father and mother, my relatives, Asheeta's parents were all at the bottom of this hierarchy. I was to later discover that my assumed hierarchy of society was fundamentally flawed.

All that I have just spoken about came about through my infusion to the world of politics. It was my new step parents at the higher echelons of the MoD that indirectly forced me to ponder politics. I became their obedient, high achieving son, until I grew up and realised who my parents actually were. I divorced them in the summer of 2002, but even today, and for the rest of my life, I will always remember and be appreciative, for all that my step parents did for me, and I particularly owe much to Mr. Richardson.

Becoming Bright

August 15th, 1999, the day my A-Level results came out. I had only recently passed my driving test at the second attempt. A few weeks earlier I had been cheated by the examiner. *("Yes, I still feel rather sore, at having failed the first time")* A few weeks earlier Asheeta and I had our driving test, hers was in the morning, and mine in the afternoon. Asheeta, in her test, had stalled several times, had curbed her rear tyre while reversing and had rolled a few feet down a hill because she had forgotten to lift up the hand brake. Asheeta passed. That afternoon, as luck would have it, I had the same examiner. It definitely was the summer of luck. If he passed Asheeta after all her misdemeanours, then I would have no problem what so ever. In short, he failed me. Apparently I had manoeuvred to close to a lorry. I was devastated, and a tad embarrassed at the prospect of telling Asheeta, and all my other testosterone driven friends. I passed at the second attempt. Dad had been kind, and I, forceful enough, to have bought myself a little Gold coloured, which actually looked brown, Mazda 323 for a whopping £500. My modelling contract was bringing in the green. Dad paid for the insurance and all the little bits and bobs it had needed. I was driving my golden chariot to college to pick up my A-Level results.

It had been an excellent summer, a summer full of luck. I had picked up the tobacco chewing Radia on the way. He put on some music, ridiculing women, I hated the stuff. If it wasn't angry music from Tupac, Naughty by Nature or Public Enemy I didn't want to hear it. I drove up Regent Road, which joined with University Road, where our college was located. As I came to the cross roads connecting them both, I positioned myself to turn right, I was travelling around twenty miles per hour, and the sun glared through the windscreen. It had a devastatingly beautiful effect. Just for a split second I was absorbed by the seduction of the sunlight when suddenly I saw a man smash his head into the front window, smack the roof of the car and fell on the other side.

The man suffered ten broken ribs, a collapsed lung and severe concussion. He nearly died. I went to visit him at the hospital after the police were finished with me. They'd given me a torrid time at the station. Radia was useless. He shivered all the way through it and went to college in a state of shock. I was cool as a cucumber throughout the incident. I was firm with the police, yet polite. I went to see the man who I had so nearly killed in hospital. He lived, and decided to press charges against me; then suddenly, a few days later he withdrew his claim, my step parents had intervened by supplying a clever lawyer to fight my case. It was resolved out of court. The gentleman and father of two, was deservedly paid £10,000 in compensation. The summer of luck had come to an end.

After having parked my car in my drive, I caught the bus back to college. There was a great big white marquee on the field where we had to collect our results. The place was swarming with students. Some were laughing, others crying and a few sitting on the pavement by the side of the road starring at their slips. I went into the marquee to collect my little slip of paper. I genuinely didn't care. I was convinced that a piece of paper could never tell me what I could achieve, and what I couldn't. It could never show my potential. All I could have done was try my best and I had done, for the last six months. Some students had turned opening their slips into some sort of ritual, and were acting, as if their lives depended on it. I stood there, people watching. It was pathetic, to see so many young people being duped into believing that these slips of paper meant their whole lives.

As I tore open the envelope, the boyfriend of another close friend leaned over my shoulder to see what I had got. It didn't bother me. Before I could make out what any of it meant, he blurted out at the top of his voice "A...A...C and C. Guys Sach has done wicked."

I continued to gaze at the slip, and he was right, I had got two grade A's in Philosophy and Electronics and a slightly disappointing C in Physics. The other C was in AS level Maths. In all the modules that I had taken in the last six months, I had received straight A's. I had taken my grades from C's and E's to A's and C's. I also knew that the only reason why I got a C in Maths was, because the college had thought me incapable to retake my first year modules; otherwise I know I could have got a minimum of a grade B, in that too. Asheeta was nowhere to be found, and so I shook a few hands, got hugs from a few girls, and I began my long walk home. I saw Jinesh, Anand and Shillon all looking worried. I knew they had struggled. Tonight wouldn't be a good time to provoke Jinesh's old man.

As I strolled home, walking down University Road, I came across the junction where I had nearly taken another mans life. I walked right by it, and re-lived the whole thing again. As I walked by Regent College and then down Regent Road, I bumped into some of Dillip's runners. We shook hands and gave each other the hard man's hug. It consisted of locking palms together, holding them to ones chest, as a sign of love and loyalty and putting our heads side by side, as one would do to hug someone.

"What's up Saint", asked Spencer.

I hadn't been called that in a while, it had felt strange. Spencer and Leroy had taken over Dillip's business. His customers were now theirs. Spencer, as I found out with a lot of Afro-Caribbean men, became really friendly and incredibly loyal, once he knew that I too was tough, and that I could give as good as I got. This may come across as a gross generalisation. I do not intend for it to be. This is what I experienced. They walked me down New Walk. New Walk is an iconic walkway that runs in parallel to the busy London Road in Leicester. It's a quite setting, with its human traffic being solicitors, accounts, students and the homeless – a strange mix.

As we slowly walked down, we spoke as if we were best friends. They asked me if I was still going to be with the Firm, to which I quickly said no. I realised that they were in some kind of trouble, I didn't want to ask, and they weren't going to bring it up, unless I did so first. This was politics. The people I knew were having problems with were the same group that had attacked Dillip, and who had slashed me; and then had beaten me with weapons. They wanted Dillip's business, and they were prepared to kill for it. With Dillip out of the way, the rest would fall like dominos. Spencer knew I could be an excellent negotiator, to bring about a truce. Spencer had responded to Dillip's killing with his own set of beatings and shootings. Most of it was reported in the news, about which they gloated. Without Dillip, the Firm would fall, and they knew it. Dillip had told me who these other people were, and that once you started with them, it usually meant one of two things. Either you acknowledged their control of all business, and worked for them as a runner, albeit a senior runner, or prepare for a bloody war. Dillip had called war, because he thought he could win. He had been wrong

As we parted, Spencer turned and asked, "So how did you do today?"

I told him my grades. He looked confused, my last words to him were, "and it means I'm a better reader than you."

He smiled, and I returned it. That was the last time I ever saw him. Two weeks later, a group of men broke into his flat and shattered both of his knees. He ended up in a wheelchair. He went through severe depression, a few years later, he tried to kill himself. He was then hospitalised, and was taken in by his aunt, who lived in rural Devon. I think he still lives there – but I can't be sure. Leroy carried on the fight, until his girlfriend was gang raped in their own home. He was so traumatised by it, that he soon threw in the towel, and began working as a runner for his new masters. Last I heard he had spent time in prison.

It was Spencer, in our last few words that had triggered off another powerful enquiry in my mind. *What was education?* Why were young people compelled to study, forcibly, from the age of three up until at least sixteen? And at the time of writing this book, the Labour Party is debating whether to increase this age to eighteen. I became engrossed by the question "why education?" Why was it necessary, who decided what was necessary; what did society gain from it; how is it utilised and what are its effects? I asked many more questions, but these are all that come to mind, all these years later.

I wanted to discover the soul of education, its platonic form. Just as with Politics, people speak about Education without ever having grasped its essence. I have spoken to senior educationalists and ministers, after they have delivered passionate speeches of change and such like; they became dumbfounded by the question, what is education? They would often bullshit their way out of it, by saying something like "it's a human right!" This is another cheap cliché that is too often used. I began to feel as I did when I was younger, during Vikas's death, when people who I had thought of as elders, as wise people turned out to be simplistic passengers upon the sinking titanic.

I wanted to understand what education was, and from where it had come. Just as with the rest of this book, I won't waste my time with the little fleshy bits, even though I have written many papers and speeches on them, I do think these fleshy bits are important, but only after realising its soul. I want to take you through my journey of realisation, of what education was and still is.

Education traditionally was seen to be the accumulation of knowledge. The more information we knew about a subject, the better informed we were. Our minds were treated as vaults of knowledge, to which only you had exclusive access. It was for the individual to use when they needed it in life. Essentially, education was based on memory. The examination model was devised, quite literally thousands of years ago to test memory, to see how well we could regurgitate information we were given. Then as the technological revolution took place with the advent of global travel and communication and mass migration across continents, a different type of education was needed.

Education became broader. From merely learning about British history and civilisation, students were required to know global history and about various languages, religions, cultures and civilisations. These changes began to occur in our education system, due to the forces of global trade and politics. Then came the 70's and the mobile technology was invented. It was in the early 70's that microprocessors, space technology, mass transit systems, cheap air travel and global trade exerted new pressures onto the system. People were increasingly put into situations where their exclusive vaults of knowledge could no longer help them. Additionally, it occurred to me that as more and more people became educated, this would quite naturally result in greater competition in the job market, if that education wasn't helping create further jobs. In other words, if the education system wasn't creating a sufficient amount of entrepreneurs, then more 'educated' people would be competing for a limited number of jobs, and if the supply outstripped the demand, then wages would drop. Quite obvious you might think. But it wasn't until the 90's that educationalists began to identify the great loss this was having on the economy. They also noticed that the traditional examination methodology could no longer show the level of understanding, a student had on their chosen subject. Besides, students began to access technology, which could memorise the information for them, meaning that their exclusive vaults were no longer exclusive nor were they in their heads. From the turn of the millennium, educationalists have started to focus not on the accumulation of knowledge; that is what knowledge to memorise, but rather, where and how to find it.

This is a major shift from the traditional aspects of education – schools are now focusing on working from home, greater emphasis on coursework, and on the utilisation of technology. It seems that things that can give us knowledge, when we need it, are the focus of all mainstream education.

It was some time later that I came across the realisation of what education was, while I ran down the Queens Promenade in Kingston, Surrey. I was now at university. It dawned on me that schooling had been the central occupation of my life. It's the same with all of us who have grown up in the developed nations. We spend most of our early lives going through the education system. I then began to think of all my friends, family and the like, and realised that they too had been preoccupied by education; in fact it had been a near identical education as to the one I was imparted.

I stopped running, and realised that quite literally tens of thousands of kids were going through exactly what I had gone through, and imparted with the same bits of knowledge. It wasn't until eighteen, that I properly understood what mass education meant. I was it; I was the product, one that went a little wrong, but near enough what they had wanted. It occurred to me that I was in a factory. A factory where blank three year olds are supplied, and after a minimum of thirteen years on the conveyor belt, they are either packaged in certificates called GCSE's to mark them as approved, or are "encouraged" to carry on down the conveyor belt to get a free upgrade. Quite literally schooling is a factory – an enlightening, totally necessary and a useful one, but nevertheless, it remains a factory.

Mass produced goods are the output of all factories, the schooling system is no different. We are all mass produced, give and take small variations. Just as on any conveyor belt flexibility is in short supply, and so any great form of variation in the production process is not a viable option. I also realised the schooling system had similar issues to that of industry – there are suppliers of raw material *(in this case human beings)*, factory floor workers *(we have teachers)*, a process *(we have curriculum)*, tight quality control *(we have examinations now for six year olds)*, different conveyor belts for slight variations *(we have options for fourteen year olds and we distinguish the better products from the rest)* and the products must be pushed on to a customer once quality control approve it as suitable. I pondered on who the customer was, for all this education.

When I got back to my room, at the halls of residence, on Kingston Hill, Surrey, I asked some of my corridor buddies, why they were at university. Most of them looked at me with a slight tickle of apprehension, they clearly hadn't thought about it – "so I can get a cool job at the end of it", most replied.

It was simple really; looking back now, the customer for all these "educated" people was the free market, of which the job market was only a part. All these products, including me, were going to be shipped off to a company or organisation, which would use us for their own ends. In return we would be paid, given a pension, praised and given the opportunity to progress within the hierarchy of the firm. This realisation, combined with my experience of politics, through the tunnels, fused my mind firmly in the further exploration of what education, in actual fact was. We were being produced; we were being educated and skilled so that we could essentially be traded as commodities in the job market. It was supply & demand – Adam Smith was right, he envisaged a society where the spirit of supply & demand would guide all mankind, it was the new Holy Ghost.

No doubt that I have over simplified the situation, because factually we have limited government control or what are called regulatory measures, on the force of supply & demand. In essence however, it was very simple. Educate the masses so that they can be commoditised by the market. It was for this reason and for no other that people had said to me, "what will you do with a degree in Philosophy?" They had all said that it would be a waste of time and that no one would value it. Indeed, the market didn't value Philosophy as much as it had valued say Computer Science back then. But what the market valued was always in flux.

It then occurred to me that if, what was in demand was always in flux, then who and how did they manage the factory? The answer as to whom, was simple. It was government, central and local. As to the how, well this became very difficult to grasp. What I had come to grips with however was that education was a factory, we were being commoditised for the *'nearly'* free market, and the factory management was the government. The management as with any industry was compelled to serve the customer, which were the corporations and the wider economy. The government essentially had to maintain a curriculum that was in sync with what industry needed. This couldn't be an easy job.

Essentially, industry itself often didn't know what type of skilled people it needed and in what supply, until the need was already upon them. A tad problem you might have guessed when it took the best part of thirteen years for a product to be produced from beginning to completion. I soon realised during my training at the MoD, which lasted as long as I was at university, that they too were in short supply of talented, unique *human goods*. They no longer had faith with the education factory to produce the type of twenty first century leaders they needed, so they set about creating their own schooling, they called it the "fast track management scheme".

It was a kind of 'finishing' school. They hand selected people at eighteen, who they believed had the innate aptitude and spirit for leadership roles. They nurtured them with the skills, which they so badly needed at the top of their hierarchy. They only used products from the education factory for sourcing staff that would be in non leadership roles. As I got older, I realised that most major organisations had their own schooling system for their very brightest, and the rest would be plucked from the conveyor belt. Anyone that has been through university and has had to 'apply' for jobs through the traditional routes will know that there is a two year Graduate training that they must complete. Essentially this is their final touch up, so that you will fit into their organisation as smoothly as possible, and will add value to their work. Companies such as IBM do not even guarantee their graduate trainees a job after the two years training, they are required to re-apply. It was from this realisation, at eighteen, when I had just begun my Aerospace degree, and my training at the MoD that I saw and recognised the value of my luck.

It also raised further questions about the short sightedness of the whole process. If, in essence we are all guided by the new Holy Ghost, then it would imply that there is no such thing as an education based on virtue. Education, I realised lacked a *'telos'*. This line of enquiry raised far more questions, which I couldn't answer. I had however, discovered that day, the schematics of education, nothing more. I just realised who the main players were, who were the pushers and the suppliers, and most importantly who sat higher than everyone else around the fire.

I am a passionate educationalist. I use the word in its broadest possible sense. Just as my parents had believed, I too now acknowledge the importance of good grades and a positive work ethic being imbibed into children from a young age. But I believe there has to be something more, our lives are dependent on this, and I believe that the twenty first century will truly test our factories to their limits. I share great synergy with the likes of Plato, who had believed, education if used correctly would be the greatest tool to free mankind from suffering. In the Indian Hindu traditions, it is said that the first twenty five years of ones life should be dedicated to learning; this is the phase where a person can be shaped and moulded to prosper in later years. Both Plato & the Indian Hindu traditions did not see education or learning as how we today approach it. They saw it as a means to enlightenment, they saw education as a tool to not only train mankind, in the art of better survival, which is, what our current education is geared towards, but they saw something else, something more transcendental. They saw education as the tool to equip people with the power to explore and discover truths. The premise being that all life ultimately should be about discovering eternal truths, Plato called it the world of forms, and in Hinduism it is called Dharma. I call it, the intellectual tunnels. As they did, I do still believe that education must help people to live better, but there has to be something more, and I believe it has to be about exploring the intellectual tunnels. This is my idealism – for I do not actually believe, that I will ever see an education factory, delivering a virtue centred individual to the corporation. *Virtue is the last thing the market needs.*

But away from virtue, education still lacks fundamentals for those who have an innate spirit, as the MoD rather nicely put it, for leadership. We must be loosing thousands of potential entrepreneurs whose innate spirit has actually been crushed by the system rather than nurtured. I was lucky. In the summer of '99, I was saved from the factory managers who would have in all honesty, if it wasn't for my new trainers, would have destroyed my innate leadership qualities. I found that we were all being well trained, and plugged with lots of mostly useless knowledge, but essentially had empty minds. A really intelligent man once put it like this, he said, *"when we are young we learn so little about so much; and as we grow older, we end up learning absolutely everything about nothing!"*

A well trained mind is nothing to belittle, but I soon realised while at the MoD that my schooling had geared me to dealing with closed problems. The problem was that the MoD was throwing me into open ended ones. Mr. Richardson made sure that I spent six months in every department and that I was continuously challenged intellectually, emotionally, and physically pushed. I was not there to be making coffee, or doing data entry, which is what I saw many other interns aged eighteen do. I was asked to deal with questions to do with decision making, not analysing sets of information. I found that schooling was excellent at making people superb analysers, but quite ill trained for making any kind of decision as to what to do next. I realised that the old men, who sat above everyone else, didn't spend their days calculating answers, they were there to make decisions that would make positive differences to the organisation. These people were the top hierarchy because they were experts in dealing with open ended questions. An other way to look at it, is that if you've spent all your time consumed in the education factory, and have excelled in it by getting high grades, this still won't help you in the slightest when it comes to dealing with open ended questions, and so you're chances of becoming the old man in the hierarchy will still be slim.

Another aspect that can be remedied immediately is that of individualism. My education was predominantly individualistic. It was only until I arrived at university, where we had a proxy little group assignment, where ones grades were dependent on others. Throughout my life, I was praised or punished based on my own actions, but in the world outside academia, nothing gets done if people do not cooperate. Basic interpersonal skills were not on my curriculum, how to present, how to influence and how to problem solve open ended issues, was something that as my university professor once said, "all that other stuff, life teaches you, you're hear to learn mathematics, and mathematics is what you'll learn."

He was right, life had taught me all that other stuff, not because it was normal for everyone to pick it up as they grew older, but because I travelled the intellectual tunnels. Most people sadly, never learnt this other stuff, to their own detriment. At the MoD, I realised that everyone was interconnected; of course I already knew this, I had come across the soul of relationships in the tunnels, but here was the practical proof. Yet, why wasn't I trained at school to deal with the interconnectedness? Was I on board the sinking titanic, yet again? Team work was something that I had developed on the football field, not at school. A sport was something that was classed as unimportant or at best, fun. It was definitely not work, and yet my core team working skills originated from it. As Charles Handy, rightly points out, that in school we are all competitors, but at work we all become colleagues.

"So you're at university learning Aerospace, huh?" said my first ever line manager in Human Resources. "I don't think that's going to be of much use here! How do you think you'll manage people that are old enough to be your parents? How do you plan to win their respect and confidence?"

Goodness, I was only eighteen, lady give me a break! I never said this to her of course, I just thought it. I was to shadow and work under her for six months. She didn't beat around the bush, she was straight, always, and she had no issues with humiliating you if she thought that was what you deserved! I was too intimidated by her initially, but after bitching about her to Mr. Richardson, I slowly came to see the logic in her madness! Ironically, she is still one of the few people I am in touch with from those days. She's retired now, and hopefully would have proof read this book. I had never interacted with anyone that was much older than me, except my teachers and other family members. I was clueless as to how I should behave and interact with them. This is another aspect that I believe schools should be actively promoting through further work experience, social volunteering at nursing homes, hospitals, at the police constabulary and so on. Young people at school need to leave knowing how to behave in wider society, and with people from different cultural backgrounds.

Essentially, what I am trying to point out is that the process of educating needs to be in greater harmony with the process of living. There are certain types of intelligence, which sadly, the educational establishment does not deal with. Every young person needs to be financially intelligent, interpersonally capable, intuitive, emotionally mature and confident in his or her own unique ability. Schooling should begin by looking inwards, not outwards. To know thy self, is more important at the early stages of life than the discovery of the world. Young people should be nurtured to mature emotionally, and this should act as the basis of all future growth. Young people should be well versed in the psychology of emotions, how to effectively manage them and how to positively influence their environment using them. Kids need to learn, at school, how they can become self motivated through understanding themselves in relation to their upbringing. They should be told that they are being trained to become commodities in the market, and that they should be looking for customers, organisations that can use their skills, rather than jobs. And as a prerequisite, every school should be given the mandate that every child leaving their school should have identified at least several key competencies, which they can build on, and use to gain employment.

My final ramble about what I think of education is that it should actively, encourage the philosophical life. Schools should be actively encouraging young people to ask questions about the nature of God, the meaning of ones life, what death is and so on. These questions are the rabbit holes that most of us, at some point in our lives fall down, but never know it! We become confused, and consequently suffer. Instead we should train young people in the virtue based ethics, not by preaching, as is done in religious schools, but through encouraging them to explore without boundaries.

In 2004, I began a session called *THINK*. THINK takes place once a week, for one hour. It is an open platform for young people to come and openly ponder on the deeper aspects of life. In these sessions, we explore anything and everything. There are no boundaries or taboos. We are there to discover, to channel our minds through this reality in order to penetrate the subtle greater reality underneath. My role at these sessions is to facilitate, ask questions, challenge their ideas to strengthen their ability to critique, offer various interpretations, but at the end of it, they should leave the session feeling as if they have travelled! They should feel more confident in themselves and most importantly with the realisation that life is far more interesting than MTV makes out!

With all this in mind, I went to work on becoming a first class Aerospace Engineering graduate, not because I could get a "good" job, but because I was in love with what I was doing – essentially mathematics. With my above average A-Level grades, I walked into Kingston University. The MoD had wanted me to study at Kings College and they had offered me a place, but I was too sentimentally attached to the idea of studying at Vikas's place. I wanted to show my parents that I could achieve what he had done, and go one step better! The MoD, Kings College and Kingston University all came to, what I later realised was an utmost curious understanding. I would officially be classed as a Kings College undergraduate student, while attending lectures at Roehampton Vale, strictly speaking apart of Kingston University. The MoD had *in-house* professors at both places whose responsibility it was that I be pushed and supported in the appropriate way. Kingston University ran a Masters of Engineering fast track degree programme, especially for those who had the academic stamina, of which I was apart, and those that were 'sponsored' by various organisations. My fast track group consisted of twenty five students of which, twenty were foreign and all of us were sponsored. I quickly realised, as I had done with the rest of life that I was in way over my head.

The students in my group were sponsored by BAe Systems, GkN Aerospace, Hindustan Aeronautical Limited, Indian Space Research Organisation, European Space Research, NASA, Lockheed, McKinsey Group, Williams – the formula one team, and of course the MoD, amongst others. I was surrounded by smart cookies, the type of which I had never seen. I was the only one from the MoD; my other "co-fast trackers" had gone to Imperial, Cambridge or University of Manchester. I had no intension of going anywhere apart from Kingston, or Imperial, because I loved the sound of it – but as it worked out Imperial had refused, even at the behest of greater powers, to accept me as one of their own. They didn't approve of the grade C in Physics. So it was that I ended up spending the next four years, with some of the brightest mathematical minds on the planet, when almost sixteen months earlier, I was advised by my careers advisor to drop A Levels, and take up a BTEC in accounts – he had thought this would be more suitable for my aptitude in maths.

I had become bright overnight because, I was in actual fact born bright but never lived up to my potential. The fall through the rabbit hole had caused me great suffering in my early to mid-teens, the world made little sense, people even less so, and I had been deeply unhappy. But as I matured and began to navigate around the tunnels beyond time and space, I could essentially grasp anything instantly, if I came across it in the tunnels. That is what happened with mathematics. I realised what it was, and why it was so penetrating, I loved it, because I knew that it would lead me to deeper tunnels and realisations about the world. So to the outside world, it appeared that I had suddenly become bright. What can be instantaneous in the physical world can be a very long time in the timeless tunnels. But this is a transcendental experience, and so cannot speak of it, but those of you who have been there will know what I mean.

My flat mates, at the halls of residence at Kingston Hill were refreshingly normal, relatively speaking. My allocated room was on the ground floor of block D, in corridor D3, right opposite the entrance. My room was at the end of the corridor. Opposite me, was Kaveeta Luthor, a British born Mauritian Hindu girl, she was reading business. She was quite intelligent but carried the Essex "ditsy-ness" where ever she went. She was a rich 'daddy's girl' who would rather drive everywhere than to take public transport. Her comments to be precise were, "you seriously can't expect me to catch the bus?"

I liked her. She had a spirit about her; she was deeply caring to the point of mothering. Next to her, opposite me, was Comfort. A British born Nigerian girl from Manchester, if for nothing else, I loved her name. I had known many girls like her in Leicester, but what I particularly liked was her attitude, her determination to work her way out of working class-ness and onto become a solicitor. She read law. Moving down from her was Imran "Dain" Parchment, a Jamaican born engineering student. Dain and I had synergy. We were both explorers of the tunnels. He too, had fallen through the rabbit hole, he too had been scared by early life, and finally he too was on a pathway to discovery the Self. Needless to point out, that he and I got on very well. He was three years older than the rest of us and was trained as a chief. My immediate neighbour was gentle *'unsure of himself'* Kevin. He read music. He had an over burdening timetable of four hours a week, plus extra tutorials. Kevin would always remind us of the extra tutorials. Kevin was from rural Devon, a town called Paignton. We shared a similar sort of humour, he and I loved Red Dwarf, Garfield and Chess *(I know chess isn't particularly packed with laughter, but it was for us)*. Next to Kevin was Darrel. I got to know little of Darrel, but he was sound enough. He worked hard, and was a good people person, he particularly enjoyed women. He studied Accounts. We became a close set of friends within a short space of time, along with others, who practically lived there. I enjoyed their company. They were a useful escape from reality. They knew little of my past and they never found out, until just now.

I was the bright spark on the block, at least which was how I felt. The only one with a scholarship, and having almost thirty hours a week of core lectures and seminars, followed by quite literally tonnes of home assignments. I saw relatively little of my flat mates because of the number of hours I had, and because every weekend I was with Asheeta. I travelled up to see her on Friday night, and would catch the coach back to London at three on Monday mornings to arrive at 9am at Roehampton Vale, just in time for lectures. Asheeta had been having a torrid time at Nottingham University, she was reading Genetics.

She hadn't connected at all well with the university life style or her new flat mates. I had recognised then that our relationship was based around us seeing each other as much as we could, without compromising our education. Asheeta was quite happy to miss her lectures for me, but I wouldn't have any of it, because I knew that if I let her miss her lectures, she would expect me to miss mine, and I wasn't going too. Simultaneously, I also realised that she needed companionship; she needed to be cared for, and loved within a structure that would allow her to flourish academically and socially. I was also well aware that university was a hedonistic place, at least in the first year. I knew that if I couldn't give Asheeta what she had needed, she would find it somewhere, and with someone else, and I wasn't about to give up my Angel. So I consciously attempted to study hard, support Asheeta, keep our relationship growing, and keep my new guardians satisfied. I also had to deal with the hedonism that was all around me, the temptations floated in and out of daily life. I could resist because I was completely satisfied with Asheeta.

If I was surrounded by temptresses, then Asheeta was most definitely in the company of men who would want more than 'a hug'! A cool cat had tried, and soon found out never to trespass again. Dillip had said that if you want people to fear you, then create your legends. And soon, Asheeta's admirers realised how real the legends could become. The cool cat never tried again and neither did anyone else! I had put a permanent night guard around Asheeta, and I would know instantly the moment when some 'nice' guy tried to comfort her through her torrid time at university. I make no qualms about it – I was not going to allow some Hyena to come and prey on Asheeta while I was away. Was I insecure? Absolutely! I too could have had girls every night, but I chose not to because I knew right from wrong, and I knew that Asheeta was the one. I knew it would take her time to become acclimatised at university, and as soon as she found her feet, my appointed night guard left. I bought her guard a plane ticket to Ibiza as a gesture of thanks. He was one of Leroy's runners, running in Nottingham. I also had my cousin Manish, who was reading Management at Nottingham. He was in his second year and a veteran of the university lifestyle. He too, intuitively noticed that I was very serious about Asheeta, and he looked after her during those days. He would make frequent visits to just say "hi", or both of them would go out together. He would inform me if there were any cats loitering. The early months of mine and Asheeta's structural relationship had been hard to maintain. I did what I had too.

Since Dillip's death, I had begun to live the experiences that I had in the tunnels. I was beginning to live the philosophy. I was still rather haphazardly falling into the rabbit holes, but my meditation techniques had improved, and I was beginning to find some joy through it. At university, I had consciously wanted a secluded life, one where I could read, think, go for long walks and most of all where I could leave my recent past behind. Kingston Hill was perfect. Five hundred yards down the hill was Richmond Park, ten square miles of woodland, ponds, wild grass and dear roaming freely. Roehampton Vale stood squarely opposite the entrance to the park. In order to strike a balance between seclusion, and the human need to socialise, I got myself a part time job behind the student union bar. It was perfect. I was out every Wednesday and Thursday night at the bar, and yet I was earning, not that I needed the money. I was discovering that money was rolling in quickly and relatively effortlessly, from the few hours of modelling I did every month. Having the bar job meant that I could socialise and get to know, by first name at least, most of the campus party animals and regular drinkers. I could effectively, from a distance, gauge the social hierarchy that existed between all the deeply insecure freshers. The added benefit, which I had missed but reaped the full benefits from, was that when everybody else cleared the bar and went clubbing, I went to my room to read; I was far too into *James Redfield's Celestine Prophesy*, to waste my night talking frivolous rubbish with people, who I didn't want to connect with. I had no recognised need for them. Hence there was no chance of a relationship developing. Besides, I was beginning to hate smoky environments. *Thank God for the smoking ban!*

I did go clubbing occasional, but only to dance and when the music was right. I found that on these rare occasions, and they were indeed rare, for I can count the number of times I went on my fingers, I found that I ended up in deep mediation. I found that soon I would be so fused into the rhythm that I lost track of everything else around me. There was no gap between the music and I. I would enter the same kind of trance that I enjoyed so much when played football or kick boxed. I still use music to meditate, but not at a club. I now prefer Wagner, Hans Zimmer or the angelic voice of Enya compared to the angry "Id"[2] driven music of Tupac Shakur. The transition from heavy hip hop to a calmer, sophisticated blend of tunes was already underway back then.

I also noted that most music was, and still is, based on sex, greed, pride, lust and all the other Id driven emotions that we all experience. I began to resent the stuff. In order for me to enjoy a piece of music, the lyrics were as important as the beat, not so for Asheeta, or most people that I know. I find this bemusing. Even today I still can't get over it. Asheeta and I will be driving somewhere and a track will come on the radio, which degrades the human mind to its most primitive nature, while at the same time degrading women, and Asheeta would bop along to it. When I would ask her, does it bother her what the lyrics are about, she would just blow it off and say, I don't care about the words, the music is cool. I found this comment indigestible. I couldn't stomach it. And I've heard this from many people, across ages, professions and the like. How can their mind not hear the words but fully enjoy the music? How are the lyrics muted in their minds? I have never been able to do this; I don't think that any human being can! In fact, what I believe has occurred is that people have become desensitised to such offensive brainless drivel. People do not mute the words, but the words become meaningless for them, but this is not the same as muting. Their subconscious is still picking up the gross depiction of the human condition, which psychologists have shown effect people's conscious behaviour.

We have a generation of people who have been exposed to such gross violent music, which they have consciously become desensitised by it, and yet are deeply affected. Let me share a clear example of what a friend of mine at Oxford did to experiment on his younger sister and step sister. Both were in their mid teens. They had agreed for one of them to only listen to pop music and Rhythm & Blues, popularly known as R&B and the other to enjoy classical, soul and jazz. This is not a water tight scientific experiment you understand, but it gets the point that I'm making across. He would invite me once every two weeks to come and see his sisters. I would just observe them and ask a set of leading questions. When we started this experiment, which went on for over a year, both were of similar mind, both dressed conservatively and held modest views. By the end of the year

---

[2] The ID is Freud's part of his theory of the subconscious mind. It is our most primitive nature, where our desire for sex and aggression stem from.

the sister that had been listening to classical had remained modest, albeit a little more sophisticated in her dress and views. She had gradually grown comfortable with the idea of smooth music, and had picked up playing the flute. Her views on sex had evolved ever so slightly and could pose decent arguments for her case, and she could still be classed as modest. Sister number two, who had agreed to spend the entire year listening to pop music and R&B, had most definitely shifted in her mindset. She hadn't noticed. As far as she was concerned, sister one *(who listened to classical music)* had remained the same, as she had believed herself to have done. She hadn't picked up on the fact that she visibly wore skimpier, tighter clothes, her views on sex had become more forth coming, and she believed that it was perfectly normal and quite right that people have sex with more than one partner. Her reasoning for this position was quite unintelligible. Whether she was right or wrong is beside the point.

Both had believed that they had changed little. Furthermore, both had thought that the other was the same as a year ago, until we showed them their answers to the questions before the experiment had begun, their gradual evolution and their answers after the year. We also took note of their wardrobe before and after the experiment, both girls noticed the difference when they compared themselves. What my friend's unethical experiment had shown, was that here were two intelligent girls of a similar taste, living in an identical home setting, who had foolishly agreed to take part in the study, without knowing clearly what they were being tested for, was that firstly both had been affected, and secondly without acknowledging so.

This was not a Nobel Prize winning psychological experiment, but it showed that there was little argument as to the question whether music influences people. The answer was very clearly yes, it does. Musical contents, whether it be rhythmic or lyrical, affects our values and the way we perceive the world. There is nothing more devastating to a young eager mind than angry Hip Hop, R&B and Pop music. Of course, I am sure, and I know from experience that in all three genres there are songs that are truly uplifting and soul purifying, but these are far too few and in between. The gross celebration of materialism, the blatant exploitation of women and the values of hedonism can only be detrimental to any society. If people want the freedom to express themselves, then with that freedom they carry responsibility. This, I believe is the flaw with modern western liberalism – there is freedom without accountability, for those who profess to be artists.

I have spoken widely on this issue and will continue to do so, so long as I have anything to offer of value. Artists should rightly be given space to express themselves as they see fit, but if their expression has detrimental effects on its audience, directly or indirectly, then they should be held to account. If their artwork does not add anything of great value to society and yet is deemed to be detrimental, then it should be stopped. Note, that I am not saying anything should be banned. What I am saying is that if artist want to call women "bitches" or other black men as "niggers", then they should be held to account. If they fail to justify themselves then the track is either re-scripted or banned. I have heard naïve *'freedom huggers'*, say to me that if you don't like it, avoid it. This is fine, but what about things that I cannot avoid like exploitative music and imagery? Whether I choose it or not, this will affect me sub-consciously at best, or worse. I believe that society desperately needs to check the values that it projects to itself, through all forms of art, and from artists who earn a great deal of money from their work, as well as the producing corporations. All need to be held to account. The challenge is how we do this?

We must ensure that we continue to live in a liberal climate, and yet attach responsibility with the freedom we practise. The danger that I readily accept is the slippery slope, which lies not too far from my proposition. The danger that we begin to morally judge peoples expression, and we equate morality as what the majority find tasteful and immoral as vice versa. A further, far scarier dream would be if the Church or Islamists jumped on this band wagon of "freedom with responsibility", because these people are not on the side of freedom, they just wouldn't want their religion challenged.

The formula as a schematic is simple, yet very difficult to implement. If a piece of artwork is constructive and genuinely adds something of value to society, even if it offends the majority, it should be expressed. However, if a piece of artwork is derogatory and it offers nothing to the growth of ideas, of a liberal society, then the artists need to be given the opportunity to justify themselves, and if their justification is inadequate, the artwork should be scrapped. I say this, not as a middle aged, white male from the Home Counties, and who happens to be a Member of Parliament. I am speaking from a life on the streets, and as someone who grew up with the angry lyrics of Tupac Shakur, who did influence me greatly, and I speak as a liberal, albeit a responsible one. Freedom is often falsely construed as being intrinsically good, it is not. Freedom is morally neutral. Whether freedom is a force for good or a force for degradation depends largely on what society does with it. With freedom comes responsibility and where this is not so, only chaos can prevail.

Music, as is everything in life, is a double sided coin. It can be a powerful medium for inspiration, for the creation, build up and release of powerful emotions. As I mentioned earlier, during my time at university, I had begun to shed my anger and frustrations of life, and with it, I began to loose my taste for angry rap. Instead, as with all dialectics, just like a pendulum, I began to appreciate Stravinsky, Mozart and Mahler. I discovered that while my block partied away their night, drinking excessively, and participating in the crudest forms of sexual foreplay, I could meditate through Mahler. I could effectively enter the tunnels, travel into the transcendental and come back to the surface of the limited, *'knowing'* something truth-bound about existence. I have found some forms of music to be so intellectually stimulating that after being fused into it, one awakes from it to find a richer, more coherent existence. I found through Mahler the medium to connect my spirit to that collective consciousness, and return back to my original state, richer, knowing that which could not be grasped through language or thoughts. It was experiential, not intellectual.

After listening to Hans Zimmer's *'breaking of the fellowship'*, I often awoke thoroughly squeezed of all emotions that had swelled in the dam of my mind. His music was a release, of a kind that I cannot describe. All I can say of it is that after it, I had shared to the full, the existential depth of an entire life. Sometimes the music became so intolerably beautiful, so rich in transcendental truths that it almost asked too much of the listener, it stretched my capacities and extended my presence deep into intellectual space. It was truly a life evolving experience to have felt such transient beauty. Saying all of this, I acknowledge that Mahler, Wagner, Zimmer or Stravinsky is not for anyone at anytime. Note that I have not claimed that they are not for everyone. In fact, I believe this music must be for everyone. It must be for humanity and not for the ivory tower alone. These musicians were true masters of navigation through the tunnels, and to be at their feet, listening to them, through the timelessness, is for those that have worked their way through the basics of the transient. There is a gradual evolution, a process of realisation, one cannot just put this book down and begin listening to Mahler, and I doubt that it would work. Try it.

Everything in the physical reality is essentially based on the transcendental, and so it too must be explored and learnt through gradation. One must appreciate the basics of the greater reality, before they begin running marathons with Zimmer or Mahler! Most people will simply not appreciate it and some even repulsed by it, if they are not already familiar with the transient. It was another form of meditation, one where I became the notes; I rode them, and surfed across to land on the beaches of transcendental truths.

It was my constant exposure to all things up lifting during my time at university, which exponentially increased my rate of exploration of the tunnels. I was beginning to find myself in them for longer and longer periods of time. Bear in mind that time does not exist in these places. What I mean to say is that the frequency, at which I entered the tunnels and lost touch with the material world, was increasing and with it my realisations about life were more penetrating and vivid. As well as becoming one with music and ones own self; I began to deeply get involved in discovering the true depths of mathematics. Now, I had realised early enough that mathematics was not transcendental. It couldn't be, for it dealt with logic, with symbols and was essentially a set of rules, and all of these things exist only in the cruder realities of time and space. This meant that I learnt language, which I could use to penetrate all that is material by day, at university, and delve into the deep pools of transient waters by night, with Mahler, Zimmer and others as my coaches.

I was becoming bright. This occurred for several reasons. The first and most obvious one being, that for thirty hours a week I was in the company of geniuses. This naturally applied significant pressure on me to perform, keep up and focus on the challenge at hand. I was most definitely the weakest one out of the group in mathematics. I was always playing catch up, everything took me longer, and I made too many elementary mistakes according to some of my group members. I felt wholly inadequate throughout my first year. Some of the Yanks often expressed their amazement that I was even remotely thought of as being capable to be in that group. They were right in all fairness. I was out of my depths, this was no new phenomenon in my life, but this time everybody knew it, and this was new.

Harpreet Singh and Yogendre, or Yogi for short, came to my aid. They knew I was drowning and must have felt sad to see a man drown in the rough mathematical waters of an Aerospace programme. Both were from India, and both sponsored. Harpreet, or as his name later became, *Little Singh*, was spotted by Indian Space Research and Yogi by HAL *(Hindustan Aeronautical Limited)*. Both were bright, but Harpreet surpassed everyone, he was a genius among geniuses. He became my Guru and Yogi my mentor. They were great teachers. Harpreet was kind and compassionate but a little impatient with me, unlike Yogi, who could sit through an entire evening with me as I tugged along; slowly grasping what was elementary to these giants. Both were physically small and Little Singh in particular had a malnourished frame for a body. He had a great big black beard which ended at his chest, he wore tiny intellectual round specs and carried a tall black umbrella around with him at all times, even on hot clear bright days. He was a very gentle creature. Yogi was small but he didn't look as if he had an eating disorder. He was deeply religious and followed the Swaminarayan sect within Hinduism. He would often come into lectures with the tilak dotted on his forehead. If I hadn't found these two to guide me, I would have failed my year spectacularly and probably lost favour with my Guardians.

    I did pass my first year, just about. I got a 58% average, which would have been respectable anywhere else, but when you are flying with jet planes, a propelled aircraft simply wouldn't do. Harpreet had passed with an 86% average, the highest out of the pack, and Yogi with a modest 73%. With managing my steady modelling career, my long distance relationship with Asheeta and completing the chores that my Guardians put me through, I had felt satisfied with my results. I was pulled into the office, however by Professor Welch, he shared his concerns about my below expected score; we spoke, and he felt that I had to prove myself in my second year if I was to remain with the geniuses. I mentioned the little conversation I had with the Professor to Mr. Richardson. He nodded and said nothing. I also mentioned that I had found two saviours and that with their help I was sure to do better.

    Two weeks later, Mr. Richardson had rearranged my study programmes with the MoD. I was to work with them through my holidays, especially summer and Easter. This would free up valuable time to study longer during term time. It proved to be invaluable. As with everything else that I had learnt in life, everything except navigating through the tunnels, I learnt from observation. I watched Little Singh. I shadowed him. I saw and mirrored the way he learnt, revised, took notes and then practised. It was he that introduced me to the wonders of the *Cornell Technique* – named after the famous Ivy League university in the States.

    It was so simple in nature that it was almost embarrassing. He introduced me to the bio-hour, it was a daily routine. He spent some twenty minutes of the hour reading ahead. He had either borrowed or bought almost every book on the reading list, totalling almost fifty. He had spent a mini fortune. Compare this to my pittance of an effort of buying three books. He would follow the year schedule given to us by each lecturer and pull out the relevant pages from the text books and skim through it. He would then always arrive ten minutes early in the lecture, to firstly find a seat in the front, and to speak with the lecturer about the upcoming class. He made prolific notes. He never stopped writing. He used, in later years, a Dictaphone to record the lecture so that he could "relive" the thrilling experience of thermodynamics. But mostly he stuck to making notes. As soon as the day ended, he would walk back to his dorms, which was twenty minutes away. He considered this his break.

Once at his room, usually around five or five thirty in the afternoon, he would make some spicy Indian chai, and drink it down over an episode of Blue Peter. He enjoyed Blue Peter, I never figured out why – it's one mystery not worth solving. After Blue Peter, he would spend as long as it took, reducing his lecture notes into smaller manageable chunks, and using his fifty textbooks to add clarity wherever he had felt necessary. Typically, it would be around eight thirty by the time he finished, sometimes longer. He would then spend an hour making something to eat, eating it and then clearing up. I don't need to point out that he ate mostly frozen rubbish. He was no cook, his one flaw, but nothing I could capitalise on, as I couldn't cook either. He must have thought of me as completely useless – a cave man in jeans. After dinner, he would begin his bio-hour. He spent forty minutes reviewing his notes, and then end by spending twenty, as I said before, reading ahead to the next day.

He did this everyday. His day would end at nine thirty, or ten. He woke up at seven in the morning to get ready for lectures at nine. He worked eleven to twelve hours, Monday to Friday and then spent a modest seven on weekends practising his weekly maths from textbooks. He worked seven days a week, seventy four hours in total. This was his secret. He was bright, but to be super bright this is what you had to do. If you compared his average day to mine, it was altogether shameful – at least mathematically speaking, and to compare his life to Kevin's, would have been simply farcical. I would wake up at eight for lectures at nine, compared to his seven. I would arrive just on time, and would have sat midway or at the back of the theatre, he would always be in front. I would make few notes and sometimes none at all and relied solely on handouts. Additionally, I would have few books to refer to for extra clarification, he had near fifty. I got home and spent time reading the Bhagavad-Gita, Nietzsche or Noam Chomsky, whereas he reduced his notes. I would relax and listen to a spot of Wagner, or Louis Armstrong, and have a chat with my flat mates, mostly eating Kaveeta's or Dain's cooked food. I went to sleep at midnight or later, while reading Buddhists scriptures. He was doing his bio-hour. On weekends, I was spending time with Asheeta, whereas he practised solutions, and spoke to the few friends he had.

Many readers may be thinking that Little Singh lived a sad little existence. I would argue that he didn't. I believe it's because we cannot connect with his pleasure that we call his life sad or lonely. If you never had to worry or were compelled to do anything, what would you spend your days doing? Little Singh would still do what he did. He loved it. He enjoyed it and flourished through it. He would get the same pleasure from thermodynamics or working in the wind tunnel as most men would get from marrying Miss World. Bad example maybe, but you get my point! I realised after two weeks of shadowing Little Singh that I could not live the way he did, because Mathematics wasn't an end in itself, it was a means, whereas for him it was an end. I wanted something else, something further. Questions of God, life, existence and death never crossed his mind. Even when I would bring such things up, he would twinge with annoyance, and politely tell me to get on with whatever it was I was doing.

With the MoD letting up some pressure, and Asheeta finding her footing at University meant that in my second year I could become brighter – at least academically. I religiously followed the Cornell Technique as Little Singh had shown, with a little twist to suit my own values and life style. It worked miracles for me. I averaged 72% in my second year. Yogi received 75% and Harpreet, a less than perfect 79%. I was no longer at the bottom of my class, I was fifth from bottom! I was beginning to prove to myself, and the Yanks that I deserved to be there. Academically, I was beginning to excel, and I was becoming sure footed.

The Cornell Technique, I realised, for it to do miracles needed prerequisite conditioning. One needed self discipline and focus, and the other is the wilful sacrifice of other activities that you'd rather be doing. In my case I sacrificed time with my house mates *(we were living in a six bedroom house on Hook Road)*, and when I did spend it with them, we played chess, spoke about life, the future and of course philosophy – even our casual chats were uplifting. I also sacrificed regular running and exercise. I put on an entire stone that year. The days of running two miles in less than eight minutes seemed like a pleasant wishful dream. Furthermore, I wasn't seeing Asheeta as much. She had moved back to Leicester and travelled the thirty minute train ride everyday to Nottingham University. To the disappointment of my flat mates, I also hardly ever went out partying. It was something that my intellect gradually became allergic to. I saw it as frivolous jovial hedonism. While my other friends were out partying, drinking, stumbling into bed and sleeping their hangover off until midday or even later, I was reading, writing and actively exploring the rabbit holes.

I had always felt that my studies, my progress, even my very existence was only a means to some other end. I never felt my life to be an end in itself. If I could distinguish myself from most other people, I would say that it would be this innate feeling that I have always carried with me, often as a heavy burden. I realised through conversations, as well as observations that most people saw their lives as an end in itself, and many of these people actually claimed to believe in an afterlife, yet their actions didn't seem to reflect their beliefs. And because I saw my life as a means rather than an end, I didn't fear losing it as much as others did. I didn't really put the same sort of value on my life as others put on theirs. And someone who doesn't really see their own physical existence as the most prized possession ends up seeing the world differently. I didn't really fear things as much as those around me. I realised after years of wondering why I didn't have the same ambitions as others, why I never wanted to work a nine to five, and above all else why I never thought like others – it was simple, when it finally clicked. I didn't fear life. Or put another way, there was very little to fear in life. It was this lack of fear that was at the heart of my free thinking. I went hurtling back into the tunnels and I remembered my realisation of fear at RAF Cranwell almost eighteen months earlier. Then as now, I began to realise the central role fear played in our lives. At Cranwell I had realised the *'macro'* effects of fear, whereas, now I was beginning to feel the *'micro'* effects.

Fulfilling Dreams

So much had happened, in such little time. I still haven't quite come to grips with how so much had changed. In this chapter, I have described how lucky I have been, and how "angels" came in all sizes. Asheeta was the first and the most life-evolving. It was through her, that I grasped what it meant to be in a 'proper' relationship with ones own mother. I learnt through observing her, how one could achieve academic success and be socially active. It was Asheeta who had made me truly happy, not externally, but from within. When she held me close, it was my soul that was being nourished. Mechanically speaking, she repaired me.

If Asheeta had repaired me, then Plato, the Upanishads, Krishnamurti, Nietzsche, Kant, Schopenhauer and Wittgenstein had all installed automated systems to keep me safe while travelling at speed on the motorway of life. The distinguished company of great thinkers had developed a navigation system inside my psyche that would take me through rabbit holes safely. I was effectively dodging the harshness of life on the material plane, and firmly holding onto the rope made from the thoughts of great thinkers as I searched the tunnels. Plato, with his reiterated insistence that only the Enlightened Philosopher Kings should rule society, due to their exclusive understanding of the 'forms', which, to this day I have associated to the same phenomenon as the intellectual tunnels that underlie our reality; then there were the writers of the Upanishads, which without a doubt is the greatest philosophical work to come out of antiquity, with its insistence on understanding the true Self, as the only way out of worldly suffering, its insights into the nature of God are striking, and something which all Judo-Christian religions could gain from, if only they would allow such *"Pagan" or "Kaffir"* thoughts to enter their cannon of text; Krishnamurti, who saw that we live our lives through symbols that we ourselves create, down to such grass root elements as concepts and visual images, and that reason itself, logic, language, political thought, custom, ritual, religion, all the arts and sciences, are man-made symbolic systems through which we try to come to terms with experience, we try to interpret it, store it, and communicate it and so, it was he that lead me to *'know'* that man is not a rational animal, or a language-using one, but instead an animal whose distinctive characteristic is the creation and use of symbols; Nietzsche, whose call to re-evaluate our values is the most challenging of all challenges for anyone, who believes that the material world is all that there is; Kant & Schopenhauer who above all else brought enlightened European philosophy to my eager mind, and who made other European philosophies look like such glorious drivel; and the Young Wittgenstein who took me to the edge of reason and logic, and left me there, alone, to gaze at the abyss that lies only in silence!

    My reason for sharing this with you, in passing, is that I grew physically, academically and socially because underneath it all, I was growing spiritually. The physical is only a manifestation of the spiritual. I became spiritually fulfilled and so my life began to flourish. At the heart of my spiritual awakening, were the thinkers that I have just mentioned, amongst many others. My regular meditations, my uplifting discussions with my peers, the positive images and symbols that I had surrounded myself with, were all playing their part in my outwardly growth. All these philosophers are so good, that if you read their work with any understanding your outlook will never be the same again, because I believe that what they say *'seeps'* into your own way of looking at things, and becomes a part of it, clarifies it, and complicates it, for the better of course. The Upanishads, the works of Plato, Kant and Schopenhauer are the only real philosophies that have attempted to wrestle with life's ultimate questions. All other philosophers and philosophies are articulations, slight re-adjustments, clarifications of these greats. The Upanishads without a doubt were the pioneering works from antiquity, of Hindu scholars to have explored the realms of the ultimate. It is said that Kant and Schopenhauer, were both deeply influenced by it, and their works were the continuation of the questions that began in the Upanishads. After reading their work, I think they have pushed the understanding of our existence yet further, which the Upanishads had begun. Since them however, there has been little progress. It's as if Plato, Kant, Schopenhauer and the writers of the Upanishads all mapped out the coastlines of our lives – the furthest limits, and everyone else has been busy mapping out the land up to their work. No one that comes to my mind has successfully mapped out the intellectual tunnels further than where they left us a few centuries back. Maybe Wittgenstein was right, for he used Schopenhauer in the light of logic, and realised that beyond the writings of these greats, is only silence – *'What we cannot speak about we must pass over in silence'*. This was the final statement in Wittgenstein's Tractatus Logico-Philosophicus. It was here at Wittgenstein's statement that I stopped asking the ultimate questions – not because there are no answers or that this quest would be unending. Quite the contrary, I now understand that life's ultimate questions are not answered verbally or logically or scientifically, instead they are to be experienced, or another way to express it is to say they are to be realised through silence.

As I travelled further and deeper into the tunnels, I was beginning to experience the world altogether differently. I became convinced that all the existentialist questions of life would be answered, but just not how I had previously imagined. So while this was going on internally, outwardly I was achieving key milestones. Milestones that I believe we all can relate to.

In 2002, I received my Bachelors degree in Aerospace Engineering with a First Class Honours. The boy aged eighteen who had arrived at Roehampton Vale as being way out of his depth, had just got to the other end with flying marks. Yet I don't remember feeling elated or in the slightest bit satisfied. At the time I was a little puzzled by this. I had worked hard. I had been disciplined and focused, and so had expected like everyone else, when the time came to collect my degree I would be happy. I felt no such thing. In hindsight I now understand that Aerospace was never going to be my life long quest. I had always known that.

My motivation seemed to come, not because I thought aerospace was a means to some other end, in actual fact I had no end in mind. It came from the idea that studying aerospace was an end in itself. I had studied hard because I was getting something out of it. I was studying for the sake of it, for no other greater or grander purpose. It was solely about learning, not achieving materially. I wanted to learn thermodynamics because it gave me something more in itself, I didn't learn it to get a qualification – at least this wasn't my sole purpose. This state of mind is truly liberating. I cared little whether I got a first or not, whether I was recognised for my work, instead, I did the work they set and revised for the sake of learning how mathematics could unravel the world around us. I guess one could argue that the end I had in mind, for aerospace was to further understand the world around me. Just as I was exploring the subtle reality through the tunnels, so I wanted to explore the cruder world above it. I knew that I had to understand both worlds – the material and non-material. I continued to study a Masters in Aerospace, and did exceedingly well at it.

By the time I was half way through my master's programme in late 2002, the Iraq War was on the horizon. Parliament was trying to convince the nation that Saddam Hussein had WMD, and was a direct and immediate threat to the UK and her interests. Commonsense, plus a little knowledge of recent history would have sufficed to know that this was preposterous. Iraq was never a threat, and never could be one. I knew from friends within the MoD, who had inside knowledge of the Middle East crises that something else was at work. It was a three letter word that began with "O" and ended in "L". To be fair, it was about something broader – it was about the global economy.

I was fiercely against the whole war agenda. I was utterly dismayed with our leaders and with what can only be described as *'the meekness of our democracy'*. In October 2002, just before the US Senate was to vote on the issue of going to war with Iraq, seventy five senators were briefed by white house officials that Iraq had the ability to launch missiles into cities across the eastern coast of the United States from unmanned flying drones. Yes, only Americans could believe such bullshit! The Senate voted in Bush's favour. Meanwhile, I was getting increasingly involved with anti-war demonstrations. A few friends and I would stand outside lecture rooms, cafés, bars and restaurants trying to persuade students to protest with us. Within a short space of time we had over thirty volunteers working on the anti-war movement. I was at the strategy end of things, mainly thinking about how we could get more people together. Meanwhile, others were writing articles, contacting student societies and most were spreading the word. It soon dawned on me watching the news one day that there were millions of people across the country, and tens of millions across the world, who were against the war too. The challenge was how do we get all these people together?

During one of my *retreats* out into the Brecon Beacons, I came across a profound realisation, one that I later realised Sigmund Freud, Karl Jung, and

Walter Lippmann had already come across. It was the idea that people were driven by simple primitive urges and desires. Many of you, who read this, may say "well that's obvious", but is it really? Do we really grasp the profound implications of such a realisation? I don't believe most people who know such facts do actually fully grasp its implications. I think most modern academics fit into this category. They know "academically" this truth, but have failed to grasp the soul of it, and so it remains as a trophy, along with their other intellectual *bits*, rather than it being a tool which actively alters their own behaviour, and the behaviour of others. The reality hit me hard. It shook my foundations. I suffered a minor intellectual earthquake. Until that moment I was rather naively thinking that people were inherently good and noble. I used to think until that moment, that society, or the general environment, in which people were raised, made them selfish. It was nurture that was the problem, rather than nature. Now, I had realised that it was quite the contrary. It was nature that was the problem. Initially, this realisation was rather disturbing. It seemed that people drove relentlessly, mostly unconsciously, towards sexual pleasure, personal security and greed, while avoiding wherever possible, fear, any form of enslavement and poverty.

As I arrived back into civilisation, and into the bustling streets of the metropolis, I began to experience people in a new light. I think it was Edward Bernays, the father of Public Relations, who coincidently happened to be Freud's nephew, in America, in the 1920's, who said that "people are irrational, and their irrationality is the drive behind all their actions". In other words Bernays believed that it was a futile exercise to inform people through facts and figures if you wanted them to behave or act in a certain way. One couldn't just speak to someone, give them purely objective, factual reasons for protesting against the war, and expect them to behave rationally. In simpler terms, I couldn't tell my friends why they should protest against the war by telling them how cruel and unjust it was. In order for this to work they would have to be rational creatures. A rational man would first listen to the argument portrayed, think about it, weigh it up against any counter arguments, and make an informed decision. The truth was however, that people acted out of irrationality, they acted from impulse and desire.

I read several books written by Edward Bernays. I found them thrilling as well as hugely disturbing. Here was a guy using psychoanalysis to manipulate the masses – successfully at that, for nothing better than greed. Bernays describes, and almost gloats of his success to make women smoke, in the 1920's. Back then in the States, it was a taboo for women to smoke in public. William Hill, a producer of cigarettes approached Bernays and expressed that culture; society and tradition were coming in the way of his profits, essentially fifty percent of the market lay untapped because it was a taboo for women to smoke. Bernays hired a psychologist for a very large fee; someone named Dr. A. A. Brill. He told Bernays that cigarettes were a symbol of male power and dominance. Women smoking cigarettes would be a challenge to that male power, and hence, a taboo was created against them smoking by a male dominated society. In New York at that time, a huge carnival was organised every year celebrating Liberty. Bernays hired a group of young girls to hide cigarettes underneath their dresses. On his signal they were to dramatically pull out the cigarettes and light up in the midst of the parade. At the same time, Bernays had told the press that a group of young girls were going to *'light torches of Freedom'*. When the time came, Bernays signalled the 'torches' to be lit and sure enough it made headline news across America. Bernays used a phrase – the torches of freedom, which deeply influenced the ensuing debate.

Anyone who stood for freedom and liberty would not condone the act, but should instead support it. William Hill over the next decade recorded the highest sales in their history, and the number of women smokers began to rise. The underlying psychology behind it was relatively simple. Women who smoked cigarettes would *feel* free, and would be rebelling against the old male dominance in society. They would feel independent and confident by smoking. This was completely irrational. It was completely untrue that by smoking, women would become more independent. But women who smoked didn't really seem to notice whether they *actually* became anymore equal compared to their male counterparts, they simply *felt* more equal. Essentially Bernays had managed to connect products with emotions. The reality wasn't important anymore. It was the feeling that counted.

It was after reading Bernays, I coined up the idea of stimulating the primitive drives of people, in an attempt to get them to protest. We approached pretty girls and got them to model in the skimpiest bits of clothing that we could possibly get away with. These girls, come models, were normal university students who we knew that other students would connect with. We made postcards and flyers with a girl modelling in provocative poses with the headline – Interested? On the back end of the postcards and flyers was limited information about attending an event, with a time and place. In the tiniest font possible we wrote something about anti war protests. Sure enough thousands of students put these postcards and flyers up in their rooms, in university corridors and gave them out to their friends. On the day of the march, approximately six thousand students attended. Now by no means am I implying that all six thousand young protesters were there because they were sexually stimulated by the postcards. What I am saying is that the word would not have spread to so many within such a short time, if it wasn't for our sex orientated PR. It made headline news, not the PR but the actual march. We'd created a carnival atmosphere. We had made banners before hand, and as people gathered we distributed them. We gave out free anti war t-shirts, whistles and other noise making devices. We got our models to appear in their outfits and walk the streets encouraging people to take part in the war protests. They gave out all the serious leaflets, with purely factual information. I thought it would be rather teasing for people, to have such beauties hand them out, what most students would have considered dry bits of information.

Once the logistics were taken care of and the speeches had begun, I decided to step back, and take a breather at what essentially a few diehards had achieved. I was expecting myself to feel pride, and a sense of victory. Instead, I felt empty and detached. As I quietly starred at our creation, I felt, what can only be described as pointlessness, emptiness and a subtle tinge of shame at what I had done. I had effectively manipulated thousands of, what I saw at that moment, as innocent flocks of subconscious primitive emotionally charged individuals, to attend something, which they would not have attended through pure factual information.

I felt as if I had cheated them in some way. If I ever saw a time when the cliché "sex sells" was true, it was at that moment. I stood at the side walk as hundreds of people walked by, many of them my friends, but mostly strangers all shouting, cheering and waving at the cameras. People were indeed enjoying themselves, and a message was being sent out to parliament, yet I felt as if it was all tainted. The feeling was driven home to me, when one of the models wearing a tiny little skirt with a white "say no to War" vest, approached me and said how much fun she was having. She thanked me for getting her involved and off she went teasing all the guys that were mesmerised by her curves. She knew what was happening, and she thoroughly enjoyed the attention. What really got to me was that all this attention this girl was getting through her sexuality was in fact raw lust. Not one of those who looked her up and down thought "hmmm what a lovely girl, that the kind of girl I need to spend the rest of my life with and be loyal too, value her, cherish her and be devoted to her."

Instead most of them were consumed by lust – thoughts of having sex with her, dreaming about what she would be like, what her breasts would look like underneath that vest, and so on and on. These thoughts and many more like it drove me towards concluding that I had indirectly exploited her. Not in a million years would she have thought that, but I felt that I was seeing something that she was not aware of. Just as the crowd was drawn to her, for her looks and body, due to their inner hidden impulses, so too, was she drawn to behaving in such a way by her hidden impulse to pleasure and tease. I felt as I had used everyone for my own ends.

All the protests that occurred before and after our demonstration were to no avail. On 20th March, we went to war with a country that was already crippled by sanctions. Yes, Saddam was a madman and a brutal dictator, but we didn't go into Iraq for the people, we went for some other darker reason. It was a clear symbol to me that democracy was not what it appeared to be, and liberalism was something altogether different to what I had naively believed it was.

I began this chapter with the arrival of my soul mate and it would only be fair that I end it with her. However, to understand Asheeta one has to firstly grasp the pretext, otherwise Asheeta would remain inaccessible. Life was a trudge. I was studying to live and living to study – for what? I need, and I believe we all need, the occasional reminder that the world is an extraordinary place, and that people are capable of truly amazing things. For me at least, Asheeta was the embodiment of what was, what could be, and what could never be. She encapsulated in her personality the reality of living. She was happiness. She was laughter. She was a breadth of fresh air, in an otherwise dark humid world. I was, and still am, prone to living in the rabbit holes, exploring all day long, the dark parts of the tunnels. If it wasn't for Asheeta, I believe I would have become rather detached from everyday life, I would have continued my search in the tunnels day and night, eventually becoming obscure to the world, and likewise the world to me.

I sincerely believe that if it wasn't for Asheeta, my life would have remained unfulfilled. I would have no doubt accelerated in travelling through the rabbit holes, I would have understood life in some areas more than I currently do, but it would have been a lonely adventure. I would have been one of those explorers on a one way trip who experiences wonders of unimaginable beauty, but with no one to share it with. In this life at least, we all need someone to share our victories with, or these joys become meaningless. Asheeta, in one word, was hope, and hope is all that I have, and it is all that I need. Through her presence and support, and with my growing awareness of the subtlety of life, I would go on to plant seeds of further progress and happiness, this time not solely for myself, or for those dearest to me, but for society at large.

Five

धर्म

Planting Seeds

THERE is a passage in the Gospel of Saint Thomas, one of the non-official Gospels which you won't find in the Bible. It reads: *'If you bring forth what is within you, what you bring forth will save you.'*

THE first significant seed I planted was in September 2000. I didn't know that I was planting a seed back then, but now, almost eight years on, I now understand its significance. The seeds that I am referring too are ideas, nothing more. Ideas that we nourish and water, and if the time is fertile enough, and we are dedicated, something real comes out of that seed – the idea in our minds become reality.

These are seeds that become something material, out of something completely immaterial. These ideas are the seeds that float around inside our minds on a daily basis. These ideas are created out of pure inspiration from our everyday experiences. These seeds contain within them the genes of your intellectualism, they represent your personality, your characteristics and always in some subtle way reflect the *'real'* you. These seeds, just like our children, if nurtured and looked after, will live long after we have gone into the surrounding darkness. They will be our legacy, our story for the next generation to continue. The raw experience and the dissatisfaction we get from it, I believe, creates seeds in our minds. Its often things that we are not happy with, things that we know we can improve, or begin which would make that experience better for everyone. These seeds once planted could become businesses, charities, political groups, cultural or religious organisations or even religions themselves, long after you are dead and turned into a messiah.

I am convinced that everyone has ideas, or seeds, as I have called them, floating around inside their minds, but sadly, most of them never get to germinate. They never materialise. They simply decay, as seeds often do when they fall on barren infertile land. We all get ideas to improve reality in someway or another everyday, but most decay before they are fully grasped. Some do fall on fertile soil, but are quickly snapped up by the hungry crows circling the land, waiting for fresh seeds to eat. These crows are other conflicting ideas or priorities, and people, often those that are closest and dearest to us. The crows are many and come in all sizes and shapes. With me at least, they come in the form of conflicting priorities – I simply don't have the time to make all my ideas manifest, no matter how simple they might be, because I am too busy investing my time in watering my other seeds. There are only so many seeds one can water and look after at a time.

With most people I have found their crows to be either conflicting ideas or other people who downgrade their idea, or simply dismiss it as a waste. Often these people, and ourselves included, have no realisation that a seed has been destroyed; a seed that essentially has been aborted. It is a reality that could have been, but we will never know its potential. Out of the many hundreds of fresh ideas experience impregnates our minds with, only a handful are born, most decay before they are even fully grasped, others fall on infertile land, by which I mean in a mind that does not have the capacity to act upon it, and finally those that are grasped, and ready to be planted are quickly dismissed by either other priorities or other peoples lack of encouragement.

Those seeds however, that do materialise, those that are nurtured, and watered everyday, looked after, those seeds that crows can't reach, well, they become saplings, and from saplings they can become giants. We are surrounded by these giants that have essentially come from someone's mind; they were someone's creation; someone's seeds. All religion, philosophy, organisations such as the United Nations, banks, charities, businesses such as IBM and Microsoft were all seeds. These seeds were planted by people, nurtured and looked after in the early days, when a living organism is at its most fragile, but in time, the seeds become plants and living things in themselves, that become independent from the founding father or mother, and still being greatly influenced by them. It's very similar to the way in which a parent child relationship evolves over time.

My seed came in the form of a football club for youths, albeit in a slightly unusual one. Before I begin to explain the idea, I should tell you what impregnated my mind with it in the first place. It had come to me when I was eighteen, and took me two years before I fully came to grips with it, and had the energy to plant it. My boyhood was centred on Belgrave, an inner, working class Indian area, where people worked as Labourers; were paid by the hour, in Leicester. All the houses looked the same, terraced red bricked Victorian, and it was truly an urban jungle. Many families worked on minimum wage, a few for even less. Unemployment or underemployment was high in Belgrave; it still is for that matter.

People worked every hour God gave them, and saved as much as possible. People here lived on a basis of need rather than want, this lead to people living rather simple, narrow lives. I can't blame them, because I have realised that necessity narrows our horizons. The need to secure the next wage blocks us from looking to see where the path is leading, or what they are missing by not widening their world. All this was true of my parents and other first or second generation migrants from either East Africa or India. Their children however, were a different kettle of fish altogether.

The term I like to use to describe second and third generation Indian youth is "Indo Brits". This generation, my generation, has multi-layered identities. The Indo Brits I refer to are British by nationality, Indian by ethnicity and Hindu in their foundational beliefs. I use the words "foundational beliefs" to describe Hindu rather than religion, for this, I will explain shortly. For now you must bear with me, or skip a few pages to understand my reasoning. These people, by which I mean the Indo Brits, have a complex mental make-up. They are composed of deeply conflicting ideas and beliefs, as well as grounding in utilitarian pragmatism that John Stuart Mill would have been proud of.

Firstly, I should explain the reality in which most of my generation, the Indo Brits have grown up in. Most of us are exclusively British in our fundamental public practices, things such as dress or outward appearance is entirely in sync with the mainstream, by which I mean British nationals of English ethnicity, and of loosely Christian or Humanistic values. Their language is almost one hundred percent English. They see their home as Britain, and struggle to come to terms with India as a country in its present state every time they visit. That's not to say that they are disconnected from their ethnicity or cultural roots, on the contrary, every time England play India in cricket, the Indo Brits mostly support one team – India! India, or at least the cricket team represent their ethnicity and cultural roots, something that they want to take pride in desperately. It does not represent a "home" team. Most will never settle in India, for they could not, simply because they are accustomed to a kind of 'Britishness', which India could not offer.

The Indo Brits have managed to integrate well with the hosts, while setting out on the mission to rediscover what it means to be Hindu in the 21st century, living in Britain. There is, I feel, a renaissance occurring in the minds of the Indo Brits, a kind of coming together of positives, combining all the pragmatism of the West, in terms of wealth creation, science and technology, while fusing themselves with the philosophical East, values of the Upanishads and the Bhagvad Gita, which are no religious holy books – they are a philosophical treatise of the highest magnitude. Of course a small percentage of Indo Brits have read either, and if they have, I doubt that they have grasped even ten percent of it. Rather the Indian East, I am referring too, comes from their unique upbringing.

Almost everyone that I knew as Indian was brought up speaking at least one Indian language at home, which means that almost every Indo Brit is bi-lingual or even tri-lingual. We were all brought up with an exclusively Indian diet at home, with a gentle fusion of Italian, Mexican and English, which our mothers had conjured up. This meant that now we were both able to be British in our language and Indian, the same was true of our diets. Next, it was the values of prayer and tradition. Most Indo Brits that I have known have never been coerced by their family *to believe*. Instead, it was the setting up of examples for them to follow if so they chose. I saw my mother pray every morning before going to work; I know this to be true for many other Indo Brits.

I saw my father and mother work hard for peanuts. This is true of many others, which was why we were actively pushed into education. If nothing else this last fact has changed the dynamics for every Brit, Indo or otherwise. We were never pushed into religion, or *being cultural*, instead we were relentlessly pressurised to study. As a result the Indo Brit community is highly educated, in fact so much so that they have taken over the Jewish community, in achieving outstanding results at GCSE's.

Whereas our parents were mainly manual labourers or semi-skilled workers, their offspring are now doctors, engineers, pharmacists, dentists, accountants, bankers, solicitors and entrepreneurs. As I write these words, I know that from my high school class of thirty, that some of those classmates have become optometrists, solicitors, programmers, engineers, teachers, investment bankers, and self employed. In one generational leap, they have become middle class to upper class, and as every economist knows, the middle class of every country effectively run it! Five to tens years from now, the dynamics of Britain would have changed forever, because the Indo Brits would account for a significant portion of the middle class. This will mean that the Indo Brits will become key political players on whose performance Britain's standing in the world will depend, not completely of course, but significantly. Their values will effect every major institution in this country, right from the monarchy down to the working practices of cashiers in high street banks.

The Indo Brits are the sugar in the milk that is Britain. These were not my words, but that of my grandfather. What he meant by this was that a migrant population should integrate with the host community as sugar dissolves in milk. Outwardly the milk remains unchanged and the sugar disappears, but the milk is forever sweetened. This is what I believe is happening with the British community at large and the Indo Brits. I often feel that other minority, and predominantly Muslim communities, would prosper if they took on a similar approach, but of course I know that they cannot. All this sounds rather rosy and paints a picture of the future that is trouble free, very 21st century, and of human evolution out of the quagmires of singular nationalities, religions and ethnic groups. With every coin, there are two sides, and the Indo Brits are no different.

Most Indo Brits were raised by parents who were in, what I like to call, *survival mentality*. These people were predominately first generation migrants, who came to Britain either directly from East Africa or India. For them home was not, and never could be, these shores. They were deeply connected to either, where they had previously come from, or India. Furthermore, many of these people came to the UK with nothing, or at best very little. They were at the bottom of the ladder. That's not to say that these people were unskilled, far from it, for they were a community of wealth creators – entrepreneurs who quite literally sustained the East African economy. But in Britain they were classed as unskilled, as they had no qualifications or any serious formal education. When in this situation, an economic crisis, people go into a survival frame of mind. It's a matter of finding work, any work, as long as it pays. They save relentlessly; they work long hours and live purely on a needs basis, on a "no frills" lifestyle. Most lived a life in those days of great insecurity. It was simply about nesting, buying a house as soon as possible; then it was about paying the mortgage for the next twenty-five years; it was about educating the children, and making sure they become qualified or skilled. These people, the parents of Indo Brits, had two core characteristics: firstly, they fundamentally believed in education, and second their faith and traditions. The first I have already spoken of, but the second, I believe very few understand, including vast majority of the Indo Brits.

I have been fascinated with all things Indian – its history, philosophy, culture, and more recently in its economy and social as well as environmental welfare. This has without a shadow of doubt come from my patriotic father. For a long time now, since the age of fifteen, I have been coming to terms with the contradictions of this generation, the generation of my parents, the first migrants into the UK. On the one hand, the vast majority hadn't the foggiest about Indian philosophy or history, and yet every adult, mostly men, considered himself to be an expert on the subject. Everyone firmly believed they knew what they were talking about. All of us, me included, have three categories to box our knowledge into; *they are things that I know, things that I don't know, and things that I think I know, but in actual fact don't.* Vast majority of Indian men come in this last category, when it comes to understanding their identity, culture or religion. They are devoted to their professed truth, and yet only after a little critical enquiry or logical reasoning, we find contradictions. They are often unable to explain to their children what it means to be Indian, with a Hindu believe system, living in the UK. They were ill equipped to answer the inquisitive nature of Indo Brits while they were growing up. Essentially, every Indo Brit that I know, has questioned their parents, and has mostly been dissatisfied by the answers they've received; things just didn't stack up. Most, simply accepted it as tradition, something which Indians do all too often I find. The side effects of this tendency are many and multi-faceted.

First the Indo Brits suffer from a diluted self identity. Ethnically they cannot ignore the fact that they are Indian. Inwardly, there are contradictory messages and values being propagated by society. Many Indo Brits do not have a clear understanding of when they are British, when Indian, and when Hindu, but most importantly how these three layers connect. Many people from this group never quite feel British, never quite Indian and never clued up, or confident with their *'Hindu-ness'*. They float around, uncomfortable with themselves. As a result contradictions rise in their value system. They become *Cultural Hindus* rather than proactive ones. Something, which I felt at the time, was a detriment to society at large. I'm still a firm believer that global society could benefit greatly, if it was to adopt some core Hindu values, not from a religious angle, but rather from a philosophical one. I saw the people who I grew up with changing identities, pending on what type of environment they were in. They could quite easily become completely British, if the environment so dictated. They could also become staunch Indians when the cricket was on, or when they were with others, who felt pride in that *bit* of their identity. On festivals, or at times of great adversity, I saw them become deeply religious, or even superstitious.

The problem with this tendency I found was that they were unable to assert themselves. The Indo Brits were passive; they still are. They were unable to contribute to their environment in any way, even when they could give positive contributions to it. They simply rolled over and became whatever the environment demanded upon them. Consequently, Indo Brits suffer from a great deal of apathy, and a lack of confidence, not from a skills basis, but from a personal arena.

Essentially, for me at least, it boiled down to a matter of leadership. The Indo Brits for all their talent and opportunity simply could not lead. They lacked any form of cohesiveness, they lacked self confidence, and they reeked of uncertainty, and as a result were meagre in their contributions to society. I also realised early on that Indo Brits were physically unable to match other communities in competitive sports, of any kind, apart from cricket. They simply didn't play football at a competitive level in the Sunday leagues, at least not enough of them. They were never encouraged too, and were far too pre-occupied with studying, or at best playing football on the computer. This physical weakness, combined with the mental meekness was essentially decapitating their inner potential, before it even got started. The Indo Brits were a talented pool for the global society, and yet we were effectively being wasted. Back in 1998, I saw it in these terms, and in 2000, this experience impregnated me with the seed of a leadership academy for the next generation of Indo Brits.

On 11th September 2000, a year before 9/11, I bought five footballs, a set of cones for £20 and went to Cossington Park in the Belgrave area, to begin what was to become Shakha Football Club aka the Academy of Leadership, or AoL as I like to abbreviate it. Shakha FC, as it has popularly been called, is a Sanskrit word meaning branch. It's a word that has been associated to groups of men coming together, to partake in a physical or intellectual activity. It simply adopted the name from a local youth group. My father at that time use to organise and run this local youth group, for kids of Indian origin, aged between ten and fifteen. I had spread the word of a football club starting through my father's youth group. I simply turned up on a Saturday morning at ten and waited. Sure enough one by one, they arrived. On that first session ten kids came. I was due to start my second year at university, and quickly realised that I would need help from someone else. I knew that he would have to be a footballer, someone who had competed at a high level. Someone who was sound in character and level headed, someone who would complement my strengths, and compensate in areas where I was weak. The person would have to be dedicated and willing to lead by example, and give up his weekend. Above all else someone who would equally gain from running a weekend football club as a leadership academy. I'm not sure how I decided to whom I should go for help, I just did it, and it came naturally, rather spontaneously.

Manish Kalia was a friend that I had shared from the age of eight. Along with Jinesh, he was one my longest serving friends, someone who I had a deep affinity for. We were in the same class during primary and secondary schools. We had grown up together, shared friends, secrets, laughs and even a few tears. We came from identical backgrounds and lived nearby one another. Manish was a quiet kid back then, while I was a loud mouth attention seeking teenager. Manish was a no frills character, what you saw, was what you got, take it or leave it. He still is like that to some extent. He too was keen on football, he played centre back. Manish was a stocky, heavy up top but a quick defender. He was completely passive as a character, until he got onto a football field. The boy could play; and he played hard. Manish's first tackle rule became infamous for its bone breaking tenacity. We had played for rival Sunday league clubs while we were growing up, and I can say from experience that his tackles were indeed worthy of fearing. Manish was never intellectual, he still isn't. By intellectual I mean the Philosopher. Manish was always pragmatic, he did what he had too, and never more, he had no great visions of success or for climbing the ivory tower of academia. He wanted to get a degree in Accounts, become an accountant, get married, have eleven children; just enough for a football team and retire with a nice sum tucked away.

This was Manish; this is still the way he is. I knew that I could often be too philosophical, too high brow and a little "airy fairy"; whereas, Manish would never be this way. I can no longer remember how I approached him; what I said and what his response was. It's a complete blur, something that my psyche has chosen to discard. Maybe it was just a formality and not really worth recounting. AoL was about Leadership, pure and simple, and through the foundation and running of the Academy, I have learnt and observed a great many things about the much debated subject.

On Leadership

There must be countless books, theories, courses which people can read, or seminars they could attend to learn leadership. Fundamentally however, I don't think it can be learnt in that fashion. *One cannot be a non leader and then become a leader through a classroom orientated course or seminar.* Anybody that believes this, I feel has grossly misunderstood leadership. Leadership can mean many different things to a great many different people. I don't really have a clear cut definition for it, and I have never attempted to create one, simply because I know that no matter what the definition is, it can never suffice or accurately depict it.

Leadership is broad, it's vast and I believe transcendental. True leadership I believe is inherent in anyone that is in one way or another, consciously or unconsciously, connected to the rabbit hole – the intellectual tunnels. Effective leaders are those that can sow seeds, water them, nurture them and create something material out of something immaterial. In other words leadership is about having ideas, which become realities, and anyone that can do this, is a leader in one form or another. Leadership is neither good nor bad, it is morally neutral. Hitler was a great leader, but a bad character. His leadership was sound for the most part, but his direction was deeply flawed and misconstrued.

To some extent we are all leaders in one shape or form. Many of us will lead our households, our children, or our social groups or friends; many will lead small voluntary organisations, others will be in religious groups, some as business leaders of varying sizes, but only *a few I believe will be naturally good ones*. Leadership is no simple trick to pull off. I believe any leader needs to have some pre-requisites. The Academy that I co-founded with Manish, in 2000, was about developing these prerequisites of future leadership in Indo Brits.

I don't want spell out what leadership is and isn't, simply because I am not sure myself; however, I do want show how some of these prerequisites to leadership can be nurtured and developed. There is a difference. I am not spelling out what leadership is, instead I'm spelling out some of the qualities that we all need to have, if we are to practice effective leadership roles in our lives. Much of the experiences I have had in this area have come from trial and error, and the inspiration has always come from exploring the rabbit holes, the tunnels that are transcendental, upon which all existence is based. I had already built a clear enough picture of what I felt Indo Brits had, in terms of their natural inherent strengths, and what were their obvious shortfalls.

Essentially, it boiled down to leadership, or the lack of it. It was through the tunnels, while listening to *Hans Zimmer's Rainman soundtrack* that I came across the prerequisites that would be required for any leader. I remember writing them down quickly on a piece of paper as the thoughts flowed out of my consciousness. I wrote at a speed that I could never maintain; it was an outpouring of intellectualism and realisation. It all seemed to fit together, in an instant, like magic; one moment I was merely pondering on the meekness of my generation, and the next I had a clear vision of what needed to be done. It's at times like this, I can come to terms with the fact that *time* has no place in the tunnels. In time and space it all looks a little miraculous, but of course, anyone travelling and exploring the tunnels will assure you that it's far from instantaneous. Inspiration has its prerequisites too – plenty of musing, thinking, meditating and observing while silencing the mind.

The first prerequisite I realised was the need to have a *healthy body*. Most research into leadership focus on the cognitive aspects of the mind; wrongly I believe. That comes later, much later. Essentially, the mind and body are the different sides to the same coin. As Timothy Warneka rightly points out in his book, *'Leading people the Black belt way'*, that great leadership begins with the body. Having a physical presence is the first step. The way in which we carry ourselves; the way we walk; our stance and the physical energy that we project are primary. This is arrived at, I realised early on during my kickboxing days, through physical confidence and awareness of ones own body. We must feel pride in ourselves, in the way we look, the way we feel about our limbs, chest, legs, even toes. As our awareness of the body grows, so too will our need to improve it, keep it well oiled, and by keeping it in good nick, we'll begin to ooze quiet confidence. When this occurs we'll naturally carry a spring in our step and have a presence.

At the academy, we created a vigorous series of training sessions that each potential candidate had to pass. Its aim was to push the individual to their physical limit, and once there, to make them push that little bit harder. Whoever achieves it passes. Note that it was never about the fittest individuals, or those that could run the quickest. It was about pushing each individual and comparing them with themselves. This meant that sometimes unlikely individuals made it through; those that were overweight, un-athletic or deeply unconfident made it through; while cocky slim confident ones failed rather badly. These individuals had no desire to be pushed. They were those, like, sadly the majority of people, who want to do only that which is enough. Leaders can never be of this nature.

Everybody, I believe has an innate ability for leadership in some form or another, but sadly, most will never become their potential, because they do not have these prerequisites of leadership. A great many kids who talked a good talk, could never walk their own talk. Some did of course, and we were deeply inspired by each one that came through the first hurdle. Every squad that the academy has had, has always been a mixture of obvious sportsmen and not the so obvious. What they all learnt was that those that made it were truly special. They had something that others didn't – the ability to push themselves to new peaks, at least physically. A trust and respect is built, between those that make it, no matter how unfit or unconfident they may look. The type of training session I am referring too is extreme; at least it is to the meek.

The boys begin with a gentle ten minute warm up jog, where they do various movements along the way to loosen up the joints and stretch the muscles. Next they run shuttle runs – short distance sprints, where they run too and fro, in total of 144 yards. They run these in teams of four or five; the team that comes last has to do it all again, in a quicker time than their previous attempt. This develops the mentality that coming last, *costs*; and when we do fail, we must attempt to do better next time; never to be content with defeat. We have always found that the team which ends up last, nearly always does better immediately after their first attempt. The kids were seeing their own performance. They were raising their awareness of what their bodies could do, things that their minds simply said they couldn't do. They begin to develop a confidence in their own bodies, and this is the beginning of developing the first requisite of leadership. After the shuttle runs, they *learn* to do over a hundred press-ups and leg-raises each, in sync with the team on a slow monotonous count, often set by Manish. Believe me when I say that Manish can count very slowly, dragging out the agony that little bit further. In the first few weeks, hardly any of the teenagers can do ten press-ups or leg-raises. They realise the magnitude of the hurdle they'll have to climb, if they want to play football. We encourage everyone to practice at home by doing twenty, twice a day. Those that do, within a short amount of time learn to do a hundred leg-raises and press-ups with ease, those that don't, well, they simply don't make it. I write this in present tense, because everything that I have just described still happens, on Saturday mornings.

There used to be a time, back in 2000, when Manish or I would lead by example and do the training with them. We would set an example first. Fundamentally, it was about showing them what could be done; they would see us in pain, and struggle, yet we would continue to do our best. Now, neither Manish, nor I are anywhere near as fit as we used to be. We've aged, albeit only a little, so now we always have Indo Brits who have been with the academy for a few years who set the example for the newcomers to follow. Essentially, it's set a legacy; everyone who plays football at the academy is super fit; they can do things that other teenagers can only talk about. We found that these kids would begin to dominate the sports lessons in their respective schools. They would set cross country records, bleep tests scores and be captains of their school sports teams. One must remember that not all those who made it were necessarily fit to begin with, in fact very few are. They were there due to their own innate ability to push themselves. This new forged attitude naturally transmitted into their studies, and so now, they were enjoying becoming excellent academics, as well as athletes. The body, was slowly, but surely created, and the academy began to instil the first prerequisite of leadership.

Once the awareness of the body arises, the mind naturally begins to flourish. I have heard my father on countless occasions say "healthy body means a healthy mind". He is right. The academy is proof, if it ever needed any evidence. Along with the rise of the body, the next prerequisite was discipline. Maybe, a softer term would be *structure*. Structure is good for all of us, but especially teenagers. I believe every leader, in any situation must have a structure, a form of discipline in his or her daily activities. Discipline is important, whether it be mentally or practically. In hindsight, I feel that I have always maintained a certain level of self discipline. I was nurtured through sports, and later through the MoD and higher level academics. It is paramount that we have structures in place, which highlight that which is expected and rewarded, and the opposite, that which is unexpected and consequently punished. The discipline that I practice nowadays is very different to those that I practiced while maturing. I regularly read, and class this as a discipline. I always take half an hour out of each day, in silence, to contemplate, meditate on the day ahead, or the one that has just passed. I keep a simple "to do" list which I write up every morning. I make sure that I'm always regularly partaking in some physical activity. A discipline that I still blatantly lack, and as anyone that knows me well, will tell you, that I can over stretch myself. I never know when I've got enough on my plate, consequently, I take on more than I can chew, and end up letting myself and others down. In my defence, I'm getting better, but still have a long way to go. A great discipline is the ability to say "enough".

At the academy discipline is paramount. We have structures in place; for example, every minute someone is late, they run that minute on top of whatever has been planned. After you've just done an intensive session, the last thing you want to do is run another five minutes. For that matter you wouldn't even want to run an extra thirty seconds if you could help it. The early days for the newcomers are steep learning curves. Within a few weeks, the whole squad arrives fifteen minutes early. The next discipline is language. We never allow swearing at the academy. Most teenagers find this abnormal; in fact most adults find it the same. We live in a society where using simplistic caricatures, in the form of swearing is far too easily accepted. Essentially leadership which uses swearing as a tool is a sign of a leader who doesn't have full control over one of the main tools –

language. Using brash, hurtful or crude language in any context de-means the situation; it over simplifies it and as a result gives off a false reality. I live by this principle, but still need to master it completely. At the academy all swearing is clamped down on with physical punishment for the whole squad, such as press ups or an extra minute added to a run, and so on. Within a short space of time, these teenagers who swear in every other sentence at school become more articulate and controlled with their tongue. They learn to channel their aggression or frustration in more positive forms, rather than shooting off a string of offensive words to someone else, as a way of venting.

The next and final aspect of structure, at the academy, is reporting in advance all absences from training sessions. They learn that their actions are firstly accountable, secondly, that they affect a greater audience, and finally, that they need a sufficient explanation for it. Leaders at all levels need to consistently justify their actions to their audience, whether it is a workforce, patients in a hospital or simply friends. I guess another way to say it, would be that it is a discipline to communicate ones actions, to those whom it affects, directly or indirectly, thereby keeping the channel of communication always active. I have found that many organisations, and the bigger they get the more they suffer, from a distinct lack of communication from the leaders at the top. We now have quite literally thousands of communication courses, self help books and technology that should make this a simple task. It's a problem that need not be there. From a leadership perspective, I think it's about being self disciplined enough to be communicative.

The next core prerequisite to future leadership is about being emotionally intelligent. It was Daniel Goleman, who I believe created the term, but this concept is as old as Philosophy itself. There are now quite literally hundreds of books and commentaries written by *"experts"* on the subject, so I don't think I'll attempt to define it – that's for another book, or maybe even another author. What is important however, in the context of what I am referring too, is its need.

We are living in a society that has never been more liberal. We are able to express ourselves, show emotions, and even vent them in allsorts of ways. We are continuously, and forever, being stimulated. We are bombarded with sexual imagery, scenes of violence, war and devastation, either in fictional or non-fictional forms. The liberal society, which we have created for ourselves, has loosened the cap on all our emotions; this is no bad thing, but only if we use it correctly. As I have *evolved*, I have found that not every person at adulthood has done so, at least emotionally. I find far too many adults being as emotionally unintelligent as a child or worse, a teenager. Maybe this is the reason why so many households with teenagers have domestic issues regularly. Too many emotionally unintelligent people all clustered up in close quarters can only be described as frightening.

We are all just bags of emotional energy underneath. But the challenge, at least for future leaders, is how to channel and manage all that energy flowing through our veins. At the academy we aim to make teenagers more channelled in their emotions, and gradually build them, at their own pace, to the point where they are more aware of their feelings. In other words we create a *"disconnect"* between the kids and their associated emotions. *"You are not your emotions"*, I have shouted quite literally hundreds of times, during early morning winter runs, when the kids would rather be in tucked up in a nice warm bed. *"There is nothing your body can't achieve, toughen your mind"*, is another favourite shout of mine. Having coached and trained teenagers, some with a wide array of emotional issues, for about eight years now, I have begun to see a correlation between a child's competence emotionally, and his upbringing. Of course schools matter too, but family more so. The family, whatever form it takes, is our first, and for a long time, only model of how the world works; how people relate to each other; or of what is moral and immoral. Attached to this is the notion of behaviour and attitude towards our world.

Increasingly, I believe, children are being over protected by parents, and the society at large. The teenagers I know get ferried around everywhere in cars or buses, guarded from strangers, prevented from playing outside in case they get hurt or fall ill, or God forbid, join the wrong crowd. Often teenagers are left with no room to experiment, to explore life by themselves. They are effectively prevented from failing. I can sympathise with every parent who is protective of their child, but they must also realise that the side effect of all their loving is severe and dangerous – their overbearing love can make their kids emotional wreaks in adulthood. Children that do not enjoy the freedom to discover the world for themselves from a young age, who do not learn to make mistakes and overcome them, essentially end up experiencing the world with a lob-sided view. Kids of this nature, I have found, end up sub-consciously believing that their life in this world is out of their hands, they believe that forces, which they can neither see nor control, effectively rule their lives. These types of kids, I have begun to identify as *externalising*. They externalise everything about achievements or failures onto others. Kids such as these have a canny way of blaming others for everything, especially receiving bad grades. "My teacher was absent for most of the year, that's why I missed out on a pass", is a classic answer I hear over and over again from students.

Another one is "my teacher can't teach properly, I just don't get what she is talking about".

I once asked a really bright sixteen year old, why it was that he only got a C-grade in his GCSE's; his answer was swift and well versed, even though it came from the subconscious depths of his mind, "My parents don't really care if I study or not, they always disturb me when I try to revise".

These kids can never become exceptional leaders, because they are not emotionally balanced. They believe that life is not in their hands; they believe that it's in the hands of others, or in the hands of forces they cannot control. They have other tendencies too. These types of kids suffer from a *crisis of reflection*. This is another term that I coined up not so long ago. It simply refers to when we judge ourselves, by how the world external to us has perceived to have judged us. In other, simpler terms, it means when somebody else thinks I'm good looking, I too will instantly *feel* good looking. When someone else compliments my dress sense, I'll instantly *feel* more confident with my dress sense. Then at the other end, when I have been criticised over something, I instantly *feel* inadequate, a feeling of rejection seeps in, and I immediately look to conform to their expectations or standards. Most Indo Brits of all talents suffer from this phenomenon.

I, on the other hand, suffered from the other end of the spectrum, that which I have labelled as a *crisis of no reflection*. This occurs in the psyches of those who have been given too much freedom to explore life, and have risen through the hard knocks of life. These kids are at the other end of the podium. They subconsciously, and some even knowingly, believe that they have the ability to change everything around them. By hook or crook, they'll manage to get what they want. These types of kids *internalise*. They look to themselves for the answers and believe they have to find it within, and never without. I used to take failure personally. I can do better; it was my fault; I let him get to me; I let them disturb me, and so on and on. These types of kids can be pretty hard on themselves. They too are unbalanced, for they believe too much depends on them. They primarily believe that they hold all the answers to their problems. People on this end of the spectrum often care little what others think or say, they are often desensitised to other people's whims and just get on with what they do best. This all may sound very dynamic, but the reality is that there is a fine balance that one must achieve. Not everything can be solved, influenced or changed by me. It does matter sometimes what people think, for example in job interviews or when

Bhavisha has a remark to make about my dress sense, which is often critical, I should listen and take her advice. I can't be good at everything, especially shopping.

At the academy we aim to get kids into a fine middle, where they have a healthy understanding of what is in their hands and what isn't. By the time they become sixteen, and too old for the club, most have a grasp of what it is that they have, and what they need. This balance of mind essentially creates a sound mechanism to control ones emotions. None of the kids that leave the academy are what I would dub as "emotionally intelligent" but they have the prerequisite to be, later in life. At the academy we plant seeds, sometimes they grow, and sometimes they grow late, some sadly never grow, but we still continue running the plantation.

The next, and probably the most important prerequisite to leadership in my opinion, is a sufficient supply of positive role models. We all need them. I think we all have them. Everyone, I have always known, has had role models, people to whom they could look too for inspiration and guidance. This occurs especially when we are young, but as we get older, we seem to loose that part of us, that looks to others for inspiration. I have always wondered why that is, and to date, no clear answers have appeared. One thing that I am sure about however is that before we step into leadership, we need leaders around us. These leaders can be family members, older siblings, teachers, people we've read about, characters in great novels, or on the television. No matter where they come from, the fact is we need them, and most of us while we were growing up, had them. The challenge our society faces, I believe, is that there are too many poor role models. Too few of us have ever had someone immediately around us, to look up too. More often then not, our roles models are in books, or on the TV and mostly too distant to really influence us sufficiently. This void of real positive role models has been filled by rap stars, movie stars and other trivial celebrities. I find far too many young talented Indo Brits imitate rappers or footballers. There is nothing wrong with this, if they really want become serious footballers or rap stars. But the straight truth of the matter is that most of us don't have what it takes to be one. Most of our talents lie elsewhere.

People, I believe, need role models who have already walked down the path that they aspire to travel up. That's not to say that we need a role model who is an accountant, if I want to lead in the field of accountancy – far from it! I mean that we need people who have the skills that we need to develop in order for us to become leaders in our particular field of expertise. Role models don't have to be walking the same carrier path, but they must be on the same intellectual journey.

Role models are those that connect with us in such a deep penetrating way that we instantly feel inspired and motivated by their presence, by their every word, and we look to develop our intellectualism based on theirs. We all need such people to plant the seeds of leadership within us. We may not become like them, in fact we may grow to be quite different from them, but nevertheless, it was they that set us on that intellectual road to leadership.

At the academy, we wanted to fill that void of positive immediate role models for the youth in the local community. Manish and I were both footballers, which gave us a lot "street cred"; besides I was only twenty, and knew all the *cool cats* in the area. I firmly believe that that academy provides a stark alternative for the kids that attend. In their everyday lives they are surrounded by people who live the rat race, for good or for bad, this is simply a fact. Once a week for two hours, all the kids at the academy are exposed to people who are footballers, first and foremost. Second, they acknowledge that we are volunteers, sacrificing our time and energy for them; next we can connect with them in a way that their parents often do not; they know we are successful academically as well as professionally; some have heard me talk on the BBC, or have seen me on documentaries. All of this combined creates an image that essentially translates in their minds as, if you want to be successful; this is what we need to be like. It works.

We actively build positive relationships with each child; we nurture, advice and guide them through schooling and personal matters. A trust is built and sustained. It is both mutual and bi-lateral. The best way I think! In the long run, these kids create a portfolio of ideas about what it means to be leaders. They raise their own expectations. They feel more confident that they have sound guides who will advise them in their best interest, for nothing in return. This form of unconditional support can act as a deep support for some of these kids. Essentially, they are left with a choice – *to be normal, or to be positively abnormal* – to become leaders. Some rise, others settle for normality, but we ensure none sink.

The final prerequisite to leadership is philosophy. I have already touched on the fact that leadership is void of morality. It is neither good nor bad. It is what we do with that leadership that creates a moral dimension. Every leader, in fact every person, has values. People have things that they accept, tolerate, or find distasteful, and that which they are adherently against. I have always been interested not in what is good and bad, but a more penetrating question – *how do I know, for sure, what is right from what is wrong?* In other words, I have always been more interested in the journey to the answer, rather than the answer itself. What is our mechanism for deciding what is right and wrong?

All the great philosophers and explorers of the tunnels have asked this question and each has given a different perspective. None have sole authority on the subject. I firmly believe that every leader accompanied with a strong physique, discipline, emotional intelligence and role models needs a philosophical outlook on life. I have found this is by far the most difficult aspect to develop in myself, as well as in others. Those who have the potential to be leaders will one day end up in that position, whether it is as fathers, mothers, managers, politicians, shareholders, doctors or judges. The question is how you fill that "value box" of leadership? What type of values will you propagate through your version of leadership? How will you decide what is fair and what is right? All these questions are unanswerable in themselves. The best we can do is to develop, build a philosophically based mechanism for creating sound values – values that positively contribute to the global society.

I am not optimistic that these aspects of leadership will ever be taken up by schools. The problem lies in the way in which we measure learning. Philosophy is never about attaining the right answers, or about ticking the right box. Instead it is a process. How the argument is developed is more important that than the argument itself. This cannot be assessed so easily. The only answers that matter in philosophy are those that you have worked out yourself, this makes it hard to grade, or set standards too. My own philosophical exploration through the tunnels has given me enough to confidently say that we must know where we stand on the big issues of morality and ethics. If we don't, we lay ourselves open to those who want to impose their definitions upon us, or to laissez-faire attitude that anything goes. I think both are dangerous in society, but especially in leadership roles.

At the academy we encourage reading; we discuss ethical questions of the day; we talk about current affairs; and we deal with real life cases in the law courts, and so on. We do this not so that we arrive at the answers, but so that we can begin to develop an appreciation in the kids, of the complexities of life. Through such exploration we develop a self governing independent system of critical analysis. Every potential leader needs this prerequisite, and I believe it is the essential ingredient to good leadership. I know that I am still very young. But often I feel that the intellectual tunnels have taken me deep into the depths of life. Physically I'm young, but I often feel very old, not in a negative sense, but from a perspective of humility towards the complexity of life and living. We are all in a continual flux of change, whether this is physical, mental, intellectual or spiritual. What changes us?

I have come to think that it is our environment – the Matrix. We take the same approach in the academy, we do not change anything – the environment takes care of that. As long as we maintain a certain atmosphere in the training sessions, the training sessions themselves will bring positive change in those that partake in them – and that includes the coaches.

Of Hardship

The Academy of Leadership is now seven years old. But for me, it has been a lifetime. The Academy is not only a school of Leadership for kids, but more so, it was my school of life learning. If nothing else I have realised that there is no such thing as the *"perfect" leader*. It seems that we merely have to "fit" the situation. What I mean to say is that leadership is about adapting, coping, and ultimately winning through any given situation, and not all of us are equally effective in every eventuality. The effective leader is one who can adapt his *'whole being'* to the situation and pioneer a way forward for the betterment of all. To me at least, it boils down to performance. Leaders are doers, not talkers!

These people perform, work hard, are disciplined, and willing to sacrifice in order to succeed. They have unbending priorities, a vision accompanied by a wide array of soft & hard skills. By soft skills I mean things that are intangible, things that cannot accurately be measured. Interpersonal skills, charisma, creativity and other such skills, I consider as soft. Whereas, hard skills are tangible; these are competences such as numerical or linguistic literacy. Throughout my life, wherever possible, I have tried to pick up this illusive "art" of leadership. I can't remember when, or in what, but I read once that leadership was the single most important aspect mankind must learn, if it is to survive the twenty first century. When I read this line, I didn't quite grasp the significance of its meaning, or fully comprehend its validity.

I don't really have a clear idea of leadership; I don't believe anyone else does either. We do however have many commentators and management gurus, who shed some light on the subject. I have read the so called *greats* cover to cover several times – management gurus like Carnegie, Charles Handy, Robert Kiyosaki and Jo Owen. I found every one of them fascinating, and from each I discovered the practicalities and theories of leadership. I came to grips with buzz words like 'path-goal' theory and 'multiple linkage' theory. They were all very clever and full of insight, and I would recommend anyone, in any form of leadership role to read these sorts of books, if for nothing else they have a knack of simplifying things we already knew, and in that process of simplification and verbalisation, we can truly "realise" the concept and begin to use it in our lives. For me however, these thinkers and gurus were only peripheral reading – they were books that I would read casually, without taking them too seriously because they were merely skirting around the edges of real leadership. To me it seems that all of these great theories of leadership only become truly useful, after we have something else; something more *transcendental*; something I cannot verbalise or conceptualise.

I guess we could say that they are further prerequisites; something that needs to be cultivated before we throw ourselves into leadership. Plato, the Greek philosopher of antiquity said that only Philosopher Kings should rule society, because they would know the truth, and only through knowing the truth, can we have justice, and it is only through justice that we can have eudemon, or in other words happiness. Whether Plato was right or not is simply not relevant, at least for what I'm trying to get at. What is important however is Plato's insistence that rulers should be there to bring happiness to society. If we take this a little further – a business leader's core aim should be to bring *happiness* to all the workers of the organisation and all its outside stakeholders. A tough job indeed! What's more is that Plato also tells us how to achieve this state of eudemon in our organisations, whether they are family units or entire conglomerates. Plato says a leader should *be just*, and he can only be just when he is in direct "connect" with *truth*. And here is where the rabbit hole is found. Truth.

How do we come into direct connect with truth? If we can manage this, we will be just in our actions, and through justice we will bring eudemon, and through bringing eudemon to everyone under us, or dependent on us, we will naturally become great leaders.

It was *Frederick Nietzsche* who spoke volumes to me about truth, and ultimately leadership. Nietzsche was unique amongst thinkers. He is controversial, and just like marmite – you either love him or hate him. Nietzsche was unique in that he believed life was intrinsically about suffering, we cannot avoid it, we cannot run from it, and eventually no matter whom we are, it will catch up with us. When I read this, I became mesmerised; his words had touched the depth of my personal experiences.

We all have dark periods in our lives. We all face difficulties that seem insurmountable. We all encounter set-backs, and when we do we are often tempted to "throw-in the towel"; to simply give up. Most philosophers throughout the ages have attempted to council us, help us face the suffering, and ultimately have tried to keep us away from unhappiness. But not Nietzsche, on the contrary he believed that we must suffer, and suffer intensely, and through this intense suffering we would find happiness. Almost alone amongst philosophers he thought it was an advantage to have serious set backs in life. He believed that we should confront our suffering, not run away from them or avoid them. It was through suffering and pain that we would ultimately break through it, and find truth, find realisation and ultimately eudemon. Suffering and pain were the tools to enlightenment for Nietzsche. The harder our lives are the better, he wrote.

    To Nietzsche, life was like climbing mountains. For anyone to get to the top, they would firstly have to climb, and climbing would cause great pain and suffering. Those that managed to survive the suffering would get to the top, and from the tops of mountains where the air is still and light, we would get the best views of life. It would be from this peak that we could truly grasp what it was that we climbed. While climbing there is little reward, little hope and the top often well out of sight. Leaders, I believe are those people, who are the minority, who never give up. When they suffer, they become stronger. Leaders I find accept their suffering and work tirelessly to get through the dark times. Giving up is simply not an option for these people. They can become single minded in their approach; once they have set off on the climb, they are going to keep moving until they arrive at their destination. Pain only makes their mental resolve firmer. The great leaders of world politics and business are often those that have had to endure much, and through it have become who they are. Nietzsche taught me above all else that leadership is not easy. It is not for the faint hearted, or for those looking to avoid pain.

    At age twenty, when I first began to grasp the challenge of leadership with the Academy, I began to realise what Nietzsche meant. To run the academy was difficult. It meant that I had to come back from London every Friday night, prepare training sessions for the following Saturday morning, and then manage the boys through a Sunday lunch time match. Then straight after the match, which often ended in a heavy defeat for the team, at least in the early days, I would shoot back down to London. I would stay up till late preparing for the lecture on Monday morning. I found myself working between nine to ten hours every day Monday to Friday, so that I could spend my weekends concentrating on the academy. By taking up a leadership role, I in effect, increased my suffering. I was no longer living the life that other students lead – a life of relative ease. My life to some extent had always reflected what Nietzsche believed. I had indeed suffered, and continued to do so, even more after having taken up this leadership position. I could no longer spend the time I had wanted with Asheeta, I could no longer spend time in bed on Saturday mornings, and had to sit through many hours of traffic every Friday and Sunday night. Within a month or two, I was feeling exhausted. I felt as if I could no longer cope with studying, and running a football academy. These were the hardest of times. Everyone around me, including my mother was baffled at what she believed was my stupidity. She couldn't understand why I was living the life I was. She worried, as mothers often do.

A year into the academy, I could no longer remember what it was like when I wasn't working seven days a week. I was the weary climber too far up to see anything down below, and far too far from the top of the mountain. I was suffering. I became deeply unhappy. My body was aching and my mind no longer felt any sort of peace or stability. My only source of comfort was Asheeta and my occasional brief retreat into the moors of Dartmoor, with my collection of books. I also began to spend less time with friends, just hanging about, not because I didn't want to, but because I couldn't. I was feeling isolated. I began to regret ever having started the academy, just as a climber might regret having started the climb.

It was here, at what I call the crossroads of leadership that Nietzsche rescued me. His words were like an invisible pull, a force that would get me back onto my feet, looking up and never down. It was Nietzsche that elevated my thinking and helped me realise that life equated to suffering, and leadership equated to even more hardship. But through it, I would one day find a release, a peace, stillness that others down below could never know. Only the man who is at the peak of the mountain can know of the view; only he can appreciate his achievement. Only he can know the fact that all the suffering and hardship he endured while on the climb was well worth it, because the views from the top are so beautiful and enriching. At the peak is where there is Eudemon, and life at the end of it all, is simply about finding peace and happiness.

So why did I pursue with the Academy, why did I continue my pursuits even at the cost of greater hardship? Simple. I was looking for Eudemon, not just for me, which I knew thanks to Nietzsche, would only come right at the peak, but for all the Indo-Brits I was serving. In effect my hardship was offset against the benefits they received from the Academy. I was in essence bringing Eudemon to them, and their growth was effectively feeding my sense of pride, achievement and ultimately bringing some levels of satisfaction. It's like a climber trekking up steep slopes, feeling exhausted, who looks down and feels a small sense of achievement at what he has climbed so far. These little "tit bits" of achievement went a long way in keeping me motivated through the hardship I was enduring.

These Indo-Brits were growing, and some of them went through impressive personality changes – they grew in confidence, they became more assertive, they began to impose themselves in their social groups and most of all, they began to take charge through the spirit of giving back. They were becoming more sensitive to their surroundings, they began to realise that they have a part to play in shaping their own world, and that it wasn't merely a ride you should get taken on! They realised above all else, that they were the captains of their own lives, and only through hard work and determination they could prosper. Nietzsche taught me that life was about suffering, but leadership in this life was about taking on even more hardship voluntarily. Life in its simplest form is like climbing Snowdonia, but leadership in life is like climbing the 3-peaks of Britain for the sake of it. Climbing the 3-peaks is infinitely harder and requires immense effort. Of course Nietzsche also said that most people will falter, and that they would rather run from the pain than to confront it. He was right. Most people spend a life time running away from hardship and pain – why? Nietzsche was convinced, and I am too, that most people will never get to experience the peaks, because they will give up at some stage of the journey, or even worse, the journey will take their lives.

Leadership was about taking on extra hardship, extra risk, and took greater effort, simply to experience the highest peaks of the mountain of life. Only leaders could experience the stillness at the peak, the deep joy at the top when their quest finally came to its end. The views from the top of the great peaks make the climb; the suffering seems well worth it. There is something transcendental at the top; something that cannot be spoken of; something deeper and more meaningful. Ultimately through the hardship and suffering leaders will enjoy a transcendental realisation that others simply will never know. So beyond all the management theories with their technical jargon, it was Nietzsche that spoke the clearest wisest message to me – life equals suffering, and leadership in life equals even more hardship and pain, but through it there is something priceless at the top. So rather than running away from the realities of life, one should confront it, fight through it and continue upwards to the icy peaks above, and there one will find something, something so clear.

But Nietzsche said more. He said that we had to learn to cope and respond to suffering – those that responded well would continue going upwards, and those that responded badly, would fall. He said that along with hardship, people must experience failure. Every one will one day or another face the bitterness of failure. Failure at any level isn't nice, and I wouldn't wish it on anyone. But it is as certain as death. At some stage, we will fail. It's simply a part of life. Failure, however, isn't significant according to Nietzsche, it's how we respond to it that counts. Upon reading these words, at age twenty, a shift occurred in my mind. The shift was powerful and immediate. One minute I was one thing, and the next, I was different. Nietzsche's words were guiding me through the intellectual tunnels beyond the fabric of this material existence, his words were transcendental, and in effect he was teaching me the deepest virtues of leadership.

As Nietzsche by my side, I suddenly felt no fear towards failure. In fact, I expected it. I knew I would fail. It was evitable, so why run from it. Rather than being motivated to study in order to avoid failure, I began to shift my thinking towards the idea that I can only do what I truly know to be my best. If my best leads me to failure, well, so be it. I would just change my approach to the problem, and come at it from another angle. I realised that leadership isn't about perfection; it isn't about being right or the best, rather it was about using ones skills at their optimum, and when little failures come our way, leadership was about responding to them in the most constructive way possible. Going back to the climbing simile, if a climber attempts to climb a particularly steep face of a cliff, and he fails, he is left with two options. The first and easiest is to simply say, "Well I tried my best, it's too difficult". The other option is to say "that no mountain is impossible", he simply lacked the skills, equipment, or experience to climb it from there. So he decides to go back down and fine tune his skills, buy better equipment, etc. and attempt it again. The leader always chooses the second option. For leaders, failure is an obstacle that needs to be conquered. It is not an object of fear.

I remember Nietzsche using a striking comparison to gardening in his attempt to drive his message home. He said that every beautiful plant, tree or flower will have ugly roots under ground, but we never see them. All we see and smell or experience is the beauty; the success, but quite literally underneath it all are the roots of the tree, plant or flower, which, lets face it, are rather ugly. He said failure is the root to future successes if only we can use failure as a catalyst for growth. In other words Nietzsche said that we should take situations in our lives that appear very dark, and grow out of them something very beautiful.

This spoke volumes about leadership. Nietzsche was not into management or leadership, but his meditations are most valuable in the type of leadership I practice and teach. His thoughts are the darkest of all, yet out of them I have reaped success; through his thoughts I have been freed from fearing failure – not always of course, but I'm getting there. I have learnt to risk, and risking I am, in my mothers eyes I am reckless, but I am following Nietzsche, not my mother, through his advice of facing challenges, I am certain that I can harvest great happiness from what little my life is.

Nietzsche, along with pointing out what was a positive response to failure or hardship, he also quite vividly pointed out what was a disastrous response. He hated the pub. To Nietzsche the pub was the underground pit where ignorance flourished through grand self induced delusions of contentment, caused by alcohol. He thought that anyone even remotely interested in experiencing Eudemon should stay well away from alcohol. To imagine that there is benefit in escaping our troubles once in a while by having a tipple is to completely misunderstand the relationship between happiness and pain, according to Nietzsche. Most readers will disagree immediately with these sentiments, not out of fact, but out of personal defence, because most of us enjoy a tipple once in a while.

Happiness doesn't come from escaping pain, because pain is as certain as old age, rather it comes from cultivating hardship, and dark times into something more beautiful. He believed, and I do too, that alcohol deceives us from our harsh realities, it helps us escape, for a little while, but it also takes our roots of future success away from us. Anything, even for a short time that helps you escape from reality is ultimately damaging to the climber. The best climbers will be the leaders of our societies, and for them, if they are to succeed in bringing Eudemon to themselves and for those that follow them, they must resist all *delusion creating substances or practices – including religion.*

Leadership is ultimately about standing out, being different, having the courage to face the darker side of life, whether it is in business, politics, welfare, or ones own life, and creating solutions for others to follow. Leadership is indeed about skill, but at its roots, is something else, something more subtle. It is the ground upon which leadership skill is developed. The things Nietzsche teaches us are the bedrock of good leadership – the ideals of accepting hardship and pain, the idea of responding to them positively, to be able to risk without the fear of failure, and to be disciplined enough to refrain from delusions that help us momentarily escape reality. I don't think any management or leadership book that I have come across has ever quite put it like Nietzsche – but then there has never quite been anyone quite like him.

Of Revolt

"Stop protesting about everything!" cried out Asheeta, followed by a short burst of crazy laughter.

Her eyes reflected more than her short outcry could ever say. This was her punch line whenever she wanted me to appreciate something, or to simply accept the status quo. She has always felt and still does, that I analyse far too much, and that for me to ever truly appreciate the status quo is almost impossible. *She is right.* I am forever in revolt. I lead a life of happy discontentment, and looking back at my short existence, I think it's quite clear that I have lived with it from day one. What's more is that I think for anyone in any form of leadership it is impossible to exist without this *happy discontentment.*

I am in an ending revolt. I am always in revolt with myself, in that I want to learn, grow and discover myself to forever greater depths. I am in revolt with my family. I see their prejudices, their closed minds and egoistic tendencies everyday. I am in revolt with my friends. They will all tell you that I *"protest"* a lot. I can't stop. I am always questioning their views about life and living. I question passionately about the ethical dimension to their existence, and I do this in the Socratic way. I firstly observe, and watch. I see their actions. I attempt to connect with their thought process and attempt to understand their past. I then question whatever it is that I have observed. I provide alternative thought processes and ethical standards, those that they have never even contemplated. I do this not to prove a point, or to show that I am truly more intelligent – because most of the time, I am not! I do it in a conversational way, where I simply ask questions that they have never asked of themselves. It becomes an exploratory conversation, and never a debate or bout of grey intellectualism where we show our mental stamina in an attempt to outdo one another. People know when I am their friend – I'll revolt against something they do or believe! I am in constant happy revolt with language, tradition, religion and politics. I accept none of it for what it is. I see deep problems with all of them; I see their benefits, and I accept them whole-heartedly, but I also see their dark side. It is the darker side of all religions, traditions, languages and cultures that I revolt against – if not physically, at least mentally.

In revolting against everything, I attempt to find the soul of that which I am attempting to understand. I try and capture it as a whole, not in bits. Let me show you what I mean with a simple example. I am in forever revolt against contemporary MTV culture. When we listen to a piece of music, how do we each listen to it? Some listen to the beats and particularly focus in on them. They squeeze pleasure from them and hence are contended. Others focus in on the lyrics of the song; some listen to the track because they find the artist sexually appealing, and others enjoy the music because it gives them the urge to dance, and so on and on. I, however, can only ever appreciate and enjoy a piece of music when I connect with the beats, the lyrics and it's meaning all at once – the complete whole. I am not going to accept the beats and ignore the lyrics, because then I am accepting something in part, which I do not really value as a whole. A track is more than just music, its more than beats, its more than the looks of the artist, and yet it's about all of these things, and more when we connect with all of them. The whole is greater than the sum of its part. I always want to appreciate the whole, never only its parts. I will not accept one part and ignore another. For me to not revolt against a piece of music or track, I must connect and value all its fragments, and draw satisfaction from the whole. Too many people are easily accepting of the status quo because they are all too easily satisfied with fragments, and lack the mental stamina to grasp the whole.

I suspect that you are thinking what do I mean by happily discontent – isn't discontent supposed to mean some form of dissatisfaction? This is how most people use and understand the word discontent. I do not. Most people understand the word in a canalised manner, which is that they see it in one form and no other, its all in one narrow direction. We say that we are discontent when we are not satisfied. It may be to do with our professional lives; we may not be at the management level we all desire to be at; or our business is simply not profitable. We can also use the word discontent when our interests are not satisfied – sexually, personally, intellectually and even I guess, spiritually. I mean something different by the word discontent, at least in the context which I am writing about.

To me the word discontent means when we are disturbed by our reality as we have understood it. Whereas, to be happily discontent means to become in a state of disturbance with ones own understanding of reality consciously – on purpose. We want to feel dissatisfaction with our perception of reality, when we are happily discontent, one isn't afraid of disturbance, instead one embraces it. Throughout my life I have seen people tirelessly walk through life being in a permanent state of dissatisfaction with one thing or another, while continuously forever attempting to be satisfied with what they have. This contradictory behavioural pattern, I believe, is deeply unhealthy. We live in a society that enforces conformity in one way or another. Its human nature I guess. To be different, to challenge the norm is always a difficult thing to do. To see what others see as obvious, from an alternative perception and then to express your ideas is a thing that only a few of us ever do. Most people are discontent because all their time is spent on avoiding disturbance, and thereby attempting to just accept the world for whatever it is. So when disturbance comes, they are powerless to effectively deal with it. When however, we are happily discontent we are always in a state of revolt consciously, and thereby, in a state of conscious disturbance. We no longer want to accept the norm, or what society, religion, culture or any other such institute enforces on us that we perceive to be fragmentary. For example, I can never accept the idea that a woman has to change her family name when she gets married to that of her husbands. Of course, if she wishes to change it, fair enough I say, but any form of compulsion or societal pressure is worth revolting against.

From a position of leadership this is of great importance. Discontent breeds a kind of helplessness, whereas, to be happily discontent creates initiative. And what is initiative? Surely it's when we start something without being prompted. It need not be anything spectacular or grand, but there is a spark of initiative when we choose to plant a tree on our own; when we are spontaneously kind; when we smile at a stranger, or pat a dog as it walks by. These types of things are the beginnings to something tremendous – the idea that once we consciously choose to be discontent and challenge our realities in the hope of a fuller understanding, we gain a fuller perception and this fuller perception allows each of us to better absorb this feeling of discontentment into a positive form – in other words as initiative. It is only through initiative that real creativity is produced.

The relationship can now look like this – *deeper the happy discontentment, the greater the initiative, and greater the initiative – greater the creativity.* It is this process of revolting against our fragmented understanding of reality that nourishes our spark of creativity until it finally becomes a flame. Surely, it is creativity that has advanced all humanity thus far, and only a few have changed the destinies of all throughout history. Where did this immense creativity come from, whether it is in commerce, education, politics, science, religion or any other field?

As I have grown older, I have found that life closes in around us. Society, the pressure of earning a wage, or to become educated, to have children, to perform some religious ceremony all ends up breaking this state of happy discontentment. I have found it increasingly difficult to maintain a discontentment that is not superficial. Superficial discontentment is when we complain but lack the will to act on it, and as I have grown into adulthood, I have found more and more superficial discontentment amongst my peers. The *pressures of life* seem to have drowned their *real passion for life*. I guess for most the flame of creativity dies when they have their own families, because the material pressures of providing for ones own family supersedes all other priority – including that of revolting, or as Asheeta has so elegantly put it, "Stop protesting about everything!"

Of Broadmindedness

If leadership is fundamentally about bringing happiness to everyone, and everything, then to be broadminded is the virtue of all other virtues. I would say that I have become increasingly broadminded as I have evolved out of my teens and into young adulthood, and now approaching the thirty mark rather quickly. But what is broadmindedness? Just like the other two virtues of leadership – that of hardship and revolt, broadmindedness has no fixed definition. It's hazy at best and downright indefinable at worst. Being a forever optimist, I will make an attempt here.

I think we all need to be broadminded, no matter what we do. Being broadminded is when we are in a state of mind that is accepting of a reality that we may not necessarily agree with, or quite understand. It seems that we can only really accept things when we have some connect with it, in other words that on some level we have *agreement or understanding*. If I have absolutely no agreement with something, then I cannot possibly comprehend it, and without comprehension how can I possibly be broadminded? Broadmindedness then becomes a tool through which we view the world. It's all encompassing, none are barred from it, and all can be attempted to be understood. Being broadminded isn't the same as having a loose stance on moral issues, or sitting on the fence. It's about seeing reality from another, altogether different angle.

I am a vegetarian. I choose to be so, not from any religious or cultural belief, but after exploring the intellectual tunnels; after questioning; after enquiring, I realised that it was immoral – *immoral for me at least*! Nearly everyone I know and care for eats meat. I am open to their actions. I don't agree with them in the slightest, but I can appreciate why they do what they do, and in a position of leadership, this is crucial. I disagree with all their reasons, in fact I think there isn't a prevalent argument for consuming other animals in the urban twenty first century life styles most of us lead, yet I can understand why people do so. It's about being broadminded.

Leadership is often about having a deeper understanding about people and their motivations. Leadership involves having ideals, and a solid moral baseline. Yet one must be able to view the world from alternative perspectives and backgrounds. This requires enquiry. Too many people, I believe, class themselves as being broadminded, when in fact, they are not. It's not that they can appreciate alternative perspectives, but mostly it's because we live in a relativistic moral climate, where we have a *"live and let live"* ethos. We often think people are broadminded, when in fact they are opinion-less, or have no understanding about the reality that they face. Hence, they open themselves up to anything. That is not being broadminded. Having little or no understanding, and not having the urge to explore, enquire about it, and hence accepting whatever people throw at us is not broadmindedness – it's a negation of truth and enquiry.

Broadmindedness is positive, not a negation. It's about questioning, challenging and exploring, in order to find truth. Once we arrive at a solid position where we feel we have discovered a deeper understanding, we will automatically appreciate other people's views, even if we believe them to be false – it's almost altruistic of me to say such a thing, but it's true. The realisation of something, to discover its soul, almost immediately brings to view all the dark areas. I guess it would be like having a schematic view of the moral landscape, where you have a perspective that few manage to have. You can then appreciate that your views of the landscape are such, exactly because of your position, furthermore, you can understand that other people hold different views because of their position, even if that position is limited.

Another aspect of being broadminded is that old ideas in our minds are lucidly replaced by new ones, without much struggle or pain, but only if these new ideas stand up against our personal critical enquiry. The new must replace the old. The right must replace wrong. And leadership is all about embracing new, sophisticated world views that will quite naturally replace old existing ones. These views could be political, social, moral, about business, or our opinions of a person. Not matter, broadmindedness is about having the ability and freedom of mind to eradicate the old paradigms with new ones. All too often leaders' demise is written in their lack of ability to shift their minds to new better ideas, and ousting with their old beliefs no matter how well they may have served them thus far. As long as we are exploring, challenging, and genuinely pursuing truth, then the rest falls smoothly into place. If so far you have agreed with what I have said, and hence have connected with these words, then the next logical step forward is to accept that there can be no authority on truth. If broadmindedness is to be a central virtue of leadership then it follows that *there can be no single authority on truth*. I should allow for that sentence to seep into your consciousness before I continue, for it has paramount consequences to the way in which we live our lives.

To say that truth has no authority means that we can no longer look at anything as gospel. That includes the Gospel – the good book; it includes the Koran; and it includes the Torah; and any other religious book that speaks of truth. I am not advocating a total disbelief, or any form of atheism. Instead my point is that we should all know that truth is not static. It is not singular, nor does it exclusively belong to anyone. Truth is, at least for human existence, forever evolutionary, our capacity for the truth is forever growing, changing, and hence, we can grasp truth in multiple ways clearing older, out of date ideas. I speak of truth not just on a religious perspective. I am also referring to business models, political paradigms, scientific theories and other such categories of knowledge. No one can claim to be the soul authority of truth. As soon as someone claims it, they loose broadmindedness, and with the loss of this virtue, the leader can no longer bring eudemon to all, but instead, at best, to a few.

Philosophers throughout the ages have attempted to get the rest of us mortals to become broadminded. It's been an attempt that has mostly been in vain – at least outside the world of philosophy. Something however has now changed. I genuinely believe that the globalised world is slowly, but surely becoming increasingly broadminded. Three reasons come to my mind, which have contributed to the growth of broadmindedness. The first is education. Especially since it is now out of the hands of religious organisations, secondly, it's to do with the internet and the information age in which we live, and thirdly it's to do with travelling across different countries.

More of us are travelling. Travelling, even when we are "protected" by tourist resorts and the like, expose us, albeit slightly, to different cultures, languages, diets, architectures and life styles. The exposure to such variety quite naturally questions and challenges our own values, languages, diets and life styles. When we holiday, we are consciously or unconsciously challenging our positions; we are travelling on the *moral landscape*. This can lead to questions, which results, sometimes in enquiry, which can become passion for that thing, which finally, brings us closer to the truth. Travelling, I believe alongside the other two developments in the last century, has contributed to a humanity that is slowly creeping towards a universal broadmindedness. It's a rather optimistic view. There are indeed many challenges up ahead, some of which I will discuss in later chapters; for now, I think it will suffice to say that the three virtues of hardship, revolt and broadmindedness are paramount to anyone, in any position of influence, if they choose to work for the Eudemon of all, and not just a few.

Six

धर्म
───────

From Peaks to Slums

"India was the mother of our race and Sanskrit the mother of Europe's languages. She was the mother of our philosophy, mother through the Arabs, of much of our mathematics, mother through Buddha, of the ideals embodied in Christianity, mother through village communities of self-government and democracy. Mother India is in many ways the mother of us all." – Will Durant

29th May 2005, was one day before a trip that was to re-forge my entire thinking, re-focus my energy, and to discover a deeper understanding of oneself. It was a trip that tested my broadmindedness to its natural limits. It was a trip that altered my world. Nothing after it looked, or felt the same. I was changed. I was forever re-conditioned by India. It was Mark Twain that said the most awesome commentaries on India and her civilisation. It was he who said, "So far as I am able to judge, nothing has been left undone, either by man or nature, to make India the most extraordinary country that the sun visits on his rounds. Nothing seems to have been forgotten, nothing overlooked".

In hindsight, I think it's impossible not to be astonished by India. I have travelled extensively, travelled to explore different worlds, with different paradigms and world views, all in the hope of discovering a little bit more of truth. And in all my travels, India presented a humanity of such intoxicating burst of cultures and religions, races and tongues, that only the mountains to the north which overshadow it are worthy of comparison. Almost three years later, I now firmly believe that the only thing more difficult than being indifferent to India is to describe or understand it completely. This chapter is my attempt at exactly that, and before I even begin to write, I know that I have fallen short.

As I packed my 60-litre rucksack, weighing around 19 kilos, but feeling like fifty, I knew that I was going somewhere that would completely dissolve my sense of being. I was nervous and a little frightened at this thought. I was worried that India would not only dissolve me, but then fail to reform my being, and so, I was scared stiff of coming back in a greater intellectual mess with deformed values. As I stared into the bathroom mirror, one that always made me feel good about the way I looked, (*its funny how mirrors have a tendency to make you look better than you actually are, whereas, others make you feel worse, but that is besides the point*), I realised wholly, that everything I was, was no longer relevant, it was the prologue to the rest of my life. It was in that twenty minute instant while shaving for the last time in Britain, that I realised the magnitude of the realisation. Everything, absolutely everything that I was, had ever been, and will ever become – the entire existence of *"me"* was to be understood, and shaped in that next few months.

I had known the feeling, in fact I had known it all too well. Looking back, I now feel humbled by the experience, rather than scared by it. I had felt the same nerves, the same anxiety, the same feelings of vulnerability, and the same intense sense of loss, of detachment. I had felt it when I was very young, the time when Vikas's demon was unleashed on me, when he had dragged me out into the summer garden and gave me a beating which I can no longer recall. I had also felt this same intense feeling of depth at his death, sitting there in the crematorium, falling through the rabbit hole, where my being was re-forged to what ever it had become. This was to be the third; and I wondered if it was the final re-forging experience of my life? It was here, standing at the foot of the drop into the rabbit hole that I starred into the abyss. In time, I was only in a trance for fifteen to twenty minutes, while shaving. But, beyond time and space, it was forever. I remember looking deep into my own eyes through the reflection, and I said "good bye" to myself, for this was the last time I was to see Sanvik, at least as I had known him.

This is the single most important period of my life to date. It was a period of great realisations in the mountains of the North, it was a period of great sorrow in the depths of the rural slums, but most of all it was a period where I was free. It was Anne Lindbergh, who I believe said "he that I love, I wish to be free - even from me."

I was free. Free from people. Free from love. Free from hate. Free from things. Free of time. Free of all responsibility. But most of all, I was free of myself. I had no expectations – of myself, or of India. It was liberating; I had known that it would be. By now I was a seasoned traveller, having been exploring around Europe, East Africa, and parts of South America. Where ever I travelled, I wasn't interested in the sight seeing, or the beautiful beaches. Instead, I was engrossed with the people, their relation to one another, and their relation to their land, and most of all to their history. I was interested in the people, not really the place. I enjoyed people watching, not to judge, but to learn. I have often said over and over again, to friends, that if I had enough money to travel all my life, and study humanity full time – I would. It had become my single most important passion, something which I connected with, I was feeling forever one with humanity. While falling through the rabbit hole, I have often felt that I was humanity, and humanity was me. There was no separation; *no duality.* In fact it was a singularity of the most profound type.

30th May 2005, I arrived at Heathrow airport, flying to Amritsar. I was flying with Manish and his sister Sangeeta. We flew with Air India, where the flight attendant at the check-in kiosk upgraded us to business class. These were the initial signs of a comfortable trip. In reality the trip was anything but; instead it was the sign of unpredictability, which I was about to experience. The flight was smooth enough and left me thinking that Air India got more stick than it deserved, but then again, I was flying business class.

Anyone that has ever been to India will have noticed the different air. I could smell it before I saw or heard anything. Even as the door of the plane opened allowing the hot dry stifling air of India mix with the conditioned air we were breathing, I felt a surge of excitement run through my spine. Amritsar didn't have an umbilical corridor connecting the plane to the airport. As I approached the door, the sunlight overwhelmed my eyes, I couldn't open them. It was nine in the morning, and the sun was in a rage. As I crept onto the stairway, looking at the airport staff signalling us towards the terminal, I immediately felt the history of the place. On entering immigration I was struck by the harsh faces at the counters. These were the bureaucrats of India, stern faced, poor looking, disinterested and making a point of it to be impolite. I felt at that moment that it was their way of saying *"you may be all richer than I could ever be, but fuck you anyway!"*

At that moment when we mortals had to show them our passports with the embarkation card, it was their one opportunity to be ahead of us in the pecking order. We needed them. I needed their nod and a glare to allow me through the gates, and upon passing their wooden docks, I felt a meditational ease somewhat instantly. I was now firmly in. I was in India, and a bag away from leaving the chaotic arrivals terminal. People scrambled to get their bags; bag attendants nonchalantly threw bags off the conveyor belts and left them on the side for people to come and take theirs away. It was a labour intensive terminal. Uniformed personnel inter-mixed with the tourist riff-raff, as British Indians became only Indians.

I saw first generation migrants, my parents generation, returning home to see family, and no sooner had they stepped a foot on Indian soil, had they lost their British manners. They became as brash and rude as the uniformed officers. They screwed up their faces, and raised their noses due to their NRI status. It was interesting to see how many of them wanted to keep their modern tag of being British, being wealthy, and better educated (*even though most weren't*), while losing their politeness and their sense of equality. They were home, it was written on their faces, and they no longer had to have the pretence of all the things that they were not. Seeing British Indians in India helped me realise the true nature of the Indian psyche – something which I will comment on in due course. It was thoroughly disorganised, with most airport staff happy to watch the chaos ensue. I too was happy to watch it unfold. I was in no rush – I was free. I didn't care if everyone got their bags first, or whether they pushed to the front door quicker, to meet loved ones who were eagerly waiting for their *modern relatives*. I didn't even know who was waiting for us outside. Manish had said that it was his *Mama*, meaning mother's brother. His Mama became my Mama. It was as simple as that. I didn't even bother to ask his name, it just wasn't necessary. I was never going to call him by his first name anyway. In the Indian culture youngsters called their elders by a title based upon the relation. So Manish, and now I too, called his mothers brother, Mamaji. The "ji" at the end is a mark of further respect.

I had landed in Punjab, and was surrounded by Punjabis; people speaking Punjabi, a language I couldn't understand. As Manish, his sister, and I pushed our way out of the airport, my eyes were sapped from the bright sunlight. It was exhilarating to see all the guileless faces scanning my face to see if I was one of their long lost relations. I looked back, without any reference, I had no idea who I was looking for, and it showed. I was third in line, and Manish spotted Mamaji immediately. While they were greeting one another, I absorbed the atmosphere around me.

The people around me all wore smiles, which were made from sincerity – a thing that we in the developed nations piety as being simple-minded. I liked the simplicity of what they wore, their cars, their roads and their mannerisms. But most of all it was the colour. It was everywhere. It was on the people, their clothes, the huge battered advertisement boards, the cars; it was on the auto rickshaws and taxis. The women too stood out. Most were in traditional Punjabi suits, sprayed with authentic colour, and their beautiful subtle nose studs, ear rings and necklaces all glimmered. Their faces shown brightly with hope, and yet their eyes showed a depth of innocence. The men looked powerful, always in front, always broad and wide. This was a man's world. The first thirty seconds told me so.

When Manish and Sangeeta were done hugging and touching the feet of their Mamaji and *Mamiji*, in prostration, I was introduced by Manish. I too, prostrated to touch the feet of Mamaji and Mamiji. I think they were pleasantly surprised. It was a mark that I saw them as my own. I have always found the act of touching feet of elders a humbling experience, while remaining difficult, and filled with an air of awkwardness before the act. It's as if everyone is waiting to see whether you'll actually do it or not. For me at least, this act is a mark of humility. To bow down to someone else, is a fight against ones on ego, ones own sense of self worth, at least in the western context of the act. I have fought hard with my own ego, my own self importance when ever I have had to touch the feet of an elder. Most in my family have discarded the act as being backward, and out of date. It's something that we all used to find hugely embarrassing. After all, we were Indo Brits, not Indians. Since however, I have realised the act of touching the feet of an elder has its place. It is the ultimate human symbolism for when we see the other in the highest possible light. I think it has its place, but not in the mainstream, I don't think I should prostrate to those I don't admire or respect or even know. But I certainly have no problem with prostrating to my parents whom I adore and owe my entirety.

We placed our bags into the boot of the large Toyota SUV, and got into the air-conditioned cabin. It was delightfully cool. It was airy and felt that I could breathe again. The fragrance of human sweat was soft and circulated the car. It was a smell that I later came to realise as the smell of hard work and toil. I took my place at the back, looking quietly out of the tinted window, while the others spoke speedily in Punjabi. Everyone seemed to speak at once. I couldn't understand much, but their faces displayed warmth. The symbol of "OM" was stuck onto the dashboard, something that instantly made me comfortable. My parents stuck the same sort of symbolism to their dashboards in the UK. Come to think of it, they even stuck it on my dashboard! I liked it. They talked away, completely oblivious to the world outside, or if they were seeing it, they didn't outwardly respond.

The journey from the airport to where ever it was that we were going began on a wide, modern motorway, lined by thirsty trees. People on foot, on bikes, on scooters and bicycles rode in and out of the traffic. It was orderly chaos.

The roads were full of sane people driving insanely. The engine roared, gears meshed with a crunching sound and the car jerked forward past a slow moving rickshaw. More than anything else what I remembered was the poverty that lined the road. As the kilometres wound past, I saw my first glimpse of the much popularised Indian slum. *It was heart ache.* I vividly remember the smell as we drove by. It was raw untreated sewage. The smell of human excretion is not only foul, but it symbolises the horror of poverty. As the view cleared and the car came to a stand still at the lights, the view was cataclysmic. I saw human misery from the comforts of an air conditioned SUV. I was disconnected from what I was confronting. There was little I could do. The gears thumped and the car was rolling again. I knew that I had to actually go to the slums if I was to truly understand them and its people. We've all seen these shacks, at least on TV, but let me say that TV is one thing, seeing them for real is another. But to live in them is the ultimate realisation of what it means to be materially poor – something that I was soon to do.

Amritsar was hard on the eyes. It was a city out of control, or so it seemed. Its infrastructure was non-existent. Looking at the electricity lines I wondered how millions of people weren't electrocuted everyday, and how they coped with fires that should have been happening by the hour. Health & Safety – what health & safety! Everyone just got on with the act of living. I had seen this kind of thing in every other third world country, but India was something else. It was the magnitude of the chaos that was striking to the mind. It was difficult to make any sense of it. It was just overwhelming. My mind shut down in those first three days. Amritsar is a city with history, marred by atrocities such as Jallianwalla bagh, where a British general named Dyer, in 1919, ordered the massacre of thousands of innocent Indian citizens. Then there is the Golden Temple, the holiest of holies for Sikh people throughout the world. Finally there is Wagah border, where India meets Pakistan in a daily ritual of puffing chests and slamming gates.

But I am not here to describe India, at least from a visual perspective. Rather I want to share my intellectual re-forging with you. It will suffice to let you know that I stayed with Mamaji, in a tiny rural community in Punjab, called Rurka. The most striking thing about Rurka was that hemp grew organically and freely throughout its streets. It was here that I saw, and attempted to understand the position of women within the rural Indian society.

SANVIK VIRJI
On Women

In order to understand the state of anything, we must understand its history, and before that, we must understand its philosophical reasoning. Women in the Indian philosophical traditions are considered different to men. I am no advocate of India's first prime minister, Jawaharlal Nehru, but it was he who said rightly *'that the condition of a nation can be judged by looking at the status of its women'*. Women within the Indian philosophical tradition are depicted primarily as mothers, as with many ancient cultures. What is of interest, and note worthy is that it is professed by the Upanishads that women create society, shape it and give it a moral dimension, whereas men are merely its custodians. Men may dominate society, but women create it, nurture its future and shape its moral climate. There is little doubt that the state of women in Indian antiquity was much better than it was in the 18th or 19th centuries, where it had hit rock bottom.

The Rig Vedas, the Upanishads, and countless number of texts shed fragmented light on the state of womanhood. Women in ancient India up until a few centuries after the death of Christ held a position of relative modernity when compared to other parts of the world. For example, we find in the Upanishads several examples of women philosophers openly arguing, enquiring into the nature of reality, God and political affairs. We also find extracts in several commentaries from Ibn Battuta, a 13th century Muslim explorer who came to India to see the extent of Dar-al-Islam, the extent of the lands ruled by Islam. He makes several references to how liberated Hindu women in the rural Indian villages were, he talks of them being allowed to openly walk the streets, attend feasts and dances. He also makes clear comparatives between the states of women in other Islamic countries around the same time, he hints that *'women here are devastatingly beautiful and free, and it is their freedom that makes them all the more beautiful'*.

Ibn Battuta was right. Indian women were beautiful, not via their looks, but rather from their aura. To stare at the Indian women is to stare at innocence. Her entire existence is driven towards attaining three goals: first, to be a good wife; second, to be a good mother; and lastly, to be in touch with God. These three aims were encoded in everything they did – their walk, their smiles, their clothes, their jewellery, their mannerism, in fact, I would say their entire nature was built around these three aspects. What I found truly astonishing about these rural women was how they saw all three foundations to their existence as one. They saw no difference between the metaphysical idea of God, their husbands and ultimately their children. Their husbands and their children were the physical manifestations of God in their lives. So it was nothing but natural for these women to care, love and cherish their husbands and children, no matter how ungodly they in actual fact were.

To see Mamiji, Manish's mother's brother's wife, was to see a women who belonged to her husband. Her physical self was not only hers; it was Mamaji's also, maybe more so. It was written all over her life. She was the carer of her mother-in-law, who was now her mother; she was the carer of her two children, and she lived through them, but most of all she was the carer of her husband. The family unit was clearly distinguished, so much so that there were no grey areas where the roles of the husband and wife intermixed. The man of the family was the alpha male. He was the hunter gatherer. He would leave the house every morning and come back with money. Meanwhile, the female was to utilise the resource the male collected for the betterment of all family members. It was her role to cook, clean, look after the elderly, the young, to ensure that the household maintained some form of discipline, and most importantly that values were being passed down to the next generation. The man was the protector and bread winner. He was also the family authority on all important issues. The woman was the carer, lover, and educator.

To live within a traditional rural Punjabi family was deeply fulfilling. It was everything that the typical family in the UK is not. That is not to say that I believe the traditional rural Indian family is better, or worse, what I want to do is highlight the differences, and thereby gain a better understanding. I want to capture the soul of the subject.

The core difference between the two set-up's was that both the man and woman had a set place, a set role within the Indian rural system. Whereas, in the UK, I have found that both occupy a lot of the same space, both are bread winners, both are dominant, or least try to be, both want independence from the other, while maintaining a sense of belonging, and both take on some caring roles. There is a great deal of overlap. It is this overlap, which breeds a lack of clarity within the British family setup. The Indian family set up is hierarchical, with stringent roles, defined and refined over centuries of tradition. If the family unit was a firm, then the Indian firm was disciplined, each member knew exactly where they belonged, and what their roles and responsibilities were. If the firm broke down, it was much easier in the Indian family system to locate the problem, and there were powers authorised to the alpha male, by consensus of society, to take charge and remedy the problem. In the UK however, we have lots of grey areas. Our firm is more egalitarian. We are all bosses, or at least strive to be. We all want to have roles that society commends, and we all run from the role of *"house wife"*. When problems occur, and you have too many chiefs, who do you look too? Who is authorised to take control and remedy the situation for the betterment of all members? Where does the consensus arrive from? Who has the ultimate decision in a flat hierarchy?

Women and men are different. They're different physiologically, emotionally, and I believe intellectually. One is not better than the other, rather they are simply symbiotic. It was in India that I came to the understanding that men are simply not monogamous, whereas, most women are, or at worst strive to be. Men are driven by their spinal cord, and so are women. The difference is that evolution has programmed them both differently. I am no longer referring to merely Indian men or women, but men and women in general. Here too, in the UK, where society is a lot more liberal towards sexual relationships and interactions between men and women, where sexual stimuli is stronger and widespread. One just has to look at the number of brothels lining the streets of every major city, and the private sex adverts in every national and local newspaper, to see that it's not only single men that visit these places. In fact I believe most men visit prostitutes, those that are young and crave experience, those that are lonely, those that are married and want to sleep with someone else, and those that have children. Of course, it simply isn't possible to accurately quantify what percentages of men have slept with prostitutes, but recent surveys show that 22% of men admit to having done so. I think this number is much higher. From personal experience I can tell you that many men I know have visited prostitutes. These men are noble, often very intelligent, successful, rational, at least for the most part, with families, who they cherish and love. Yet, after everything is said and done, these men that often love their life partners, who cherish their children, can't resist the call of the Id, that part of the mind which craves relentlessly for sexual gratification.

For most men I believe it simply is sexual gratification, nothing more. It's sex without any emotional baggage. Many women I speak to find my views difficult to accept, their rationale is often the same. Why would men want to pay for sex when we live in an age where one night stands are common place, and women are more liberal and sexually active? I believe it's simple. It's simple, because men are essentially simple creatures. It's sex without emotional obligation. Most men I believe find it easier, even more honest; to pay for sex, rather than pick up a girl in a bar, play with emotions in order to get something physical. Besides, for most men it's easier to pay for sex, and skip all the emotional foreplay involved in one night stands. Furthermore, just like the Bonobo monkeys, most men use emotionless sex to vent aggressive build up energy. Its pent up aggression being released safely, relatively speaking. In a world where we are conditioned to believe that sex stems from a boy-meets-girl situation, rather than boy-pays-girl, the latter is always considered seedy and driven underground. Yet we all know that boy-pays-girl relationship has existed since human society began. Why is it a taboo, when we all know of it? We are a species that I believe is altruistically schizophrenic – we all know, and a significant portion engage, in boy-pays-girl relationships, yet we ignore it, and make ourselves believe that it's an activity for a seedy few. The truth is strikingly different, and I believe its time we face up to facts. Most men do not wish to be emotional vandals, and hence, paid sex, is the best way for them to balance their need to vent sexual aggressive energies, and not vandalise anyone. The boy-pays-girl is simple, all too simple. The girl does it for money, and the boy for sex. The girl exchanges emotion for money. Its money – the one thing that displaces emotions, frees men from bondage, and responsibility. The money to some extent also helps men distance themselves from contemplating the wider effects of their actions on the girl. Money, it seems, is the great neutraliser of natural emotions.

I suspect that most women reading these pages are feeling a little uncomfortable with the thought that their husband or partner has, in all probability, engaged in a boy-pays-girl relationship. A little dose of discomfort is a price well worth paying to connect with the truth that men are simply not designed to be monogamous. Saying this I do not cast judgement on men that have engaged in a boy-pays-girl relationship. To *some* degree, (and I emphasise the word *some*), I think it's rather responsible of men to vent their sexual energies in a controlled manner. My comments are not to be taken as an endorsement to visit prostitutes, or that I do not understand the tragedy lurking just beneath the surface of most of these girls, who I truly believe are victims of their own existence. I just want to point out the core truths about human, or should I say male nature. I also want to point out the simple fact that love and sex are two different beasts, which do not necessarily like each other, at least in the minds of men. A man can sincerely love a woman, and then visit a prostitute for sex. I think this is a rather alien concept for most women to grasp, for whom I suspect that sex and emotion, if not love, go hand in hand.

The challenge that most men face is that they are continuously bombarded with sexual stimuli from the moment they awake, to the time they nod off. Rather than me rambling on, I just ask you to count the number of sex orientated images you see on your way to work tomorrow – I bet you'll be surprised. Then there is fashion. The number of women in tight jeans that a man comes across in a day simply adds to his sexual frustration. Most women's fashion directly or indirectly, consciously or subconsciously, stimulate men. Every man is programmed by evolution to continuously scan women. So when a woman is in clothing which enhances her sexuality, or simply her curves, the result will be that more men, whether they wish too or not, will glance over the figure in view. If the man dislikes what he sees, then there is no problem. However, all too often, men particularly enjoy what they see; society, as well as morality, puts restrictions on their natural impulses. They cannot act on the sexual stimuli they've just received. This builds quiet subconscious sexual frustration within the male psyche. Over time, this builds. Eventually, every man will reach his peak, and unless he can vent his sexual frustrations and fantasies with his partner, he will seek to do so anyway he can. Hence, we have the boy-pays-girl scenario.

Some people right about now may be wondering whether I have engaged in a boy-pays-girl relationship. The answer is "no I haven't". Not because I am moral, or that I do not suffer from the same impulses as all men, but rather because I have learnt to dissipate my sexual energies in an altogether different way. From a very young age I have been fascinated with the movements of my thoughts. As far back as I can remember I have always disconnected myself from my feelings. I remember the mantra I used to condition myself with – *"you are not your emotions and you are not your feelings"*. I have always attempted to understand my thoughts and feelings from a presumption that they are in some way separate from me. This type of psychological conditioning has always meant that I analyse the sensations entering my consciousness, whether they are physical, emotional or intellectual. When one is sensitive to the stimuli and its related sensations, we can begin to understand why we feel the way we do. From understanding the relationship between stimuli and sensation, I ended up rather naively learning how to effectively dissipate emotions that I didn't care for.

The first thing I do to remain sexually in control, from an emotional perspective, is to ensure that my mind is engaged in productive activity. I see the mind as a tool. It is not me, but a part of me. From that perspective, I take it upon myself to make sure that it's never idle – at least for too long. When the male mind is idle, it is at its most devastating. Also the type of activities that I engage it with is always intellectually stimulating; I absorb my mind into information and environments where it will learn new skills, new traits, and new thinking patterns. I read uplifting literature. I'm a persecutor of comics that disguises itself as newspapers – I keep my mind firmly away from triviality such as the Sun, News of the World, and the increasingly popular trend of buying "lads' mags". Instead I'll engage my mind with Time magazine, journals, I'll write poetry, read serious newspapers, and generally ensure that even when my mind is officially on a break, I'll relax it with a dose of Stravinsky or Mahler, or even play chess, rather than watch the latest video from some over hyped, over sexed girl band. I'll certainly keep it away from "hardcore" pornography, which I deplore from a moral stand point.

No matter how much we try to absorb our mind into non-sexual activity, sex is always present – if not directly, then most certainly indirectly. In fact most advertisements are built around stimulating our primitive sex & fear driven subconscious. There is nothing one can do about this, part from renouncing the material world and becoming a hermit in some lost forest. This is not for me – at least presently. So I have devised another way. I accept the sexual content that enters my mind on a daily basis, I watch it, and I pay particular attention to the types of thoughts which are created as a result. Then I simply meditate on them. I allow them to burn in the depths of my thinking when I meditate, I allow my sex stimulated thoughts to go where ever they like, and eventually just like all fires – they burn themselves out. Meditation, whether it's through silence, music or visually based, help to dissipate thoughts that may otherwise adversely affect daily actions.

In India, my mind was deprived of sexual imagery for the most part. Spending the first few days in a tiny rural community in Punjab was exactly what I had needed to detoxify my mind. I understood why it was that in the Indian tradition, men and women played such different roles. I understood why women didn't show their curves, cleavages, legs or neck so readily. I found the Indian system to reveal the simplicity of the male mind, and the repression it caused for women. Women were absolved of their right to show their sexuality in public in order to preserve what little sanctity remains of the collective male psyche. Is this right? Are women repressed if they are unable to show off their sexuality? I truly do not have any clear cut answers. One thing however is certain – the issue of Western liberal freedoms as somehow being superior to the restrictive traditions of the east is far from clear cut.

SANVIK VIRJI
Beyond the Punjab & into the Shallows

    I left Rurka ten days later than I had scheduled for two main reasons. The first reason was due to the hospitality of Manish's family, it was too irresistible to leave, and secondly, because it took me a lot longer to acclimatise to the Indian climate, its people and life style. It was now early June, and we were well into the Indian summer. Sweat was the order of the day. Rurka suffered from daily power cuts during which time temperatures outside soared to 40 degrees centigrade, and hovered at a moderate 36 degrees inside. I spent the stifling afternoons doing as little as possible. I read; I mused starring at the cement filled walls; I thought about everything that I had seen thus far; I reflected on my life, my journey. The last six years had been an incredible thrill. I had gone from a disgruntled, aggressive, under achieving adolescent to a confident, well travelled, well trained, academic success story. It was quite a transformation. Yet, I felt empty. Life was good. It had begun to treat me kindly. I was beginning to live up to my potential, and I knew that my potential ran deep. So then why did I feel empty? What was I missing? I pondered all afternoon on the 4th of June 2005, lying on a hardened mattress on top of a bed with creaky springs. As I heard the second hand tick from a nearby rusty clock, I realised that I was searching for something, but couldn't put a finger on it. I continued to dream with my eyes wide open. I was taken to another place, of another time. I peered through a rabbit hole to see that which lay ahead. It was this moment that spurred me to leave the relative comforts of Manish's family behind, and continue my journey, alone.

    I left Rurka, leaving Manish and Sangeeta behind with their loving family. In the few days that I had stayed, I had felt at ease with everyone in the house, and was readily accepted as one of the family. This feeling of instant warmth and hospitality, I was later to discover ran right the way through millions of families in rural India. There was something in the culture that made the people of this ancient land inviting, and trusting. The ideal of feeding the stranger before oneself was so alive and sacred, in a time when all ideals have been forsaken, and to speak of sacredness is to be blasphemous to the God we worship – money!

    I left Rurka and headed east towards Delhi. I had no particular intension of going to Delhi right away, but simultaneously I hadn't the foggiest about where I wanted to go either! I have mostly travelled unplanned. "Let the chips fall where they may, allow the wind to take you where it blows", and other such romantic phrases assisted in un-shaping my mind. After all, I was free, with no one behind me, no one in front, and nothing in particular to do or see. I arrived at the bus terminal early in the morning, just past eight. It was heaving full of morning commuters, farmers transporting their vegetables, mothers carrying babies looking to visit their relatives, school children in bright red uniforms rushing to catch the last bus before school, and random bystanders watching the morning unfold. Stray dogs paraded the terminal in gangs of two and three, patrolling invisible territories and barking at other rival dog gangs. Cows lethargically strolled into the main bus compound chewing on last nights graze. The main road where the buses waited had dust laden tracks on either side. Litter roamed the terminal, courted by a subtle breeze lifting bits of paper and crisp packets off the filthy stained floor and into the air.

I stood there in my trekking sandals, khaki combat shorts, white kurta top and a buck hat, with a small rucksack attached to my front, and my main wardrobe on my back! I certainly thought the bus terminal looked a mess, but equally I think the bus terminal reciprocated the same feeling back towards me. I glanced around to see if there was an information post, or a ticketing office mixed in with all the fast food vendors surrounding the terminal. I hadn't a clue as to which bus to catch. In fact I hadn't a clue as to where I was even going? I just knew that I wanted to make my way north into the mountains. I pulled out my rough guide and began to scan the state map of Punjab. Rurka wasn't even on the map. The nearest place was Jalandhar, a large military town about forty kilometres away. I asked a passer by in my weak Hindi which bus I had to catch, and as do all Indians when it comes to directions, he pointed somewhere vaguely with his eyes and mumbled something under his breadth.

"Shukriya", I said, meaning thanks in Hindi. He didn't acknowledge it, and strode off in the opposite direction. I stood there starring at him, watching him dodge people traffic and slowly merge into the whole. I had written the following piece about the mumbling stranger:

He came across my path,
At that place, at that time,
By coincidence or fate, by destiny or dumb luck,
Was there any other place or time where I could have met him?

I captured him in my life, if only for a flicker of light,
He will never again re-appear, nor will I remember him soon after,
Who is he, where is he, when is he?

Millions of strangers come and go,
Millions of flashing lights in another wise dark night,
Each stranger is a firework in the night of life,
They will flash with a radiant beauty, but for only a second,
Enjoy the bang, enjoy the flash,
For in a second it will be dark again.

      I jumped onto the only bus that had Jalandhar written across the front. I didn't have a ticket. The bus was already jam packed with no seats left, and people had already begun to queue down the bus securing their standing position. I too fixed my spot. It was just like travelling the underground in London, except the smells were different and amplified by the heat. The labour classes don't have 120 rupees to spend on deodorants, and hence, their toil was on display for all to smell. I didn't really mind it so much. In fact, I rather enjoyed the rank smell of human sweat, because here it didn't represent what it represents in England. Here it represented the working classes, labourers, young children, the elderly and the poor, all of whom worked hard. Human smell was as normal as being human. Rather refreshing really when we think about it. What could be more honest than the smell of your hard labour, or even your human condition? I took the backpack of my back and decided to lay it on the floor of the bus, and sat on it. I spent the next three hours sat on my rucksack, with my eye level no higher than the waistline of a rather overweight shop owner who stood in front, moaning to himself about the poor condition of the bus. He stood out on the bus because he was dressed in a clean sky blue shirt with sweat patches on his upper back, and armpits. He had a gold plated pen neatly clipped onto his breast pocket. We were the two recognisable anomalies on the bus. Whereas, he groaned and moaned throughout the journey standing, I sat there quietly equally sweating if not more.

      The three hours to Jalandhar flew by relatively quickly. The bus jolted to a halt. The only advantage of sitting where I was was that I could get off the bus right away. As I stammered out of the door the intensity of the sunlight quite literally hurt my eyes. The heat of the sun was unbearable and my sweat soaked white kurta was firmly stuck to my chest and back. I needed a cold soothing drink. I walked as quickly as I could to the nearest little restaurant I could find and parked myself underneath the fan. I ordered a cold Miranda and sat there for a full five minutes with my eyes closed attempting to cool down. My bags were blocking the gangway, which lead to the rest of the seating area, but no body cared, people were quite happy just to step over them. This would have never happened back home. I pulled out my map and spread it across the table. Now I knew where I was, and knew I had to make for the mountains, if for no other reason, than to simply escape the heat. As I scanned the map my eyes fell upon the name Dharmsala, a town in Himachal Pradesh. If you've never heard of Dharmsala before, then you probably also know little about the state of Tibetans living there, or their spiritual leader, the Dalai Lama. Tibet is a hot topic, and one that is close to my heart.

Tibet is a large country sandwiched between the ancient cultural giants of India & China. Even though the vicinity to the two awakening giants is too close for comfort, it has always been distanced, and for thousands of years been protected, by its mountainous terrain. Tibet is probably one of the few civilisations which can truly claim that technology has lead to its downfall. For thousands of years it was protected from invaders, looters, and self righteous, truth proclaiming religious fanatics. This has meant that Tibet and its people have quietly got on with the task of building a culture in relative isolation, in peaceful co-existence with one another. Indeed this is a romantic picture, and it is equally true that Tibet has had its fair share of bloodshed, but relatively speaking Tibetan culture has been far more peaceful than others, and I would go as far as to say that to some extent it has been a beacon for the rest of humanity when it comes to the matter of spirituality and peaceful living. Then in 1904 came the British from India, and as usual forced the Tibetan people to open its borders for trade at gun point. Eventually, after the fall of British rule in India, China invaded Tibet in 1951. The Communist government in Beijing dealt with the Tibetan Buddhist culture with an iron fist. The Chinese military destroyed well over one thousand eight hundred monasteries, executed thousands of monks, and arrested millions. China ever since the twelfth century has claimed sovereignty over the 'roof of the world'. I am no historian, nor do I know all the facts about the issue, but aggression is aggression and it stinks just as bad no matter how you mask it.

The Dalia Lama left Lhasa; the capital of Tibet soon after the Chinese atrocities began, and since has lived in Dharmsala, India with his exiled followers. My passion for the Tibetan people comes from the fact that they are victims, they have been made homeless, exiled from their own land, and they have been brutally forced to abandon thousands of year's worth of culture. China is no mug! It knew that Tibet has vast reserves of copper, and other precious minerals needed to re-build China as a global superpower. It has systematically encouraged Chinese settlers to migrate from China and into Tibet. Soon, it is feared that Tibet will become a majority Chinese population, and according to democratic principles, which China will eventually adopt, when it serves its own interest best, it will declare heroically that the people of Tibet have elected a Chinese representative, to which no doubt the west will applaud. I have always feared, and still do, that soon Tibet will be forgotten. Its people will find a new home in India, and they will become Indians. I applaud India, its government, and its people for embracing Tibetans by the droves, when India struggled to feed itself. At a time when we speak of human rights, equality, the rule of law, and spreading democracy, where we are willing to fight "just" wars in order to propel humanity into higher states of consciousness, in other words, humanity must be capitalist and democratic – where is Tibet on our radars? If we talk of fighting oppression and brutality, and if we in the West are the vanguard of the downtrodden, then why aren't our countries confronting China? Just as Saddam was an *evil* dictator, a brutal oppressor who wouldn't reason, so "we dealt with him"; well so why can't we deal with China?

The answer is simple and it reeks. China is a trading partner. It's an economic force, not forgetting a huge militarised nation. It scares us, and our greed suppresses our humanity to do that which is right. Our fear and greed is the reason why we cannot stick up for the little guy. I suspect it's always been like that, and I equally suspect it always will! I know I have just ranted for a page and a half about Tibet and an emotional rant is always incoherent and rather watery when it comes to hard facts and logical reasoning – yet underneath my rant, I believe there is a subtle fact, a fact about human nature, and if you are like me, you'll find it disturbing.

Once I was impregnated with the idea of going to Dharmsala, all I was bent on doing was turning it into a reality. The only things standing in between Dharmsala and I was the immeasurable heat, and the chaos at the bus station. I strolled out of the narrow restaurant with both my bags attached to my body, knocking every customer from where I sat to the door along the way. After a stream of apologies reeling off my tongue as if I was giving away sweets, one lone customer at the front of the restaurant said in perfect English "hey NRI, you don't need to keep apologising, you're in India, and we have the commonsense to see you can't help but brush us by. We accept it without any fuss."

The gangway was so tight that I couldn't even turn round to see the person who made the comment. So I walked on by. I couldn't help but say "sorry" to him as well.

I crossed the lawless main road, dust piggybacked on every air molecule, carbon from the kerosene guzzling cars, settled on my white kurta. A cocktail of dust, black carbon and sweat created an atmosphere that was rather overwhelming, to the point where all one wanted to do was check into a nice five star hotel, and laze in the clean cool pool for an hour or two. But having decided on Dharmsala, Dharmsala was where I wanted to be by nightfall, or at the very latest early next morning. Old rickety buses lined the terminal, one after another. I couldn't make out where the ticketing office was, or where any of the buses were heading. I asked several people if there were any buses headed for Dharmsala. Eventually I found a group of tired old, battered looking, Tibetan monks, all dressed in saffron robes sitting on a patch of ground that once upon a time must have resembled a tiled floor. Upon seeing them I felt my heart warm. I instantly felt an affinity towards them. I wanted to protect them; I wanted to give them every penny I could afford to give; I wanted to cover them in cotton wool and make sure that the poison of the world could never reach them. It was pure emotion. I gently asked the group of old men whether they were heading for Dharmsala, one of them nodded and the rest ignored me. So I took my pack off, and sat myself down next to them.

I arrived in Dharmsala after surviving a gruelling 15 hours journey on a bus that seated 35, but transported well over 50 people – transported being the operative word. We were cattle, nothing more for the bus driver and his trusty conductor. Their combined monthly salary is probably as much as my daily amount as a poor tight pursed student, and so whenever they can make an extra buck and a half by letting people on whenever they can, they do so. It's all illegal of course, but I guess as long as its not harming anyone what does it matter? Just at that moment, as I thought transiently, I heard a massive bang and the seated passengers behind me all wailed to the conductor. I hadn't a clue as to what all the commotion was about. Out here the locals spoke Pahadri, meaning mountainous, another language in the pantheon of Indian languages. The bus came to a rolling stop, and the conductor snapped at the passengers nearby, they in return snapped back with fingers being pointed in several different directions. No sooner had he strode off the bus, had he popped his round dark face with white glowing teeth back in to shout something at the cattle. Everyone simultaneously moaned, and began to dismount the bus. It was ironic how cattle like we really were. I eventually got off the bus to find that the rear tyre had blown. I suspected that our cattle herders had miscalculated how much extra weight the bus could handle, and had packed their bus with one too many animals.

For me this was a welcomed stop. Jalandhar was now six hours behind us, and Dharmsala was another six hours ahead. But it would be longer, no doubt, because our herders were not up to date on vehicle tyre repair, nor were they the types to have someone doing it for them if it cost them a single rupee. What's more was that they couldn't officially report this back to their masters because then they would be found out about their illegal herding business on the side. So while they toiled over what to do, I wandered off down the road. I was free, and I loved it. When we are free of expectations, we find ourselves being accepting of reality, we learn to make the best of out of every situation, and no situation is better or worse than another, it was merely a situation! We were now in shallows. This was Himachal Pradesh, and the flat green lands of Punjab were well and truly behind us. I was now in the high hills of India. The terrain was rocky; the dust was red, and people considerably poorer. As I stood at the front of the bus starring at what appeared to be a small village about five hundred metres up an inclined slope, a hand tapped me on my back.

"Come", he said, just as a dog owner would instruct his poodle. As he walked on by with another group of passengers up the inclined slope, I did what any obedient poodle would do – I followed. As we entered the hustle and bustle, I quickly realised that I was surrounded by market traders all selling identical things. The quiet hills were radically submerged by the loud colours and narrow lanes leading up to what was a temple complex. Every market stall had idols, garlands, incense, holy water and postcards of yet more idols. Traders tried to make eye contact, grab my hand to lead me to their stall, some even attempted to scare me into submission by telling me that I would incur bad luck if I went into the temple without an offering to Mata, meaning mother. The story went, as I was to find out later that an idol of Mata had suddenly appeared around the 1970's, carved out of the rock face of the mountain. Since then the small temple had become a cosmopolitan worshipping centre, where hundreds of thousands of people came to offer their prayers, and money.

The temple had since grown in size and wealth, but clearly not in infrastructure. People shoved and cajoled one another. Little old ladies elbowed their way past me, and little boys and girls ran stepping on my toes as they zoomed by. It felt as if I was entering a night club rather than a place of worship where apparently God had appeared. The atmosphere was far from divine and the people even less so. One thing did shine through, and it was abundantly clear – faith. People had travelled hundreds of miles for this, and it was their blind faith which was on display. Not necessarily a bad thing for the ignorant; blind faith is better for them than no faith. Ignorance and no faith leads to meaninglessness, and that is a one way trip to self destruction of self and spirit. As I got closer to the idol of Mata people became increasingly frenzied, and emotions ran high. The idol was protected by the in-house Poojari and a security official with a big stick made out of bamboo. His job was to look ferocious, wave his big stick around and make sure no one prays for too long. He would tap people on the shoulder with the stick if they held everyone up; followed by a snap of harsh words indicating it was time to move on. It felt as if we were all on a conveyor belt in a large worshipping factory, where at the end of the ride we had to pay ten rupees for the privilege of being pushed around. I admired Indian civilisation, and its philosophy hugely, but this was so far away from that image it was almost surreal. I felt annoyed.

As I left the temple complex without giving my designated ten rupees, a man gently grasped my arm from behind, and as he pulled himself closer to me, he looked flatly into my eyes and said, "nastic, don't worry, I put ten rupees in for you."

Before I could respond he and his buddies were off dashing through the crowd, elbowing old ladies out the way. The term *"nastic"* means atheist. This was one of those incidents that vividly show the submerged layers of stupidity and humanity, intertwined in a cocktail of blind faith and backwardness. Being an optimist, I like to look at the positive. Here was an absolute stranger, whom I will never meet, who felt that I would incur bad luck not having given ten rupees to the temple, and in turn he paid it for me! In which country would this kind of thing occur? What kind of deeply stupid, ignorant, but warm, kind loving humanity is this? That was his selfless deed for the day. He, in his heart felt that he had saved an ignorant foreigner from getting bad luck. Would I have done that for him? Would you have done that? Probably not!

As I walked through the main temple square and blackened archway there were a sharp set of stairs leading down to the main road from where I had entered the complex. The stairway was lined with little girls, all poorly dressed but clearly in their Sunday best. People upon leaving the temple complex walked over to these girls and prostrated to them, physically touching their feet. These girls with their big round white eyes would bless them by patting the victim on the head. He or she would then rise, and leave a few notes at the feet of the girls. Blessings from these destitute girls were retailing at twenty rupees a pat – not a bad business I thought. It was meagre sustenance for the poor of course. Within this wired portal in between the Himalayas and Punjab, there was a smallish oasis where the poor girls of India were quite literally seen to be divine. In any other place and time they would have at best been ignored, and at worst abused verbally, if not physically. On seeing this I felt an array of mixed emotions. I was angry and softened; I was immensely shocked at the ignorance of people, and yet saw the lively hood this very ignorance provided for the neediest. I felt drunk, I felt overwhelmed by the contradictions of the Indian mind. It was simply too much.

There was no consistency; as soon as one judged, that judgement would be contradicted. I guess it was like attempting to decipher a pattern out of an infinitely complex series of zeros and ones. It's all *gobbledegook* but somewhere in the mess, you know there is a pattern, a visible thread which binds it all together. I barged my way through the crowd and took a deep breadth as soon as I returned to the shallows. The air felt cool inside my lungs. I felt a release. I was out of the mad house, and back into the world which made sense – well kind off!

As I climbed back onto the bus I found that my seat had been taken. So I did what we Europeans are best at, I politely informed the old man that he was on my seat, which was clearly marked by my sweater, bag and water that he had rather unknowingly thrown out of the window. He ignored me completely. And so did everyone else. I removed my tourist like buck hat to reveal my face. I widened my eyes, and I have been told that I have huge balling ones. I have always used them to good effect to show when I may be about to strike. Was I going to hit the old rude impolite wrinkled man? Of course I wasn't, but I wanted to scare him; besides I could feel the angry adolescent Sanvik growing inside of me. He was arising out of his deep slumber, and I knew that if he were to come to the surface, there would be violence, and only one of us was going to get hurt. So I took a deep breadth, swallowed hard and began to insist that if he hasn't got a ticket, he ought to move. At first he said that he needed a seat, he was an old tired ill man. As a young man I should understand. I walked off the bus and asked the conductor to do something about my dilemma. He asked for a fifty. I gave it to him. He in turn took it to the old man, spoke to him harshly, threw the fifty at him, and magically he got up and vacated the seat. The conductor looked at me as if I was an insolent boy who had needlessly disturbed him. I didn't care. I had my seat back!

I spent the rest of the journey to Dharmsala in silence. I didn't read any of my books, I didn't write in my journal and I didn't acknowledge any other person on the bus. I was in myself. My mind was exhausted with the outside. I starred out of the cracked window looking at the view outside. The hills rolled by, gradually becoming steeper, trees became taller, and I began to see snow on the peaks afar. Cold air seeped through the window pane, and the fresh air softened my anger. I thought hard about my experiences, and my optimism, passion, and enthusiasm for the trip ahead wavered. I had travelled to South America, a continent far harder to backpack than India, at least so I had envisaged. My expectations of my own people, my own heritage, it occurred to me was far greater than what I was experiencing. I had envisaged India and Indians in particular to be humble, gentle, welcoming, polite and intelligently religious. I had indeed seen snippets of this in Punjab with Manish's family, and little incidents throughout the trip constantly reminded me of this, but by enlarge I had seen the complete opposite. Indians were egoistic, cruel, aggressive, disrespectful and ignorant. I felt bruised. I was finding it increasingly difficult to connect with what I had known of Hinduism, and Indian civilisation and its contribution to science, technology, philosophy and language.

Were these really the descendents of a civilisation that produced greats such as Aryabhatta the fifth century astrologer and mathematician who had already proven that the world was spherical and gravitated round the sun; Sankraacharya in the tenth century who developed a philosophy and an understanding of God that I believe still has to be matched; the Buddha who in the fifth century BC professed ahimsa and vegetarianism to humanity and an philosophy of non-attachment; the writers of the Upanishads where between the fifth century BC and eighth century AD developed human knowledge in every area conceivable? How could have such a great civilisation become so decadent, so bankrupt and lost?

As the roads meandered their way higher and higher into the shallows, we passed tiny towns and villages like Chintpurni and Dera Gopipur locked between great wide open valley's, rivers and lakes. The air here was thin, people had faces that were chiselled from the harshness of life, and yet radiated an aura that was gentle. People, as I was to later find out, in these areas were simple to the extent that most hadn't ever been more than twenty to thirty kilometres away from their homes. They had travelled as far as their legs had carried them. I would find and stay with people who had never sat on a motorised vehicle before; people who had never seen a city, or solid buildings. My trip was to become truly life changing, with my trip to Dharmsala being just a warm up.

The bus pulled into the lower end of Dharmsala. Upon leaving the bus, and collecting my mangled rucksack which had been thrown off the bus, I instantly realised that Dharmsala was not at all what I had imagined. I had, as is my usual flaw in life, romanticised it. Dharmsala in its lower side is like any other town in India, there wasn't a hint of spiritualism in the air. What was noticeable was the air itself. It was light, and clear. Hills surrounded us all around. I knew rather instantly that my trip had begun. All my euphemism was back. Flat land was a commodity here, everything was at an incline. The road ahead in to the town was steep. On my right there was a stairway spiralling its way up a ridge. I passed a taxi stand at the top of the stairs where all the drivers were ushering me to take a taxi up to the higher part of the town. Being a man of resolve, I proudly declined. I would make my own way up to the Tibetan quarters. I was directed by the information centre on the high street where I found all the usual amenities such as a bank, restaurants, hotels and bazaar.

town was deeply Buddhist and Tibetan culture had made its mark. I made my way up to the Dalai Lama's residence. The tourist inside me wished that I'd taken a taxi up here! My calves were aching and my chest and back were soaked through with sweat. His holinesses residence is on the south side of the town, it's rather humble, surrounded by government buildings; in front is Dharmsala's most famous temple Tsuglagkhang. It shelters three images. Each was in a posture of meditation. The first statue was *Shakyamuni* (another name for the Buddha), *Padmasambhava* (the saint who took Buddhism to Tibet) and *Avalokitesvara* (the ideal of compassion); all surrounded by offerings from worshippers. People were leaving anything and everything as offerings, from biscuits, fruit and vegetables, to clothes. As people came out of the temple, people tap the wheels behind the temple, setting them turning to scatter their prayers with the wind.

As I stood there absorbing all that was around me, I felt alive. All my pains and aches vanished. My anger had subsided, and I was filled with what I could only call *"hope"* in my diary. As I approached the temple, I saw monks, some of whom were settling down in the courtyard outside, who had travelled with me from Punjab. I walked over in their direction in the hope that they would recognise me and give me some guidance as to where I could spend the night. To my sheer delight as I walked into the courtyard, it wasn't the temple that captured my spirit; it was the activity that was happening right in front of me. Monks were seated, whom I later learnt were from the nearby Namgyal monastery, and debating fiercely. It was so apparent that they were discussing religion, philosophy and life. Most of it was in Tibetan of course, but I picked up the occasional name of a thinker which I latched onto. Each afternoon, monks would come and debate in the courtyard opposite the temple, amid shouts, claps and gestures that make up the traditional Indian art of discussion.

I was filled with an inner joy, and my face lit up like a lamp. I had read in Amartya Sen's book appropriately titled 'Argumentative Indian', that this sort of open debate was what distinguished eastern philosophy. I couldn't hide my happiness. I was in India, I was finally here! This was what I had searched for, and my trip to Dharmsala was worthwhile. Everything that I had wanted I got in those few seconds in the courtyard. I sat nearby the group of monks with whom I had travelled. A few faces turned to see the bearded foreigner approach, but most were too absorbed to notice me. I unloaded my rucksack and sat in that courtyard all afternoon. I could hardly understand a word that was being said, but it didn't matter. I was thoroughly absorbed with it all. I sat there concentrating on the body language of the main debaters, and even though it was all alien to me, I wanted to be apart of it. I was participating in a philosophical tradition that spanned across the history of humankind – the idea of scholarly, spiritual men coming together to discuss the truly meaningful things in life – those aspects that are the true mysteries of our existence. On this day I was apart of that history, I could feel its weight on me, and I loved it. I was a part of something great, something living, and something so honest and revealing. I may not have understood much, but I was learning. I was learning from the aura of the place, and its people. I was learning from the feelings it created. I learnt by *being*, not doing. It was here in the hot month of June, in 2005 that I learnt what it meant to grasp something by being. I was one with the debate, and that's all that mattered.

Soon it was dark, and our debate was ended with the abbot of the temple reciting a prayer, and to bless the participants with honesty and wisdom. I still hadn't found a place to stay the night, and dusk was already upon us. I looked around to see if any of the faces in the courtyard were open enough for me to ask them for assistance. At a quick glance I saw an elderly monk rolling his mat, ready to depart back to his resting monastery. I walked over and asked in Hindi whether he knew of a nice peaceful place where I could spend the night. Before I had even finished my sentence he walked right by me as if I was a ghost. After such an enlightening afternoon I felt a subtle disappointment at the reaction of the monk, which in all honesty lasted a split second. I shrugged it off, and made my way out of the courtyard, and back towards the main bazaar. I walked into several guesthouses, all of them tacky, which I didn't mind, but the atmosphere was wrong, and I felt a discomfort in them. It was a commercial outlet, it didn't have even an ounce of spiritualism, and I was not willing to compromise on the mood of the place. The afternoon had been too perfect for me to stay in such dry lacklustre place. Time waits for no man, and soon it was nine, pitch black, and I was still without a bed. I sat on the pavement and noted in my journal, *"If I was ever to be homeless in life, then I would ask for no better place to be homeless in."* I wondered off the beaten road, and headed for the woodland just past the temple courtyard, and thought I'd make camp there. All I needed was a fire and sleeping bag. As I crossed the courtyard a gentle hand tapped me on the shoulder. It was the old monk who had ignored me.

He bowed, and so I reciprocated the action. With a tinge of a smile appearing on his old wrinkled Tibetan face, he ushered me to follow him. He led the way to Namgyal monastery. As we approached the entrance he removed his worn slippers and walked inside. I copied.

As I entered the stone walled austere monastery I was welcomed by another monk, "Namaste, stay with us tonight please, you are most welcome."

"Thank you", I replied, and bowed to him lowering my eyes.

"My brother didn't mean to ignore you earlier, he has taken a vow of silence until Tibet is freed, and he hasn't spoken in over twenty five years", he continued.

I turned to face my guide once again, with added respect. I was taken through a maze of corridors that were poorly lit by candles. I later learnt that electricity was in such short supply here that it made Rurka look sophisticated. We entered a hall where I found lightly padded mattresses laid out on the floor. A few monks were already fast a sleep. Others sat cross legged praying, swaying too and fro as they recited old prayers. I was taken to an empty mattress which was to become my bed for the next two nights. I rested my bags next to me, took my sweater off to use as a pillow, and immediately lay down. It had been a long day, but what a day! I had travelled for an entire day and a half without proper rest. I had travelled well over two hundred kilometres, leaving the flat lands of Punjab and into the shallows of the Himalayas. No sooner had I lay down to rest, and smiled to myself, feeling contentment of a sort that we experience only a handful of times in our lives, I dozed off into the abode of sleep and peaceful dreams.

A gentle hand awoke me early next morning. My eyes opened to a beam of light flooding through the large bay windows directly opposite. The face was gentle, it was young, and resembled the calmness of a typical monk. But there was something in his young eyes; he had a spark, a fire, a passion of some sort. For the rest of the day he was my guide. I did everything he did; I ate what he ate, and I recited what he read. I fused myself into their world. I did everything I could to lose myself from my past and my world in England. I became Goba's disciple. Goba meant eagle in Tibetan, I don't think he could have had a more fitting name. His eyes said it all. He spoke perfect English with a tinge of the sharp Indian accent we know, and one that I have come to love.

"Tashi Delek bhaiya", he said as he bowed with both hands clasped, in the same way in which all Indians greet. I too acknowledged his greeting, reciprocally.

He told me to wear things that were loose but covered my entire body, and to remove my watch. *"Time has no place here"* were his exact words to me. He also told me to wear slippers. I already knew why. Just as in Hinduism, and generally within the Indian culture one must remove shoes when walking into certain rooms. There were no women in the monastery, and monks were only allowed to leave in pairs to buy any rations they may need. Goba took me through several corridors and through a large door which lead to the vegetable garden. Here the monks grew their own food. They maintained a low fat vegetarian diet, mainly composed of whole grains, proteins, and seasonal organic fruits and vegetables, a lot of which we grow in the organic gardens. They made granola and soy milk, and baked fresh bread daily, along with simple desserts. The garden radiated an aura of freshness. The wind carried with it the smell of all the plants, herbs, and fruits that were grown there. I worked with Goba and helped him water and then clean the garden. It was a beautiful morning surrounded by the haze of mountains and the air of spirituality that encompassed the monastery. We worked mostly in silence. I liked it. Goba carried a subtle Buddha-like smile on him at all times, and being around him made me smile too. I had no idea how long we had been in the garden before Goba signalled the end of our work, and took me around the monastery where monks washed themselves before going to morning prayers. We each had a small bucket filled to the top with lukewarm water. I followed Goba. I have always found it fascinating how child like we become when we are surrounded in an atmosphere that is completely alien. I behaved as if I'd never washed. To some extent it was true. I had never washed in India with a bucket of lukewarm water and a small used soap in the great outdoors surrounded by monks. I did exactly as I saw. The lukewarm water was soon cold, but it did the trick – I felt great, all my senses were hypersensitive, and my mind felt sharp. Cold water has a certain potency to wake the senses, something that I have never been able to take advantage off on a daily basis. A cold shower in England takes willpower that I simply do not have presently. But one day!

      Namgyal is more of an academic institution than a monastery. Goba showed me around. There were two hundred monks resident there, most of whom were training in Buddhist philosophy, debating, memorising rituals and prayers, and building the mind so as to reach the ideal state of detachment from worldly pleasures. Most monks also took a course in English and Hindi. Goba was a third year student. He had another ten left before he could be considered a Rabjampa, or *master*. He spoke little, and for the first time in my life I too had little to ask. Throughout the day monks were active. They were either in classes, or working in the garden, washing, cooking, playing musical instruments, or in the courtyard debating. Soon it was breakfast; we sat on the cold stone floor, ate a small portion of fruit and left. No sooner had we gotten up did two younger monks, mere boys, quickly hobbled over and took our plates away. I spent the rest of the morning attempting to recite Buddhist rituals. There are quite literally thousands of rituals and Goba had committed a lifetime to memorise them all. Some rituals were dedicated to bring rain, a good harvest, free Tibet from China, bring peace, but mostly all the rituals were centred on deflating ones own ego, and reconnecting with humanity.

The atmosphere was surreal. A cocktail of incense, candlelight and synchronised chanting created a rabbit hole through which we all took a journey. I was the last to close my eyes and fall under a spell caused by the chanting. I went to another place. I felt my body grow light. I was floating on water, with waves gently cradling me too and fro. My mind grew still, and soon even the chanting faded into the background. My mind grew silent, and the stillness released an energy I'd never felt before. The tips of my palms tingled with a type of *pins & needles*, and I felt connected to something bigger and yet within. Coolness flowed down my spine releasing my lungs to breathe air of a type that I'd never experienced. The rest I cannot even begin to explain, but I travelled an immense distance across intellectual space. At some stage the chanting must have stopped but I hadn't realised. It was silent.

As my eyes opened, I felt stillness in my heart. Goba was smiling ever so slightly, while starring at me. I didn't speak. I had extended beyond myself, my spirit had travelled and I came back to my wake state with more of *it*. I do not know how to begin describing this *it*. All that I can say is that words are our prisons. Any attempt here to describe it would only be equivalent to a blind mans attempt to describe colour. It simply cannot be spoken off, but only experienced. The intellectual space I had travelled was vast. I awoke with a new sensation deep within. I had found a signpost in my journey. I awoke with a sensation that I recorded in my journal as "serene".

I was happy.

I spent another day and half with Goba and the other monks. I debated, I listened, I explained, and I meditated. I travelled lands far over the mountains of my mind and beyond. I travelled to distant lands in my mind; places that I didn't know existed. I understood me better! I understood my life better, and with it – I understood my destiny better. But mostly, I sat in silence. And just as suddenly as I had arrived, I knew it was time to leave. It was now mid-June, and I'd been at the monastery for two days. It had felt longer. I had spent a significant part of life there, but not if you understand life by time!

Goba took me to a procession where hundreds of Tibetans were lined up waiting for the Dalia Lama to arrive and bless them. Goba took me to the front of the line, always looking away from the great Lama's eyes, and spoke something in Tibetan. The Dali Lama blessed him, and he walked off back to the monastery. I never saw Goba again, nor do I think I ever will. We had shared our spirits, and it'd been long enough for him to have taught me a depth to life that had always eluded me.

"Did you enjoy your stay", he asked. It took me a while to answer.

"Yes", I replied. He then tapped me on my head, and said "God bless you, and may you find light in your life."

I looked up and saw directly into his eyes. He smiled. I felt radiance and a humility that I had never felt. I looked back down as an acceptance of his authority, of course I didn't say anything, but he knew it.

"Have a safe journey", he concluded.

And just like that the Dalai Lama moved onto the next person in line. I stood still starring at the soft ground for quite a while not quite sure what to make of it. Just as everything else in Dharmsala, it had felt surreal. Eventually someone knocked into me and I awoke from my trance. I picked up my rucksacks and headed back down the hill and into the main bazaar. There I bought a few essentials for the trip ahead, and took my last look at the monastery and the Tibetan Buddhism that I had come to love. I walked back down to the bus stand. I felt like crying, but I didn't. I felt like a child that was leaving home, never to return again. The loneliness crept into my being. I sat on the edge of the road and took my map out. Where to next?

My eyes landed on Shimla, and then on Rishikesh far to the east. Even though the bus stand was noisy, dusty and dirty, I felt still. The world around me seemed to move at a thousand miles per hour, but I was still. Nothing mattered. I looked around and saw human beings; I saw stray dogs; and I saw birds in trees, but not as I'd ever seen them. It's difficult to explain. The experience of the Dharmsala bus stand on leaving was totally different to my arrival. Yet, it was the same place. I had changed, not it! There was only one major route leaving Dharmsala heading towards the east. Rather than waiting for the bus, I decided to walk. I said my final goodbyes, and headed off. It was roughly a seven hour bus ride, if not more from Dharmsala to Shimla. I had no intention of walking the whole distance, but at least a part of it – albeit a small part.

I arrived a few hours later to a tiny settlement called Tang Narwana, a place I found to be full of back packers and trekkers. It was the starting point of the Guntu Got trek high into the mountains. It was a four day trek. I had no intension of being diverted. My own trek was approximately ten kilometres. I passed beautiful lush slopes, full of evergreen trees, clinging onto the edge of steep sides. I passed locals carrying firewood on their back. I passed through a valley of majestic beauty, and the scenery was simply orgasmic. The air was fragranced by the mountain tops, and every breadth cooled my inside. My mind was still, nothing mattered; Me, Myself and I – no one else. Only I existed. Everything else seemed like a gentle dream.

Dreams have a quality. They are real, and yet exist in the realm of the unreal. In dreams I feel, but I can never quite seem to touch. In dreams everything is based on the real world, and yet they are a fantasy. Anything is possible. Our imagination and *our will* seem like our only barriers to the impossible. My trek from Dharmsala to Tang Narwana was done in a state of mind where anything seemed possible. I felt as if I was watching myself. Before I'd even entered Tang Narwana I had left it. The road ahead meandered downwards. A few hundred yards directly below me the road turned on itself. The road quickly narrowed, and there was barely enough width for a single bus to pass. Then there was me, not the biggest creature in the world, but I knew that if a bus came, I'd be a sure road kill. The road swerved to the right and I knew that I was in a blind spot for any oncoming traffic, but I knew that most drivers horned as they came steaming round bends.

My assumption was flawed. I didn't include European tourists who hired cars and never horned as they came round bends. Everything happened in a flash. One minute I was minding my own, walking in the land of nod, and the next I was flung off the road, smacked against a tree trunk, hit the ground and rolled twenty odd metres down a steep decline. I wasn't hurt, but only shocked. It took me a few minutes to realise what had happened, it felt as if I'd been in a boxing ring and had been out boxed by a tougher man. I was dazed, and it had happened too quickly. As I got to my feet I realised that apart from a few cuts and a grazed knee, I was unhurt. I climbed up the slope to find a bearded man and a woman in her sixties looking down the valley. The wife, at least I assume it was the wife, turned and saw me shake off the dust and leaves that covered my pristine white sweat soaked clothing.

"Oh, my goodness", she yelled, letting loose a healthy dose of relief from the fact that her husband hadn't killed a poor coloured soul. "Are you ok?" she asked.

"Yeah sure, I'm fine, lucky escape I guess", I reassured.

The nice German couple ended up giving me a forty minute car ride to the next town from where I could catch a bus to Shimla. They had hired a car from Delhi and were on a road trip to Jaipur, in Rajasthan, a few thousand kilometres to the West and into the desert state. I guess a forty minute detour to help a young man who they could have so easily killed was no big deal in the context of their entire trip.

They were kind, generous and found them to be rather deep. He had a background in teaching psychology at the University of Bonn for thirty years, and she had been a clinical psychiatrist for the best part of her life. Both came from a generation when Freud was still venerated and respected. They deplored the modern state of psychology. I found their views on the subject matter striking and perceptive. They both argued that modern psychology in theory and practice had been built around a gross underestimation that the human psyche was purely built by chemistry. They spoke mostly, while I listened. Their talk was passionate, and it was obvious that they spoke from a level of expertise and experience. They also made points, which I have only later come to appreciate; the fact that modern science is geared towards only that which can be measured, is one such point. The Freudian model is inherently immeasurable and therefore modern psychology dismisses it, to its own detriment. If Psychology wants to be classed as a science, then that's fair enough, however, our society needs to acknowledge that science is inherently limited and we mustn't use science as the ultimate arbitrator when it comes to things which it cannot measure. *Not all truth can be measured.*

It was after I'd left the intellectually stimulating company of my German friends that I realised what they meant. After all there were three clear areas where science had no grounding at all; firstly in all areas of values, science becomes rather toothless. How can science ever explain the phenomenon of one rose looking prettier than another? Secondly, when it came to morality; the problems of judging right and wrong, good and bad, just or unjust are all spheres of thought where tangible science is lacking in answers. Finally, science is way out of its depth when it comes to the metaphysical – on questions of God, consciousness, the soul, etc.

Science then clearly has it place, in the realm of measurement and not an *inch* further. It's arrogant and foolishly naive, I believe, for scientists to dismiss areas of knowledge beyond the field of measurement. In particular, I'm thinking of areas in alternative medicine, where often academics and medical practitioners "pooh-pooh" the idea of Ayurveda, Homeopathy and other such ancient approaches to health. Why?

Well, after asking several doctor friends of mine, and keeping in mind that Asheeta is now a medic too, it seems that they have all been trained to measure, and anything that cannot be done so just isn't worth relying on. On the other side, is my dad's eldest brother, Arvind uncle, who I've always called "Bhai", meaning brother in Gujarati, is a Homeopathic practitioner. His take on the matter is altogether different. He believes, as do other Homeopaths that an ill person can be treated using a substance that can produce, in a healthy person, symptoms similar to those of the illness. He believes that serial dilution removes the toxic effects of the remedy while the qualities of the substance are retained by the dilute. Often he has diluted the remedy to such a level where only sugary water remains, yet I have seen, and experienced first hand how this sugary water effectively cures illness. When I ask him how this occurs he simply answers by conceding humbly "I don't know. It just works. I can't seem to quantify it."

My point in all this is simple, and I have to thank the German couple for leading me to it – that there are real things out there that cannot be measured, but yet understood and mastered to improve all our existence, and for anyone to play down ideas that are intangible as being mystical at best, or down right "mumbo-jumbo" at worst is plain arrogant and shallow. That's not to say that every idea that is immeasurable is worth considering, far from it in fact, ideas such as teaching school children that the theory of evolution is wrong, and that some creator super being called God created everything in seven days, deserves to be shot down and mocked.

I was grateful to be dropped off in a pilgrim centre called Mandi. I said my goodbyes to the kind German couple, whose names I regretfully cannot remember. Mandi was a small town trapped between the mountains and river. It was a pilgrim centre, full of temples, ashrams and tourists looking to escape the Indian heat. I didn't particularly connect with the place, and caught the next possible bus to Shimla. From Mandi I passed hundreds of villages built out of mud and cow dung, banked on the side of slopes. Worn faces stared into the bus, we met eyes for a moment in eternity, and I could feel their aura in the moment of oneness with the stranger. The faces of men were happy, but worn, with eyes full of enchantment, and desire. The women were fair skinned with beautiful round eyes, smooth faces and covered in colourful ornaments. Their eyes were deep, and strong. As my eyes met theirs I felt connected, a sense of responsibility overwhelmed my journey to Shimla. The roads meandered up and over the mountains. The air was cool, and the sun glared through the window gently tanning my skin on one arm. I passed small semi urban settlements such as Sundarnagar, which means beautiful city in Hindi. Indeed the surroundings were beautiful, but the city itself – well lets just say I didn't even get off the bus! Sundarnagar bus station was covered in a stink, with open sewers on either side, complimented by rubbish heaps left behind by passing traffic. The Indian habit of littering was all too apparent here. I was grateful to have left it behind. After another two hours, I arrived in Shimla – the famous retreat for British aristocracy in the hot summer months during the infamous Raj. Shimla was full of memories, especially of its colonial past. The town was sprawling with tourists and its enchanted streets and alleyways were now truly a museum piece. I left Shimla behind no sooner had I arrived. I crossed state boundaries entering Uttranchal, passing Mussoorie, Dehra Dun, and arriving after a twenty hour journey to Rishikesh, meaning the *place of sages*.

With Love, from a Cave

It was here and now that the bulk of my spiritual development took place. I was to embark on a journey of a lifetime, where I would stay in Ashrams, meditating, taking an early morning dip in the holy Ganges. I would wonder the surrounding hills for hours, alone, reading timeless classics such as Kant, Schopenhauer and the Upanishads. I would spend three nights with a Naga Sadhu; a man who has renounced the world, who wore no clothes, and lived in a cave, 2800 metres above sea level. Here we would discuss philosophy, ethics, politics, the future of mankind, and above all he would give me a signpost to the rest of my life, and my destiny. He would set me nightly riddles keeping me up all night in deep concentration. I would see ice caps from which the Holy Ganges takes form, I would see thousand year old temples, and countless Sadhu's living in quite isolation from the world, deep in Yoga and meditation. I would stay with a princely family who barely had enough money to feed their children. I would become enchanted by the valley of flowers near Kedarnath. I was to set upon a journey that millions of Hindus wish to take once in a lifetime. It was to be a journey across four holy peaks, which have been spoken off throughout Indian history; a place where the teenage Jesus is rumoured to have visited and explored; a place where the Buddha is to have found enlightenment; and where Lord Swaminarayan is to have walked at the age of twelve.

Rishikesh was no longer a small hermitage where people found isolation. Rather it was a bustling town full of temples, ashrams and tourist lodges. I had been told to stay at Parmarth Niketan – an ashram founded by what I can only call a semi renounced holy man – Sri Muniji. Rishikesh was a town split in two. On one bank was the actual town with its vast residential areas, chemical factories, and endless number of restaurants. And on the other side was a strip of ashrams, bookshops, and cyber cafes wedged between the Ganges and the mountains. I stayed in the *"spiritual"* quarter. Parmarth Niketan was not what I had expected. I'd always regarded ashrams as being austere and somewhat simple. Instead Parmarth Niketan was equal to an immaculate five star hotel. It had over 300 bedrooms for guests, a luscious green courtyard, two temples, and a Bunyan tree that must have been hundreds of years old. The atmosphere was sober compared to the noisy cramped street outside, the ashram offered allsorts of therapies, meditational classes and an array of other spiritual services. I didn't take any of them up.

I stayed at the luxurious ashram for a night only, merely to recuperate. The next morning I took an early morning dip in the holy Ganges. The water was ice cold but refreshing. Even at five in the morning as the sun rose in the east, people were quietly doing their prayers, deep in self contemplation. My dip in the Ganges lasted a whole thirty seconds, to be frank, even that's an exaggeration. I staggered up the steps on the bank of the river, only to find myself completely, and fully awake. All my senses were alive. My mind became hyper vivid. Things appeared sharper. I was more sensitive to the environment. The early morning rays from the sun suddenly felt warmer, my sight became sharper, but above all else, my mind was still. These things I write are immeasurable, and the sensations and feelings I wish to communicate are beyond the realms of language, at least mine. But nevertheless, I have made an attempt of some sorts.

I gathered my rucksacks and left the ashram, not knowing that I'd return a changed man. A porter who worked at the ashram escorted me to the bus stand from where he found a rickety battered stinking bus that would take me to a tiny settlement 2800 metres above us; a settlement that only existed for six months of the year; a settlement that was built around a pilgrimage site, which millions of Hindus visited at least once in a life time. The site was an old temple built next to the source of the Ganges. The bus ride to Gangotri was a rugged affair. I'm not the tallest guy in the world, and even I struggled to get my legs in between the rows of densely packed seats. The bus was grossly over loaded with "human cattle". By now I was familiar with all the smells that come with such an experience and I was no longer phased by it. The journey was vigorous, which was meant to last twelve hours, for me however, it ended in ten. Upon seeing the peaks above and catching infrequent scents of the fresh air that one can only be found in mountains, I decided to get off the bus and walk rest of the way. It was rather spontaneous, but then I have always let the force guide me.

By the time I reached Gangotri it was dark. Small roads were lined with make shift restaurants, which created an atmosphere of expectation and enchantment. All around us were shadows. The mighty Himalayas dwarfed us. The array of lights created a reservoir of comfort in an otherwise starless night. My immediate concern was accommodation. I had no where to stay. It was cold, and I knew the night wasn't going to tolerate me sleeping outdoors. I drifted past shops, focusing on rows of shacks, for anything that resembled a hostel or even an ashram. As luck would have it, I found a Gujarat Ashram on the opposite side to the bus stand, slightly elevated by an inclining slope, overlooking the rest of the settlement. By the time I'd found the Gujarat ashram, I had already been refused by three hostels. Apparently they were fully booked. But I had a suspicion that my overgrown dark beard and shabby hair didn't do me any favours. The Brahmin at the ashram didn't look to me kindly. He was suspicious as to my true identity. He asked me several questions as to who I was, where I'd come from, why was I alone, and I had to prove to him that I was Gujarati – well at least a part of me was. Eventually he let me stay the night. I slept with my jacket and combats on. It was a cold night, and heaters are an invention yet to reach these peaks. I left Gangotri early next morning. The sun was rising and I headed upwards to the real source of the Ganges, to the ice cap known as Gaumukh. I intended to trek to the icecaps, and then to its eventual peak called Tapovan, a mere 4463 metres in height. From here I would make my way to Kedarnath, the next peak on my list.

When I came across the mountains I became enchanted, spellbound by their rugged beauty. Walking through the mountains was my prayer, my meditation, and my solitude. It was in the depth of solitude that I fell once again through the rabbit hole, and I began to travel across mental space that I'd always known off, but never quite realised.

God is nature, and nature, is my God. I realised that in the reverence of the natural beauty that lay before me, I was experiencing Gaia, our mother Earth. Whatever name we chose to give her, she is the Earth and all that pervades it. My reverence for Earth had started a long time ago, when I was a mere boy running up and down Bradgate Park; a natural woodland reserve on the outskirts of Leicester. The mountains of India became in that instant my wild paradise. I saw them in ways that I knew most never could. I was a child of the urban streets, and the grey jungle. And after the death of Vikas, I had asked many questions about life and death. I had spent many years wandering the moors of morality. As I walked into the holy mountains of Gangotri, I felt for the first time in my life that death was no bad thing. It was nothing to fear.

Bird songs echoed across the valley. I stopped to rest a while. I listened to all the birds sing. It was here where I realised my violence, and the violence of humankind. I came to understand the Buddhist and Jain claim of Pacifism. I had read many volumes on the subject, had put it up against intellectual vigour, and I always found Pacifism to be a flawed idea. The idea of non-violence at all costs was simply unrealistic in the world of human beings. At least I had thought so until that moment. As birds soared high above, the wind hissed in my ear, and as I felt the weight of the mountains, I knew what violence was; it was wrong and unjustifiable. I also realised its anti-thesis – Pacifism. Sitting there on the slope high above Gangotri, violence was wrong, in all its forms. Violence towards others, violence towards oneself, and violence towards nature could never be justified, not for power, not in the name of God, nor for the economy. On the intellectual sphere where words are king – Pacifism was admirable but ultimately limited. But in reality, the world beyond the here and now, beyond words, I knew that violence had no place in my mind. What's more, I came to realise that there could never be peace until we learnt to make peace with Mother Earth – with Gaia. As I lifted my backpack, taking in a deep breadth, I concluded to myself that I would spend the rest of my life serving Gaia – the mother of Humankind. As I write these words almost three years later, I feel content that I have kept my word.

As the hours slipped away I inched closer towards Kedarnath. I was walking on the roof of the world, where the air is light, and the land becomes barren and cold. The evergreens were no more. In their stead lay huge boulders across the valley intimidating the landscape. Compared to some boulders I was only a tiny amoeba. But it wasn't the land that made me feel small. It was something in the June sky. What initially appeared like a dark aurora coming and going, swaying in the twilight, what appeared as a giant organism floating high above, I realised was birds – millions of them. They darkened the sky, if only for a moment. Small is not only beautiful, but I realised then in its full glory, it can be powerful. I was indeed small, but not in its negative form. It was humbling to know as much. The birds lifted my spirits and warmed my heart with every pass they made over me. The collective noise of their wings was rhythmic and possessed hypnotic qualities.

I had come to the mountains to breadth its air, which cooled my soul, for the aroma of evergreen trees, and the holy water of the Ganges. I had come for peace. As I walked in the direction of forever, I came to understand that these mountains, for millennia knew only but peace. Antiquity was better connected to peace than modern man. Antiquity understood it better. I realised that for the Sanayasi peace was a way of life. They were one with Gaia, and respected her moods. They were wise, and I knew why the wise men from all over the world for centuries had travelled these very mountains. Folklore in these parts spoke of nature's spirit as overlooking these mountains and protected them. I could see how these stories must have come about, for indeed in these mountains of old, one could feel a spirit. The mountains which dwarfed my soul were like great poets, and their majestic beauty was their poetry. One has to travel these mountains to know from the depths of ones soul that we do not need to look elsewhere for peace and paradise, it is right here on Earth, if only we could lose our politics and economics for a moment. It was our pursuits solely for power and wealth, which inherently limited any chance of peace in our lives. In these mountains there was no power, nor was their any need for money – and here there was peace. Life became vibrant and resilient. For the Sanayasi, the mountains were their temples and the cathedrals of nature. These mountains were millions of years old, pieced together by geological time. As I trod amongst them, I did so lightly, for I knew they had stories of their own to tell, but I knew they'd never tell.

With every sun rise and sunset my only companions were the mountains and the great river Ganges hurtling towards the sea. The noise of rushing water became my constant companion. Her waters reminded me of my brother. In 1996, my mother & father had travelled to India to scatter Vikas's ashes into the Ganges. My broken parents never came this far up into the mountains, but nevertheless, the river below had at some stage carried whatever remained of my brother. It evoked great sorrow, and imagination. I dreamt up happy times we'd shared, and I imagined a future where the abyss hadn't taken him, a future where my mother and father had their oldest child. As I walked, time stood still. The thoughts of a future which could have been captured my soul. What would have life been like, had Vikas lived? Where would he have taken all our destinies? The thoughts hurt my heart, and yet it was a pain I wanted.

The Ganges below gave wise council to what was then a lost mind. It called me over to drink its icy cold water. I left my bags up on the slope and headed towards the river bank. It was a steep climb down. The water was crystal clear and terribly cold. As I drank it, I felt it run down my body until it fell into my mid-section. It made me happy and I said a prayer to the river.

"*Please wash away all my sorrow, anger and attachments.*"

If the Ganges is holy and worth preserving, then every river on this planet is the same! Water is the matrix of life. Without it there is no life. There is no civilisation with all its overhyped, shallow notions of politics, economics, and justice. Water, which we sacrifice for instant wealth is what gives us life, and so why was it that we traded it so cheaply? Seeing the mountains rise way above me, I realised that this water nourishes all life, animal, insect, plant, bird and human. All were doomed without it. I could deeply appreciate why it was that ancient human civilisations worshipped water and the rain. Yet, with all our clever understanding of nature through science, which should make us value water even more than our forefathers did, in fact has made us devalue the Holy Grail itself. How is it that more knowledge has lead to this? Isn't knowledge meant to enlighten us? Then why has humanity with all its knowledge turned water into a commodity that is to be traded in the same way as we might trade cars? As the clouds below began to merge, I thought of them as wondrous. I revered the clouds at that moment as I used too, when I was a child. Water is precious, the way we use it, is a measure of us. In those few moments I realised that it was an ecological imperative of our times that we as a human race re-connect with water. We abuse water only at our own peril. As my consciousness absorbed these realisations I began to feel a pathway opening; a pathway to the rest of my life. I gazed long and hard into the sky, and began to make my way to the bags. I gathered my things and continued up the path to Gaumukh.

As I got closer to the Ganges the pathway became an obstacle course. Mammoth boulders lay before the ice caps, which were now in sight and the route to the pinnacle – at Tapovan. The next two hundred feet took best part of the day to cross. As I conquered the last few boulders I saw the magnitude of what lay before me, and what I had already been through. I was familiar with mountains, and I knew what to expect at the peak – but nothing could have prepared me for what I saw. As I arrived at the summit of Tapovan, ones eyes become overwhelmed with Mount Shivling & his partner Mount Meru. Both were closer to 7000 metres in height. They dwarfed Tapovan at a mere 4400 metres. The sight is truly a wonder, and a sudden swell around my tear ducts built up releasing a gentle stream of warm water flowing down my cheeks. The sight was Godly. I stood their, for what seemed like an eternity. My tears warmed the peripherals of my face. As I looked onwards the barren rugged beauty of the trek miraculously became green. A lush meadow surrounded what appeared to be the base of Mount Shivling and the amphitheatre of 7000 metre peaks. As I made my way towards the green meadow, I realised that it was from here that professional climbing expeditions begin their journey to peak at Shivling, otherwise known as the *Matterhorn of the Himalayas*. I found basic tent accommodation up there, where I had just missed a group of Swiss climbers making their way to the top. The Sherpa's were kind enough to let me stay and eat for free. I spent dusk starring at my own theatre of dreams sitting underneath a tree. I felt a sense of healing taking place deep within. Gaia had been a gracious host, but had I been a gracious guest? I extended the thought to encompass all humanity. The answer sprang forth with a gentle but clear "no". Neither I, nor humanity was gracious towards Gaia.

The next morning I was told by one of the Sherpa that the only way to Kedarnath was heading back to where I'd come from, heading towards Gangotri, right the way back until I came to a small junction called Malla, from where I could begin my trek up to Kedarnath. The only other way was to climb Mount Meru, which if I were to be honest was as appealing, as jumping in a pool of sharks right after I'd cut myself.

I headed back. Hours passed, and the trek became an endless tiresome passage back to civilisation. The sun had almost set, and I began to see Gangotri into the distance. I had walked relentlessly for over fourteen hours. My feet felt heavy, while the rest of my body had been numbed.

I had seen several renounced men along my trek but all were either in meditation, doing yoga, or looked far too out of this world to approach. Some looked out right frightening. As I sat there recuperating I saw a figure not too far behind. It was a tall thin man, with a walking stick in one hand and a saffron robe on the other. As he approached I realised he was a Naga Sadhu – literally translated means *naked good man*. He was covered in ash and had long dreaded hair that came to his ankles. His beard came down to his chest and his body was lean but muscular. His skin was darkened and worn. His walk oozed confidence and his eyes beamed radiance as he directed his stare directly at me. His stare frightened me in a way I'd never been before. There was something in his presence that told me he held a strength that I couldn't even imagine. In hindsight, I can't understand why I felt as frightened. I was no mug! Furthermore, I'd been in many a sticky situation and had managed to fight my way through it. But this was different. Here, I was at the mercy of the old man approaching. What's more is that I think he knew what I was thinking; he sensed my anxiety.

"Aap ko meri saath bhait karni hai", he asked, now only a few feet away.

I was speechless, and must have looked gormless too. He spoke in Hindi, asking whether I wanted to speak to him. Indeed I had. Before I could get my mental bearings he invited me to spend the following evening with him. He pointed towards a cave a few hundred feet above the path we were on. He increased the intensity with which he starred into my eyes, and said "come only if you want to", in Hindi of course.

And just like that, he walked off in the opposite direction. I watched him climb up the slope in the direction he had pointed. It seemed like an easy enough climb. It was getting dark, and I was still five kilometres away from the ashram. I timed how long it would take me from this very spot to get back, so that the following evening I could retrace my steps. I also left a five pence coin near a boulder, ensuring that it wouldn't be noticed by any random stranger. By the time I arrived at the ashram it was pitch black. Furthermore, I was exhausted. I threw my rucksack off, quickly jotted the following line in my journal – *'unbelievable day'*.

I collapsed on my hardened bed and fell into a deep pleasant dream.

I awoke to find a beautiful fresh morning sun beaming its radiance upon my tired face. I felt as if my feet had been amputated. My heels were badly cut, and the front of my toe was badly blistered. I felt like an Afghan fighter fighting the Russians in the mid-eighties, at least its how I imagined it then. I literally pulled myself up, staggered across the cold room, undid the latch and pushed the wooden flimsy doors outwards. Sunlight consumed the room. Before me lay the Himalayas, I took in the freshness that one can only find in the highest of mountains. Instantly I felt alive. A sobering happiness replenished my spirit and I remember smiling at the group of old men who too were staying at the ashram. I hadn't had a bath or shower in days. I looked rough. The expressions on the faces of the old men told me as much. It was barely past six in the morning and the town below was heaving with quiet activity. There were no cars, just people and horses. I saw young and old make their way to the temple, the heart of the settlement, the place where most Hindu's who come here end their pilgrimage. If only they could see what I had. The temple they worshipped in was fine, but the cathedral of nature I had just come from was something else. As people took a dip in the Ganges, in waters that was probably just above freezing, I realised that I must bring my parents here. It was a mental promise I made to the powers that be. It's a promise that I still need to fulfil.

I managed to get half a bucket of warmish water to take a quick wash in the great outdoors, for the whole town to see. Privacy is a commodity in these parts. People just got on with it; so did I. I had an entire day to spend wondering the surrounding hills, if my legs permitted. I was awaiting dusk, so that I could go and find the Sadhu. I bought some batteries from the market below, and spent the day pondering on my life; on the act of living; on the phenomenon that is death; on luck and destiny; and of course thinking about home. After all I was no hermit. I spent best part of the day underneath a wooded area overlooking the ashram and the entire settlement. I wrote pages into my journal attempting to capture my emotions and feelings that I'd felt at Tapovan, but I have always known that such things can never be given justice by words. Soon morning had become noon, with the sun beaming down on the Ganges rapids; and noon became a lethargic warm late afternoon. I took a little nap underneath the conifers, birds keeping me company as I rested not only physically, but also emotionally. The world that afternoon became a gentle place. I had felt safe. Everything moved slowly, and watching time became a soothing act for my inner self. I watched the sunset over one of the peaks and soon it was dusk, and time for me to walk into the dark.

    I left all my belongings at the ashram, everything apart from a torch. I headed back up the slope in the direction of Gaumukh and Tapovan. I walked in darkness keeping an eye on time. I knew that in approximately forty minutes I'd be in the vicinity of the cave. My pulse must have soared well beyond the hundred beats per minute mark as I steered my battered feet up the mountain in total darkness. The moon provided what little light it could, and the stars lit the sky in an array of glimmer; holes to heaven. It was cold. The wind swirled, and the Ganges below sang its usual song, one that I'd become so familiar with. It's not very often in the West, at least those of us who are city dwellers, we find ourselves in total complete darkness. The feeling of vulnerability can overwhelm us. I was heading several miles up the Himalayas in darkness, to see a man who lived in a cave, wore no clothes, and no one knew I was going. My torch created just enough light for me to see where the next turn lay. Eventually I found my five pence piece. I knew I was close. I looked up and the surrounding hills. Indeed at eleven hundred hours I saw a light. That must have been it. It appeared to be a fire. I eventually plucked up enough courage to make the climb up. I could hear the sound of the Ganges fading as I went higher. It was as if I was leaving the hands of a guardian for the first time. I'd become so accustomed to the sound of rapids, that to leave it was frightening. Eventually, the fire got bigger, and I caught sight of the small cave. It was getting cold, icy winds swerved past my face sending an uncomfortable chill through my body. I arrived at the cave to find a *havan* – a holy sacrificial fire; a trident marking the entrance, and a small austere looking idol of

Hanuman, the mythological God like character in the Ramayana. All around the cave shadows of trees lined its boundary. The sadhu was no where to be seen. I dared not enter his cave, so I stood outside patiently. I could see that he'd been expecting me. A small patch on the ground had been cleared of foliage next to the fire, at right angles to where he'd sit. A few moments later he appeared out of his cave. He seemed immense. He appeared to be far taller than I'd remembered, and his eyes communicated a strength that was formidable. Before I took any steps closer I began to remove my shoes, as a mark of respect, something that I always did when I went to anyone's house. He stared and asked in a sarcastic yet authoritative tone "are you a sadhu?"

Words wouldn't come out of my mouth. I guess even they must have been frightened. I just shook my head to say no.

"Then why are you removing your shoes, you're in the Himalayas, you'll freeze, keep them on", he ordered.

We both sat at right angles around the fire. It was warm. My body was sheltered by a thick outdoors jacket, which I'd picked up from the air force, thick boots, a shawl, and a buck hat. I'd still felt the chill. The Sadhu was practically naked. A thin saffron cloth covered his genitalia. The only light we had was a welcomed gift from the fire; its radiance was all we had to keep us warm and to keep the dark at bay. I couldn't see anything a few metres away. It was pitch black. Behind him was the entrance to the tiny cave where he must have slept. After a few moments of silence, my pulse slowed, and I felt at ease within. Something told me that I hadn't anything to fear. He starred into the fire. I was frequently glancing at him and the fire. He was still, I was not. He was calm, I was getting there. He was in the known; I was in the unknown. He knew; I did not. I sat there cross legged, as he did, in silence. So many questions raced through my mind; why was I here; why had he approached me; what did he want; what was his name; how had he become a sadhu; what motivated him; what did he do all day; and so on and on. The list was endless.

There was silence, we didn't say anything for half an hour, and I was beginning to think what I was doing there? The only sound came from the sacrificial fire as dry acorns, and pine needles burnt, and were swept up by the thermal air and carried away by the icy mountain winds. The crackling from the fire was soothing, and broke what would otherwise have been an unbearable silence.

"Ask only that which is valuable. Don't waste your time asking questions about me. I'm just a passing character in your life. Today I am here; tomorrow I will no longer exist. Your life however, is with you as long as you live. So ask about you, not me"; and just like that we entered into the most thrilling, metamorphing two day dialogue I'd ever encounter.

Before I spend the next twenty odd pages going through my amazing experience with the sadhu, I should explain a few foundational points that I picked up along the way. Firstly, he was illiterate. Second, he had become a sadhu at the age of twelve after an argument with his parents about him wanting to read scriptures rather than go to school. Next, he claimed not to have a name, and he came from humanity; he never mentioned once any geographical location. He had not spoken to a civilian in over four years. And, he'd lived in these mountains for over twenty five years. His master lived somewhere on Mount Meru. He had no exposure to television or any form of media as you or I would know it. He only spoke in Hindi. Occasionally, children from Gangotri came to give him boiled rice; he held a strict vegetarian diet. He practised yoga and mediation for most of his day. On the second night of our conversational double bill, I saw him perform a hand stand with his entire body inclined vertically, with all his weight on his little fingers. My assumption is that he must have been at least in his seventies. He had a sharp temper, and he never held back when I asked irrelevant questions, or if I ever let my mind wonder. I spent two evenings with him, either in deep conversation or silence – both were illuminating.

On Time & Being

We are all in a matrix. A matrix is anything which shapes or moulds something else. We are all being moulded ever since we were conceived, by the matrix in which we exist. This matrix could be our physical environment, our emotional climate, and our intellectual pursuits. We are a mere spec of consciousness in another wise dark universe. We are a mere observer who is the product of the whole movement of time, right from the very beginning. So, you and I are exactly the way we are, and are where we are, because the entire past before this moment has brought us here. The sadhu made a point of it to expound the fact that by the past he didn't mean just our lives, but the entire history of time; something which by its very definition means beyond not only our lives, but that of everyone and everything we know. All that reservoir of time; reservoir of moments, has lead to this very spot of you reading these words. Back then in June 2005, all the reservoir of moments had lead me to be in the presence of a mountain hermit deep within the Himalayas. He went on to explain that everything we experience is through the screen of the past. All the moments of the past right from the beginning of time infringe on all our experience in the present. In short, he meant that you, dear readers, are reading these words, and when you interpret them to make judgement, you do so with all that past that's locked up deep within your psyche. Some of you will instantly connect with what has been said, others will remain confused, some will feel that I am talking rubbish, whatever the result may be, the fact is that these words have been observed by you in the past. You are not experiencing *'now'* independently. You are experiencing *'now' from the past.*

If we are unaware of this subtle state of affairs, we the observer are unaware of our conditioning; and if we are unaware of our conditioning we create a division between *us* (the observer) and that which we *experience* (the observed). Hence, as long as we experience the world through the filter of the past, we never quite experience the 'now' in its *'real'* state. Therefore, we never quite see reality as it is, but rather as our past determines. Let me bring this point home – basically what the sadhu was implying is that we are all a little neurotic. We all possess a natural mental imbalance. Every person on this planet has neurosis. None of us see or experience reality as it really is, instead we see it from the past. As you read these words you experience them, understand them, make sense of them, ultimately judging them based on the things you already know; books you have already read; places you have already been; ideas you already accept; and so on and on. The question is can we experience reality, can you read these words for what they really are without the bias of the past?

It seems obvious that the 'now' is determined by the past, and that the future will be created by this 'now'. The challenge we all face is that time is forever in motion. It never stops. Hence, by the time we see something and process that information, the moment is already gone. I wondered what action is required to end this motion of time, hence of continuously living in the past? It seems that in order to completely free oneself from the past, and therefore experience the 'now' without the past, we need to break off from it altogether. But how on earth can I experience something and make sense of it, if I abandon all that I know?

As the sadhu spoke, I listened. But not in a way of ordinary listening, rather I was in perfect tune with his message, and his message wasn't the words he spoke. The words were the carriers of his message, not the message itself. It was there, on the ridge next to a cave in India that I realised that words are vehicles we use to transfer messages, yet how often do we take the word itself as the message. Most human miscommunication occurs because words that we use misrepresent what we actually mean. The speaker uses inaccurate words, and the listener takes the words on face value. Both cause conflict through misunderstanding.

When I use the word anger, what am I actually saying? Can I feel anger without the word? If anger as a word didn't exist, would I still be able to feel anger as the actual thing? Clearly I could. We can all feel things that we cannot conceptualise. If anger didn't exist in my vocabulary, I'm sure I could still feel it when it grew inside me. Of course I wouldn't be able to think about it very well. The feeling of anger without the word would be rather confusing. I'd feel it without being able to express it verbally. Without being able to verbalise the feeling of anger, I couldn't think about it.

All this is true, but just because I cannot think about something doesn't mean it's not there. And it was here that I realised a fundamental truth; we think with words, but words are limiting, hence our thinking is limited. I can experience things that are outside the realms of my vocabulary but I quickly distort that reality by attaching an inaccurate word that I already know. So if I was a Martian, and I'd never seen the colour red before until my first day on earth, I'd be rather fascinated. I saw red. But I'd have no way of expressing it to other people or myself. The word red doesn't exist for me. However, on Mars we have a colour orange. My mind instantly refers to the past, pulls out the closet previous experience to the colour red, in this case, it was the colour orange, and I create a new word – *"orange-ish"*. I know it's not orange, but how else can I possibly process it in my mind without associating a word to it? It seems I can't. So I do the next best thing. I create a word that originates from a previous experience of something similar. This allows me to think about my new experience but in a distorted way. Red isn't orange-ish. It's the colour red.

It was here that the sadhu brought the two items together; the past and our language. It was our words, which grounded all our experiences in the past. We are continuously experiencing a wonderful new world everyday, but we are trapped by our words, by our thinking, and hence we experience reality from the past, never quite grasping it for what it is. His answer to my question of how can I live in the moment; how can I grasp reality for what it really is, was simple. *Don't think was his answer.*

I remember there being a lengthy silence after his final point. He had shown me the entrance to a rabbit hole. He held my hand and showed me which tunnel to catch, and once I'd caught it, he let me go off, deep into intellectual space. My experience went something like this; *we are all a little neurotic because we are incapable of grasping reality for what it really is, because we live in the* past; we see today based on yesterday; we judge others based on previous judgements. All of this accumulates as previous experience and knowledge. This knowledge creates thoughts, and thoughts are created from language. We think in a language. Our language is limited by our past. This inherently implies that our thinking is limited by our past. The 'now' is being experienced but as soon as I think, or I apply thought upon my experience, the reality is diluted; it has lost its purity, and is in fact tainted by my past. The only way to end this dilution of reality, according to the sadhu, was to stop thinking, and therefore unhinging the 'now' from the past; to experience reality without thinking. To truly understand the world we must merely observe, not think, not judge, nor interfere. The reality before us; the 'now' that is here has infinite possibilities, but we only have finite words to cope with this reality. Infinity doesn't fit very well into what's finite, hence by using words to think we lose bits of reality that doesn't fit into our vocabulary.

The implications of this are immense and wide ranging. There is a popular story, and I'm unsure of its validity or accuracy but nevertheless exemplifies the point I am making. The story goes something like this; when Columbus' ship anchored on one of the Caribbean Islands his first officer kept a daily journal to log events as they occurred. In his log he mentioned that a strange looking coloured man in unusual dress starring directly at the ship. His reaction is unusual in that he doesn't react at all. He just stares. He doesn't call anyone either, he just continues to stare. He did this for four days when suddenly he screams in some form of shock and horror, runs back into the forest grove and brings back an army of men with spears a few hours later. They begin to scream and perform some kind of dance around a fire.

Some time later Europeans discovered a journal kept by the village Wiseman. Someone had it translated, as in all probability the person to whom it belonged was killed. But that is another point and I wish not to dwell on it. When translated, it read something remarkable. On the same day as they had anchored, the author of this journal mentions how the sea and waves at a specific point were behaving extraordinarily. He writes how he threw stones towards the patch of water which looked strange. The Wiseman initially thought that a creature lay still underneath the water; he writes how he dismissed that idea. After four days of searching, thinking and starring he writes that a great wooden monster suddenly appeared out of no where, as if by magic. He then runs to tell everyone else of this wooden monster on the horizon. Everyone else saw the ships instantly because he had already conceptualised his findings into a language, he passed on those ideas, and so the other villagers saw the ships right away. Only recently have quantum physicists caught up with philosophers like Plato, the writers of the Upanishads, Schopenhauer and Krishnamurti; who have disseminated this knowledge for centuries.

Quantum Physics now tells us that eyes pick up everything that resonates within its visual limits, which is a heck more than what we *actually* see. The problem is that our brain – the visual cortex only imprints that which it can conceptualise. The Wiseman from the village couldn't see that ships because his brain had *no 'idea'* about anything which even remotely resembled that which his eyes were seeing. Consequently his brain filtered out the ships altogether. So it seems that the brain only captures what it has the ability to deal with, and filters out everything else that the eyes maybe picking up. This idea which now Quantum Physicists have cottoned onto has some powerful implications. It means that right now as you read these words there could be things around the place, which your eyes are seeing, but your brain is filtering out because it lacks the ability to capture it. If my brain can only see what it can conceptualise, and what it can conceptualise is completely dependent on knowledge, thought and previous judgement, then I see *'now'* from what I already know of the past. Hence, we all seem to live 'now' from the past, consequently missing out 'bits' of reality which we cannot grasp. We are all missing things exactly because we live in the past.

By now I was truly in the rabbit hole and the tunnel was getting deeper and darker. I arrived at realisations at a speed, and with intensity as I had never done before. I was away from the sadhu; I was away from the Himalayas; I felt nowhere and yet everywhere.

It occurred to me that we were reality creating machines. If what I experience is only a fragment of what's really out there, and I create my reality based on my own brain and all its previous experiences, thoughts, emotions, feelings, and judgements; then surely we are all creating, or should I say experiencing a *'self-made' reality*, which is distinctly limited from *the real*. Another major implication of this fact is that it brings into question how much science can actually tell us about 'reality', as in science we are still the observer. As long as we remain the observer we are inherently limited in picking up the *'whole' of reality*. Is science the pursuit of reality? Well if it aspires to be, then its always going to fall short because the final observer, who is human, is always living in a self-made creation; a self-made reality, one that has been manifested from its own past. Additionally, if we are all self-creating our experiences that are inherently limited, then it would mean that there is nothing "out there" (outside of us) that is independent of us. The *'out there'* that we are all experiencing right now is subject to what's happening 'in here' *(I'm pointing to ones own brain)*, and it seems that I cannot distinguish from *'in here' and 'out there'*. I need to make clear here that I am not saying that there is no reality and that everything is inside our own brain. What I have realised is simply that the "real" reality that is out there is something which we are not experiencing. Rather we are only experiencing that which our brains have the capacity to pick up. What's more is that our brains limitations come about from our words, our language, our thoughts, and our conditioning through the matrix; in other words our lives.

To grasp reality we must break with the past; not just our past, but from all the past; from the past of our parents, our communities, our religions, our cultures, our languages, our traditions, our beliefs, and so on and on. That is not to say that everything we know is wrong, or delusional – no far from it! In fact much of what we experience is 'real', but we miss a great deal out due to this mental conditioning of the past. When we can dislodge 'now' from its past, we will begin to experience the 'whole' reality.

Then just like that my senses re-engaged with my body and I felt a sharp pain of pins & needles throughout my legs. I had to uncross them and shift my body a little. No sooner had I moved slightly did the sadhu snap at me, "What are you doing? Where is your mind, bring it back here", pointing at the forehead. "You must detach to experience what's really there; you must forget little pains that occur. If you search for reality, you must loose the body."

I was shocked at what he'd said. Was he following my thoughts somehow? How did he know that I was exploring reality? We had been completely silent for at least half an hour. He had sat still starring at the fire; I had been physically looking down starring at my feet, in deep contemplation. I had to defend myself.

"Ji, mere pare dukh te he", I said meekly, careful not to annoy him.

He starred deep into my eyes, he was silent, and so was I. I'd told him that my feet were in pain, to which he responded unsympathetically. Soon he went back to starring at the fire, and I tried to find the rabbit hole.

Within a few moments I was back in them. My next enquiry began with the question *'what is reality'?* If I accept that what I experience is only a limited version of reality, I still had to know what 'real' reality was. Traditionally scientists, of whom I was one, as my background was in Aerospace, approached matter – that thing which everything else is made out of, as being static, predictable and ultimately at the heart of everything else. At least this is how I'd understood it to be. But I was heading down a rabbit hole, which was to break with my knowledge and understanding in order to experience 'real' reality.

I'd already known that at the quantum level every atom was made from three sub particles; namely a proton, a neutron and electron. In between these particles was immense empty space. In fact most of an atom was empty. If most of an atom is empty, and everything is made out of atoms, then most of everything is empty space. This is rather strange, and if you do not think so then you haven't clearly connected with these words every well. Everything around you, even this book is mostly empty space. Yet my experience and yours too, of this book, is far from it being empty. In fact it feels rather solid. If physical reality was mostly empty, fair enough, but time too, seems problematic.

It occurred to me that I have a distinct connection to the past, limited connection to the present, and absolutely no connection with the future – why? Not experiencing 'now', is what I have spent the last few pages explaining, but it gives little to no understanding as to the past or the future. In physics, I knew that there was the mystery of the direction of time. The laws of physics make no distinction between past and future i.e. they don't change over time; they have no bearing on time. What puzzled me was that *why should I remember the past but not have the same epistemic access to the future? What made time flow in the direction that it does? Why do we think that by acting 'now' I could affect the future but not the past?* These things can only be explained by understanding causes of the flow of time. Yet modern physics tells us nothing. These things are so fundamental in the way we experience the world that not to ask these questions sooner was to feel somewhat dead until that moment. Apart of me was born when these questions were raised deep within me.

My next major journey through intellectual space was in attempting to understand the future. The future seemed to me, to have an infinite number of possibilities. Anything could potentially occur at any time from now. Yet, I could quite comfortably predict what actually *"will"* occur. How could I be so sure about the outcome of the future when so many possibilities lay ahead? I couldn't logically; yet my feelings told me otherwise – albeit illogically. Life would be a rather maddening place if each of us didn't have a sense of what was to happen next in our lives. In consciousness it's always true that we move forward in time – why? Why could I not move backward in time? Furthermore, why is the future predominantly predictable in an array of infinite possibilities?

Physics tells us that most of the universe is empty, and time for an unknown reason, always seems to flow in one direction. Quantum Physics and certain Indian philosophical schools have expounded the idea that in fact time itself is a man made delusion, or at least its direction is. They say that it's perfectly possible to have the same epistemic connection to the future as we already have with the past. My journey through this intellectual space led me to the following realisations.

Essentially there is no real past, nor is there any real future. The notion of time exists due to the fact that we are never experiencing the present holistically. Now before I continue I must tell you that what I am attempting to write about is reality – *a reality that is timeless*. Yet I do so with these words as my only tool, a tool that by its sequential nature exists in time, and hence, is already projecting inaccuracy. Nevertheless, I should at least attempt it here the best as I can. May I suggest however that you, dear reader, attempt to physically visualise the pictures I attempt to draw for you. This is the best way for you to see the rabbit hole, and thereafter all I can say is "bon voyage".

Time is the side effect each of us experience due to our state of being. We are forever in the past, as I have already explained. We experience a limited 'now' due to the conditioning of the matrix in which we exist. In reality, there is no time. Hence *what was, is now, what's now, is now, and what will be, is also now*. I need you to grasp this point from the offset. This is the rope that will guide you to your own rabbit hole where you will personally experience these realisations. If what I say is even remotely accurate then why are our experiences so different?

To explain this lets pretend that my cousin Kalpna *(who badly wanted to feature in this book)* is presently reading these very words right now. In her experience she reads these pages, eventually gets bored, and burns the book, tells all her friends that it's a complete waste of time, and that it's inaccessible. From 'now' it is also equally possible that she gets bored, and stores the book, tells all her friends that it's a complete waste of time, and that it's inaccessible. It is equally possible in the 'now' that she gets bored, leaves it on the table and her five year old daughter rips it apart, tells all her friends that it's a complete waste of time, and that it's inaccessible.

I have given three small possibilities out of infinity of what could happen right now. But Kalpna who is conditioned by the matrix, who forever lives in the past, who has limiting conceptions, ideas, feelings and judgements ends up selecting, unknowingly one reality out of infinite possibilities of what to do right 'now'. Let us suppose she stores the book after getting bored. For her that was the only reality that existed, but in 'real' reality, which she is completely unaware off at least holistically speaking, any number of things could have been manifested.

The longer she breaks away from the matrix of the past, the longer she would remain in the 'now', and living in the 'now' is to experience *infinity right 'now'*. It is in the 'now' that everything that did happen, could have happened, will happen, and could happen exist simultaneously. We collapse this reality, this wave of possibilities into a singular particle driven reality. Hence, we pick on a single version of events to live our lives through. It is through this phenomenon that the delusion of time, its flow towards the future are created in our minds.

Sub-atomically speaking, there is right now a wave of possibilities that exist simultaneously of what Kalpna might do with the book once she is bored. As soon as Kalpna experiences boredom, all her past infringes on the experience and she collapses the wave of infinity into a singularity, in other words, into one possible outcome, and continues to live with it. This idea, I believe in Quantum Physics is called *Quantum Superimpositions*.

The idea of Superimpositions says that a particle can exist simultaneously in multiple positions, and then our consciousness collapses onto one such particle position, which we experience as reality, and miss out on all the other places where the particle could have, or did, in fact exist. The realisation of such a bizarre world has some bizarre consequences. A superhero could use superimpositions with the world being nothing but potential shifts of reality until they choose. Heroes choose what they want; being in many places at once, experiencing many possibilities all at once, and then collapsing on the one. Those of you who have managed to keep up are indeed correct at what I'm ultimately getting at. The idea of time travel, the idea of being omniscient are all real possibilities, we just need to de-condition ourselves from the matrix. The fundamental shift in thinking that was required was to acknowledge that the reality we experience is due to our mental state, it would not be so, unless we were such. The entire material world is experienced according to our shifts in consciousness.

By the time I had reached this point of my silent enquiry, staring at the fire, I was suddenly told to leave. He was gentle in his instruction, but very clear. He acknowledged the progress I had made in the tunnels beyond space and time. He smiled as if he'd known exactly what I was experiencing. I had spent four hours with him, mostly in silence. The night was cold, and the fire was slowly decaying into another nights slumber. The sadhu took his leave without a word and retired into his cave. I left moments later struggling to bend my legs and in sheer agony. I made my way back to Gangotri.

It was dark and terribly cold. I jumped the ashram gates as they were locked and quietly made my way back to my room. It was pitch black. I brushed my teeth and fell onto my bed looking up at the stained ceiling. I knew that something fantastic had happened. I had personally experienced some form of human communication without any verbal statements. I had no doubt then, and I have no doubt now that what I experienced on that first night with the sadhu was extraordinary.

I continued my exploration of all that was. I had explored time, but I wanted to know more about ones state of being. I wanted to know what made me the way I was. I wanted to know what made every human being different, and how in time we all appear to be such different creatures, when at a sub-atomic level we are all created out of the same thing – whatever that thing maybe. The night was cold, but I didn't feel it then. I was alone, yet I didn't think so. With this in mind I lay on the bed. Sleep overcame me, and I drifted into an enchanting limbo.

The next morning I awoke to a freshness I'd never felt. I wondered around nearby foothills. I was lost practically the whole day in deep thought. The previous night had been a deep exploration of time which, I realised was rather meaningless without the observer, in other words people. I wanted to know people. I wanted to know what 'Being' human meant. I was seated underneath a tree in a dense quite woodland a few metres above Gangotri. I remember starring at my hands as I went through the following journey.

For anything to be different from anything else, in other words for my hand to be different from this tree, either space or time has to be presupposed, or both. In the case of material objects such as my hand and the tree, it was fairly obvious. For one object to be different from another it must either occupy the same space at different time or a different space at the same time, or a different space at a different time. After all, we live in a four dimensional universe – the universe of length, width, depth and time. All this is commonsense. You can distinguish your hand from this book because it occupies different space, in the same time. Looking around your room you'll find that our universe is built around this principle – all things must exist in a different space or time in order to be different. This is less obvious with subtle things such as numbers or the alphabet.

Numbers in themselves don't exist in space or time as we traditionally think. Numbers occupy no physical space, and seem timeless. But are they? Well, it seems that even numbers exist in time after all. Numbers are different from one another, one is different to two, and two is different to three, and yet this entire concept is based around a sequence, an order of some sort, and any order or sequence implies time. One comes before two, and two comes before three, and so on. Hence even our abstract thoughts and ideas seem to be bound by time, when we think a little deeper.

Our language as I have already said is grounded in the past, hence it exists in time. What about poetry and music, these things exist in our universe, do they take up space or time?

They do indeed.

Poetry presupposes succession of words, and so does music, in terms of musical notes. These things are built around succession, and hence time orientated. It seems that we can't think of things if they are not bound by space or time. What is there that is space-less, timeless, and yet distinguishable? As the sadhu had pointed out the previous night – *don't think*! But how could I not! Everything around me was full of thought, full of time – if I can say such a thing. Every physical thing occupies space. If it wasn't for space or time, everything would be one big whole.

Here is where the penny should drop.

Everything would be a unified whole if it wasn't for time and space. Whatever is out there that exists without the observer, i.e. *without you and I*, the realm of whatever exists in itself independently of experience, must be in a state of *spacelessness and timelessness*. It's not a particularly large step from this point to then state that differentiation, the idea of duality, the idea that things can be separate from one another, can only exist in a world of experience.

Let me clarify this notion a little better. My explorations through this philosophical journey led me to the understanding that what ever I can experience with my senses, and intellect, can only be done so in time and space; that which is beyond my language, my thoughts, my thinking, my senses, and ultimately my imagination, must be timeless and 'spaceless'. There is this world, which you and I experience, as you are right now. But there is also another *extended world* – the world that you and I cannot experience, or at best haven't experienced yet. All those things, all those possibilities that we have never thought of is in this other extended world; it's in an extended reality. This extended reality is timeless & spaceless. Furthermore, it's timeless and spaceless exactly because we are not there; not there physically nor mentally. The moment we extend ourselves physically or mentally to this extended reality, we *"discover" it*, and as soon as that occurs, we bring with us the baggage of time and space. This creates differentiation; a duality between things, fundamentally because we see ourselves as unique differentiated things.

Right about now many of you will be feeling sore, certain parts of the brain will be throbbing; for this I apologise whole heartedly. My situation is this; I am trying to describe experiences that are beyond language – and the only tool I have for describing it to you are these words, which are grossly limiting. My aim is not to clarify everything for you; in fact this is impossible, at least with words. My intentions are far less ambitious.

All I intend to do is to make you aware that our lives are only a spec of dust in this otherwise expansive universe; to show you that there are alternative things you can physically, emotionally, and intellectually experience, which only you can ever know about; theses are things that you can share with no one else verbally. To know about this extended reality is to know truth, and surely to know truth is to find a deeper meaning to our lives, and by doing so we find a little oasis of contentment in an otherwise unhappy existence. Believe me, your headache is a price well worth paying!

Just like you, my head too was hurting that day, as I sat above Gangotri. I knew that I'd stumbled into something truly fantastic. It was a rather strange sensation, a sensation that some of you will be experiencing right now. You know what I mean, and you know that it is truly experiential, and yet you can't rationally think about it, you can't make sense of it, and traditionally we'd dismiss anything that doesn't make sense; but not today dear reader. Today you should stick with the sensation. It's this sensation that is the gateway to your own rabbit hole. I can't tell you anymore, all I can say is try it, and see how far down the rabbit hole goes.

After a brisk walk into town and a quick bite to eat, I headed back to my spot underneath the tree. My thoughts continued. The question which raged within my mind was could anyone actually experience this extended reality, in the normal sense of the word experience. Could anyone 'know' this extended reality?

I'd already known that Hindu & Buddhist philosophies had expounded what I had just discovered, thousands of years ago. Furthermore, I had known of Kant & Schopenhauer, both of whom had discovered what they called the noumenal world. Whereas, I have used the words "extended reality", they used the word noumenal. In fact Plato, the ancient Greek philosopher too had told us about a reality upon which our experiences were based; he had called it the 'world of forms'. Each one of us had arrived at the same point from alternative paradigms, alternative shifts of consciousness and time. It was quite an honour to have known that the greatest minds humanity has produced had walked these same paths that today you are treading. They are no smarter than us; they just got their first. But let us continue down these trodden paths.

Schopenhauer and Kant had both asserted that we can never have any direct experience of this extended reality. The problem that later Schopenhauer had extended was regarding the idea of *knowing* something. He had said that to know something by definition implies that there is a two, a duality – there is a knower and a known. We return back to the subject-object scenario. In an undifferentiated reality where there is a single unified whole, it would be unable to know itself, simply because there is no knower and known. In a single unified whole; there is only the whole. Knowledge in itself is dualistic, since it presupposes differentiation. It follows that there can only be such a thing as knowledge in the phenomenal world alone, and that world which exists in itself independently of being experienced is 'knowledge-less'. Therefore, we know about things only so as long as there is time and space. As soon as the foundational items of time and space disappear, all scope of knowledge disappears with it.

Sitting under that tree was blissful and it was the bliss that was allowing me to explore reality to such depth. A fact that I could recite Schopenhauer is a testimony to that point, as anybody who has read his works will tell you that he is almost impossible to remember, and yet underneath the tree his ideas came alive. And yet, I felt that there was a bit of a contradiction – how could I say that we cannot *know* the extended reality, and yet claim that it must be a unified whole beyond time and space? Wouldn't this imply that *I know* this extended reality? Or was it a question of *knowing about*, and *actually knowing*?

For instance I know about Einstein but can I claim that I *know* him? I may know every fact that may exist regarding his life and values, and yet can I claim that I know Einstein? Clearly I cannot claim to know him. But I can claim to know 'about' him. So there is a difference between knowing about, and actually knowing something. I can *'know about'* the extended reality, but never come to *'know'* it – in the same way that I might know my mother, or Bhavisha, or myself for that matter, of whom I have personal experience. Come to think of it, I suspect that most of our knowledge is about things, rather knowing them directly.

My explorations ended that day on the foothills above Gangotri with a deeper understanding of reality. As I walked back to the ashram I attempted to collate all my thoughts, in an attempt to create a fuller picture of my discoveries. All the pieces seemed to interconnect. There is a reality that we all experience. We call this reality our lives. The problem was that we experience our lives permanently from the past. It was our thinking that fixed us there. Our words, which create our thoughts consistently restrict our "now" experiences. We could never quite appreciate now, because we think. As soon as we loose our words; our thoughts when we experience "now", then and only then, can we experience the present for what it really is. The challenge was to become thoughtless, to see now, and attach no words to it, thereby unhinging the past.

It also occurred that the entire notion of time was an illusion; an illusion caused by our conditioning. If we could experience now as it really is, then all the past and future would disappear, and what we are left with is the wave of infinite possibilities. This wave of possibilities collapses into a singular particle driven reality as soon as we apply thought onto our experience, and return back into the dimension of time.

Just as time in reality is not there, but only a stream of infinite possibilities, as a unified whole, so it was with things. All things in the phenomenal world seemed different by either the space they occupied, or time at which things existed, or both. But if we took our thoughts out of the equation, if we stopped thinking, and began to only observe reality, then along with the disappearance of time, all things would loose their differentiation. That world, which is beyond our senses, beyond our imagination and intellect, that world where timelessness exists, must also be space-less. It is our conditioning, the fact that we live inside the limits of our own language, and knowledge set that binds us down to experience the whole as separate bits – separated by time and space. Somewhere beyond the world which we experience is an extended reality that is neither in time nor space, and thereby cannot be differentiated, and so by logic must be a *unified whole*.

This was all rather mind blowing stuff. Our world, our universe, our lives could be so inaccurate and misrepresentative of what's really out there that I thought it scary. I was seeing a tree, my hand, the sky, and people far below getting on with their daily chores. All that appeared different. But technically if it wasn't for my knowledge, language and thoughts, all these separate things could just be segments of a unified whole, to which I have no direct access too, but can only know about.

Soon it was dusk; the sun had set after another exhaustive day. I had travelled a million miles, and I felt exhilarated. I was there with Schopenhauer, with Plato, with the writers of the Upanishads, Nagarjuna, and Krishnamurti; I had experienced what they had discovered. I had read their thoughts and philosophies, but now I had just lived what they must have experienced. It was a feeling of immense joy and satisfaction. I felt bewildered as I came out of the rabbit hole. The world looked the same, yet different. I slowly drifted back to my ashram looking at things in a whole new light. I collapsed on my bed and fell into a gentle light sleep, flirting with sleep but never quite giving in. I was waiting for my time to go back into the dark.

Rabbit holes can be Dark

I made no notes in my journal as to which day it was; but I was intending to leave Gangotri, and head towards the other peaks of Kedarnath & Badrinath. I didn't leave of course; how could I? Instead, I packed my small rucksack and left the ashram to go back to the cave.

My second night was much darker; not only was it starless but also bare of moonlight. Even intellectually, it was darker; much darker. As I reached the cave cold and breathless, I found the fire glowing, spreading its light and heat in an otherwise icy night. It was comforting. I kept my boots on this time, and sat at my place as quietly as I could. The sadhu was just sitting in his yogic position, deep in contemplation. I sat there too. I stared, almost mesmerised by the fire. After some time he spoke.

"You've come, very nice", he spoke in Hindi.

I nodded with an awkward smile.

"Are you a good man?" he asked.

"I try", I replied, quickly but meekly.

He closed his eyes and went back into himself. After a few minutes I realised he was not going to say anymore. I stared; first at him; then at the sacred fire. I'd never been asked so poignantly whether I was a good man or not! In fact I find most people never get asked such a straight forward question. These are the hardest of all enquiries to satisfy. I have always found their simplicity too penetrating. Am I a good man? Are you a good person? How can we begin to answer such questions? From where do we begin? How do we define what is good? What is our point of reference – is it our religion, or our cultural values? Is good relative? Is good framed within the structure of our psychological states, or our understanding of right and wrong? From which premise does one begin? Is there anything tangible that can be unquestionably tagged as *good*?

After an hour or so of searching, I found the rabbit hole to the question of ethics, the idea of good and bad, just and unjust, and right and wrong. It was here that I found the darkest of all realisations. What I realised that night was to change my outlook on life, it would alter my relations with people, and most importantly open up new ways of perceiving reality – a reality that I was to discover was locked away behind the door of cultural repression, societal despotism, and religious orthodoxy.

I entered intellectual space through the question "am I *naturally* good?" What, if anything, can it mean to be natural, one might ask. The word nature derives from a Latin root *Natura*, meaning *'the course of things'*, and so we can re-interpret the question as "is the course of my life good?"

The only way in which I could answer such a question was if I knew where it was that my life was heading – but of course, I had no such idea. The previous night I had discovered that time was an illusion, and that it was I who created reality from moment to moment, effectively collapsing infinity into a singular reality. So to answer the question depended not on some unknown future, but on what there really is – *the now*! Is the course of my life good, presently; in other words right now? When the question is posed in this way, the word *good*, whatever it may mean, becomes dynamic, in that I can be good one moment, and then not good the next. Am I a good man; can only be answered on the course, which I have taken at this very moment. In other words if my actions, thoughts, or even my entire being, at this very moment is on a good course, then I am indeed good. Equally so the other way; if my being is on a course that is not good, then I am not a good man. Neither state is permanent. I am a *good man now*, but I maybe equally *not good tomorrow*, or in the next moment. It all depends on, at what moment I judge myself. Regardless of what Good actually means, this notion is still true. The notion that a man could be "all" good or "all" bad was simply not naturally true.

So naturally was I good? Well, at that moment in time, on the edge of a cave in the foothills of the Himalayas, I certainly felt good. But what does it mean to *be good*? What was good? I'd realised that goodness was a state of being, one could be good one moment, and then bad the next. But to understand 'good' was genuinely a difficult proposition.

Society, in the liberal West has a relativistic notion of what is good. Good means different things to different people; what's more is that what can be good for one person may not be so good for the next. When a woman leaves her husband for her new found lover, it's clearly bad for her husband, difficult for her, but ultimately good, and wonderfully good for her lover. How do we begin to judge whether her action was good or not? It's good for her, and her new lover, but disastrous for her husband (*if we assume he loved her dearly*). In her reality she has done an honest act, she has been true to herself, her lover and, even though painful for her husband, nevertheless honest. So is the act right? Is the act good? Well, to me at least, it became all too clear that night.

Yes, if and only if, they didn't have children.

It was here through exploring human relationships that I ventured into the meta-ethical dimensions, which ultimately lead me to understand good and bad, right and wrong, with such clarity. It was through the exploration and understanding of love, marriage and compassion that I discovered the meaning of an ethical existence. I also discovered that the ethical life was ultimately unattainable for the vast majority, and in all likeliness me included – I was no better! The discovery meant that we mortals, with all our human limitedness were forever doomed to suffer due to our inherent lack of understanding about the true nature of things. I came to understand that through our limited understanding, and emotional retardation, we were likely to continue acting badly, wrongly, or whatever word you would rather use – I just hope you understand my point. And yet through all this, I saw that each of us had the innate potential to *rise above our humanness*, to grow beyond our emotional retardation, and begin to live correctly, and thereby were indeed capable of a better existence – the challenge lay in the journey.

I have already gone through what I believe love to be – the idea that all our physical, emotional, intellectual and spiritual needs are satisfied effortlessly. I have also discussed the nature of the male psyche, in that it is fundamentally not suited to monogamy. With these fundamentals in mind I wish to return to my previous example; that of the woman leaving her husband, for her newly found lover. I made a rather brave statement: *"It was indeed right for her to leave her husband, if and only if, they didn't have children."*

On that cliff, next to a cave in the shallow Himalayas I discovered what marriage was. Marriage, it seems, is a man made construct to make men live up to their responsibilities of providing responsible parenthood for their offspring. Without making this book into some anthropological study of the evolution of human society, I want to show that the only purpose of marriage is for a couple to procreate, and when creating within the confines of a marriage, the children conceived have a better chance of surviving. Not so true now days of course, but any anthropologist will tell you that it was certainly the case in days gone by. Marriage was created because human society in the days long gone realised that it increased the chances of survival for the new offspring, and provided emotional stability, if the man was committed to them. If men were allowed to engage in sex, have children, but had little commitment to them, then that society would crumble. *Marriage is a pragmatic solution to a male problem* – the problem that men are not naturally monogamous.

Marriage ensures that the future security and prosperity of the society is kept at the forefront of any personal short term desire. Marriage ensured that if men wanted children, and inevitably most men are programmed by genes to have children at some stage, then they must get married. In marriage, they are bound to provide welfare for all concerned – and the *'all concerned'* are his family. Marriage was the doorway to creating this much desired stable family. With the women creating new life and the men providing for it ensured stability, and prosperity for any society.

Love, as I have already spoken of is temporal. We can be in love, and fall out of love at any given time, mostly driven by circumstance, and whether our needs are being satisfied. Marriage is a pragmatic solution to creating a healthy society. The needs of society supersede the short term desires of the couple, for the sake of their children – not because children are inherently good, but rather because society is safe guarding its own future. Our children are in essence, our future!

The harsh reality is that love and marriage do not necessarily go hand in hand, and there is no formula that states that one should be in love throughout the course of a marriage. Love is a psychological phenomenon that can elevate us to higher conscious states; marriage is a pragmatic solution to rearing healthy offspring; they do not necessarily go well together. The truth is that most people fall in and out of love all the time, but remain in a marriage.

For those readers who are married and already have children, will agree with me when I say that once children arrive, the relationship is infinitely more complex between husband and wife; and that a greater tolerance for one another develops. What I mean to say is that once married with children, the idea of separation becomes physically and emotionally far more difficult to even comprehend. Marriage creates families, and families in turn create communities. I believe in community, hence I believe in marriage. As much as I believe in marriage, I'm also of the opinion that no one should be compelled to spend their lives with people who become a barrier against their happiness. After all, each of us can only reach our potential when we are in a state of happiness, contentment, and at ease with ourselves *holistically – mind, body & spirit.*

The fact that most men and women want to bear children at some stage in their life inevitably means that marriage is a must. But what of those who choose, consciously not to bear children, but still engage in the act of love? Is marriage 'naturally good' for them? As I went ever deeper into the tunnels, and further away from societal conditioning, a new vision began to emerge within my psyche – a vision that I knew most would be unable to connect with. I began to see that for those few who did not want children, marriage was no longer a need, but became a luxury; something which they could chose to enter for the intense sense of belonging. Was marriage 'naturally' good for them? I think not. Yet, I think as most people want a deeper sense of belonging as you enter mid-life, even if they have a "no children" policy, marriage becomes an increasingly viable option.

What felt like hours drifted by. The crackle of acorns in the dark fire broke the silence. The air was cold, but held at bay by the heat around the fire. I stared at the sadhu who now had his eyes tightly shut; his posture was straight and his gut sucked right the way in. I'm not sure where it came from, or what triggered it, but somehow the idea of *Dharma* seemed to enter my thinking.

I had come across the term throughout the Upanishads and several Buddhist scriptures. The idea of Dharma was the ultimate arbitrator of moral judgements; but I'd found it incredibly hard to pin the meaning of Dharma down. In fact, I suspected that many thinkers had tried to grapple with the meaning of Dharma, but never quite conceptualised it in their words as it must have appeared in their minds. Was I good?

From a Dharmic perspective it would translate as "was I Dharmic?" Was I following the ways of Dharma? But what is Dharma? Until that night, I had always *known what Dharma was*, but *never truly had I known*!

Yes dear reader, I know I've just contradicted myself; but somewhere in that irony is a nugget of truth and it's for you to recognise it.

"Was I a good man?" I realised that I had to know something about the principle of Dharma before I could begin to answer such a question.

On Dharma

Dharma is often confused by many pseudo Indian intellectuals to mean religion. This couldn't be further from reality. Religions are institutions with hierarchies, rituals, places of worships, a mythology, and a host of other complicating practices. Dharma, on the other hand is intangible; it's abstract; its beyond, I believe, even our vocabulary, hence so many thinkers have failed to pin a clear definition. In the pantheon of definitions and explanations that have emerged over thousands of years – I discovered my two pence worth!

Dharma, as I have later come to conceptualise, (*which isn't 100% accurate*) means *when one fulfils their individual, societal, human and universal duties. These duties arise from the purpose of our lives.*

Simple really, and rather uninspiring with a tinge of "oh that's it then", but if you can really absorb what I've just said then we can explore such powerful notions with depth and clarity.

I discovered innately on the mountain above Gangotri that in order to answer the question, "was I good", I'd first have to understand the point of reference; an over arching principle; something with which I could draw comparison and judgement. I'd already discovered that *being good* was a relative term; there could be no tangible 'law' from which good could be drawn. Yet ironically it's impossible to know 'good' from bad without some foundational concept. I think to some extent each of us has foundational idea(s) in our psyche of what is good and proper – in all probability it derives from our culture, or environment. Nevertheless, to make such broad judgements such as "am I good", we must have something deeper; something that permeates throughout human nature; otherwise all moral judgements would be made on superficial foundations.

Dharma was that over arching principle:

"When one knows the purpose of ones own life; then they acquire natural duties that assist in achieving that end, and the fulfilment of those duties is good, and the opposite is bad."

The reason why I believe that ultimately most of us are incapable of making accurate moral judgements and living morally astute lives is because we'll never come to discover the purpose of our lives.

The premise that I have based this definition on is two fold; both of which I do not intend to explain here, for this is not a book of meta-ethics but rather a description of my intellectual journey. The premise is that *each of us has a unique purpose to our lives, and that ultimately this purpose is good*. The second premise is that *this purpose permeates throughout our lives and is individual (personal), societal (as we are social animals), human (our natural positive evolutionary instincts), and universal (those that are timeless and apply to all things).*

"Ji nahi", I said.

Two hours had passed since he'd asked me the question. He opened his eyes. There was a gentleness that I'd not yet seen. He knew that I knew. I hadn't the foggiest as to the purpose of my life. How could I answer his question? I couldn't. I had no way of conclusively answering such a simple question. But I wonder how many of us can answer such penetrating questions conclusively. Not many I suspect.

Silence once again surrounded us, the fire grew cold and the wind began to penetrate my back. I grew cold. Soon however, the mind drew within once it had filled it's lungs with much needed oxygen.

What was the purpose of my existence? How could I conclusively know? My mind travelled deeper and deeper into intellectual space. I thought about everything that I'd done, I'd experienced, I'd felt, and had come to know and love. I thought about my parents, Vikas, Dillip, Rene, Asheeta, and all those that had shared a snippet of existence with me. What did any of this mean? What had been purposeful? What had been morally correct? If most people throughout existence hadn't known their purpose, were they *immoral*? Could they be immoral or moral if all that they were doing was through the unknown?

Let me simplify it.

Lets suppose that I do an act "x" *(whatever it may be)*, but I'm floating through life not knowing my purpose – can I then ever be classed as a "bad" person, if my act "x" was bad?

I think not.

At best I can be classed as ignorant – and it's through my ignorance that I do wrongful acts. Note, that I am not imposing that people are good, or that there is no such thing as a bad person, or that people aught not to be punished; because that would be a preposterous proposition. Rather I'm talking about everyday approach to making judgements. I think most of us do things that are wrong, in varying severity and frequency; all that I'm suggesting is that I discovered another way to approach the very idea of right and wrong. I think what we can class as right and wrong depends on our individual duties towards ourselves, towards society, towards humanity, and towards those things which are universally right – something Freud called the *"collective unconscious"*.

So what's right for one person, no longer means that it's right for me. What's wrong for one person doesn't necessarily mean it's so for me; additionally, majority of our acts fall into individual and societal categories. If we can come to know our duties towards oneself and society at large, via our purpose, then we will mostly be a good person. I think most of us make mistakes and do wrongful acts because we are lost. I firmly believe that most of us lead semi-meaningful lives. Having little meaning to life is like a sailing boat having no sails. The boat would just float along according to where the tide would take it. Most us float through life, experiencing fleeting moments of meaning – like when we get our degrees, or when we get married, when we have children, and so on and on. These are passing moments, albeit powerful passing moments. They are meaningful for a moment, which push us in a direction with a great thrust and then fizzle out leaving us at the mercy of the currents of life.

It was this night in 2005, above Gangotri that I realised it was my Dharma to find my purpose – it was the duty above all other duties. I think it's likewise for all of us. Our first and most pertinent responsibility to the rest of our life is to discover our purpose. This should be our "real" education – it was certainly mine. The sadhu was fast tracking my life. He was shifting my entire paradigm to the extent that the great walls of my life were tumbling down – he was shifting the direction in which I was travelling; not directly of course, but through his simple question.

How do you come to know what the purpose of your life is? How do we begin to explore such abstract questions; and more importantly, how do we know when we've discovered it?

On that mountain top, I discovered the purpose of my life. I don't really know how it happened. An overwhelming feeling sprang from deep within; a feeling that I'd never known – and just like that I knew.

I'd realised that my purpose was to explore, understand, and assist all the millions of people who were already dedicated to making this world a little better than they'd found it. I was to join that ocean of souls that had dedicated their lives to bettering humanity. I'd realised with an overwhelming conviction that at any *personal* cost, I must live so that I may leave this planet better than I'd found it. How I did it was not important to me at that moment. Rather it was a profound personal revelation that told me I was not designed to be a pilot in the air force; or a senior diplomat with the Foreign Office; or an academic; rather I was to work independently; to use my creativity and vision; to propose new original ideas for society, which would add value to life. I was not to work for any one mission, nor any one race, community, agenda, or political ideology – rather my purpose was to find the unifying thread across humanity.

I'd pushed away several powerful incidents in my life where I'd had snippets of this destiny – this purpose. This time however, I knew it was different. I knew it was here to stay. Ultimately I knew that my happiness lay at the centre of this purpose – for without it, I'd never find peace, contentment or satisfaction.

The Grey Warrior

I left the cave that night knowing that I'd never come back; nor would I ever see the sadhu again. I arrived back to Gangotri exhausted. I was twenty five going onto fifty five. I was done for. I crashed onto the rock hard dusty bed, and fell into a deep dark slumber.

The next morning was a dull grey affair. Cloud and mist had descended from the high peaks onto the ashram. Visibility was poor, and the hot water rations were reduced to a quarter bucket. I felt uneasy. Following a snappy Indian breakfast consisting of Idli Sambhar down in Gangotri, I headed back up to the cave. I never reached it, because I couldn't find it. I tried for hours.

I parked myself on a shallow ridge overlooking the bustling pilgrim town and wrote the following; I'm unsure as to its origin. The following words just spewed out from the cocktail of emotions, exhaustion, and intellectual ideas that were present that foggy morning.

The march towards the enemy has begun,
My heart beats un-rhythmically,
I feel true towards my way,
I know, and I enjoy
I have been happy, I have been content,
I have tasted laughter and touched joy,
My enemy took it away from me and has taken for himself,
It's worth a fight,
For the enemy is wrong & seeks my obedience,
I shall not surrender nor speak of him in my thoughts.

(The march abruptly halts)

I am in trees,
I am in the green,
I am in his world,
This is the world which I despise,
For it is filth, cruel, it lacks comfort & peace,
It is savage,
This is a world I do not understand,
Nor is it worth understanding,

SANVIK VIRJI
My heart rages,
My mind burns,
And my body boils from within.

I wait silently,
Silence is unbearably loud,
It deafens my senses and frustrates my being,
There is no sound, no music, no dance, & no happiness,
My thoughts talk; getting louder and louder,
There are a thousand voices,
Speaking a thousand tongues,
The silence is driving me insane,
SILENCE – I scream.

All goes quite,
All is still,
The trees are covered in white shadow,
There is a glow in the air,
Moisture I had not felt,
The breeze is warm,
The white shadow comes all around,
I see,
But I do not see,
I hear silence,
I smell the scentless air,
And touch the invisible shadow,
The silence is serene,
The trees sway,
I gaze at the soft earth.

I suddenly see him,
He is in white shadow,
I check my eyes,
And in a blink he is gone,
But I feel his presence,
He disturbs the air as he moves,
Heart beats beat faster,

Shoulders grow heavy,
White shadow blurs my sight,
Hands fail to find strength,
My heart fails to burn,
My mind fails to rage,
My body no longer boils.

I command for the hatred to rise,
I command my hatred to come in my hour of need,
Where is my anger?
Where is my frustration?
Where is my enemy?
Damn this earth,
For it has stole my emotions,
It's drained me of all that I am,
Where is my victory?

The thousand conversations reignite,
But now they are a thousand fears,
And a thousand insecurities,
I see him again,
Shadow thickens,
I fail to see,
He floats through the trees and the white shadow is his stead,
My stomach churns,
My legs shake,
My arms stiffen,
My eyes smell fear,
My ears see my enemy,
I feel his shadow,
I taste his footsteps,
And I sense he is near.

Breadth is heavy,
I draw my sword,
I see him,
Through the mist he rises,

SANVIK VIRJI
I await him,
I am fearless & fearful,
I am strong & weak,
I know & I do not know,
I am sure & unwise,
I live & yet I die,
I see & yet do not see,
There is silence & there is chaos,
There is only us – my enemy & I,
Yet a thousand voices scream.

He is here,
My heart thumps,
My chest hurts & my limbs shake,
Lord, give me strength!
Shadow is larger,
The mist no longer conceals him,
There is total chaos,
I fail to know myself,
I release my sword,
My eyes close,
But I still see him,
I don't want to see him, take him away,
I feel my enemy,
He's in my mind, body & soul,
There is pain,
It's sharp; it's hurtful & chaotic.

I fall.

The soft earth catches my knees,
My body tumbles onto the ground,
My cheeks rest in the mud,
I lay,
Dead, but still alive,
In mist, in shadow under fallen leaves,
There is silence.

The battle is over,
And I have fallen,
Fallen through mist and shadow,
I rest in limbo,
There's a stillness I can't feel,
There's a silence that's joyful,
Peace runs through the depths of my soul,
I lay,
On the moist earth as if in the hands of my mother,
How I have dreamt of being,
& not being,
How confident was I of my vision & my life,
Where is the 'my'...I ask?

I lay forever in the softness & moisture of sodden earth,
I felt a comfort that should not be disturbed,
I was one with the earth,
Through silence I hear a single voice,
A vivid tone,
A subtle sound,
My voice, but not how I remembered it,
It's the voice of my enemy,
I see his feet holding his proud self before my fallen body,
I stare into darkness,
And I see light,
I touch my enemy with my broken will,
His feet boast strength & yet there was softness,
There is power & yet seems egoless,
There is anger & yet I feel compassion,
He has victory & yet it's not over.

I blink,
And he's gone,
I lay among trees,
I abruptly turn & see I'm alone,
I rise,

SANVIK VIRJI
And see nothing,
Yet I see everything,
I'm a little confused,
Yet clear,
I know not much,
Yet know everything,
I have seen only for a brief moment,
Yet I have seen for an eternity.

What did I see?

I fully appreciate and understand that this *'thing'* that I have written is analytically a *semantic monstrosity*, but if you can't get past the analysis, then I'm afraid you've missed the point of my rapture on that ridge.

Seven

धर्म

Left Wondering

I returned to the UK in late August 2005. I had returned a changed man. I think very few people, with the exception of my father, were none the wiser as to my inner transformation.

I write these words in October 2008, in a Star Bucks, in Barcelona's entertainment village. It's quite here. I'd set out to explore the prologue to ones own life, with the understanding that without such knowledge one could not possibly comprehend ones own destiny. The prologue to my own life has been mainly philosophical, and to some degree mystical, with snippets of unusual experiences and coincidences. These experiences have become a *veneer* on the underlying cause – a cause that has deep philosophy resonating within it.

I am who I am, because of all that I have discovered through the rabbit hole – through philosophy; through conversations with masters of logic, epistemology, mathematics, linguistics, metaphysics and the such like. I have become who I am, and I am, what I am, because of the great intensity of pain and suffering I have endured from a young age. The suffering has been like a great furnace where hammers strike hard and repeatedly, at iron that has been softened by great temperatures. The suffering is the softening up, and the hammering are my subsequent pleasures and successes – both are equally valuable to me.

Ultimately, this is a book about exploring and living philosophically. A book of ideas, but more importantly it's meant to be about living practically. I have merely scratched the surface of my realisations, and the experiences I've had during my travels; during intellectual journeys, and most importantly during interacting with human relationships. By twenty-five I'd experienced excruciating pains of death and loss, but also of the deepest bliss and contentment. I'd been exposed to great heats and had been softened up at an early age, followed by years of blissful hammering, which have subsequently shaped my being. I have become learned; but am I any wiser?

Well, the blunt answer is "no!"

Wisdom it seems, likes to ferment for years; solidifying when most of our living is complete.

Wisdom comes reassuringly late.

I have been asking the ultimate questions ever since I can remember, and I do not intend to repeat myself here – but I've realised that the challenge is *existential rather than intellectual*. The Upanishads along with Kant, Wittgenstein, Nietzsche and the long array of Greek thinkers, I believe, have mapped out the coastline *(synoptically)* of all human thought. None, I believe have surpassed the Upanishads. Some of the best philosophies of the past millennium have probed the limitations thus implied in the hope of characterising them accurately and acquiring a better understanding of their implications. There is always hope that the boundaries as drawn by the Upanishads will be pushed further back. Additionally, there is endless scope for criticism and correction of the Upanishads, and plenty of room for development. Thinkers such as Kant and Schopenhauer too reached the same coastlines as drawn by the Upanishads, albeit arriving from another paradigm. Have they surpassed the Upanishads?

I think not.

Hindu scholars, and by enlarge the entire Indian philosophical tradition to the detriment of all humanity have assumed that the Upanishads cannot be surpassed. One of the greatest mistakes of the writers of the Upanishads has been to assert that none can go further. In principle, I see no reason why the Upanishads cannot be surpassed; indeed I cannot even see the possibility of them remaining as the pinnacle of human understanding. I can't possibly predict what the next philosopher of genius will do; and how he or she will look to surpass our current limits of human understanding.

Clearly I'm not that genius!

Every hundred years, a great philosopher emerges, someone who adds, clarifies, extends or enhances our present understanding of reality – and I have no reason to think that this will end. Maybe, just maybe, the next genius is already born. We shall not know until the great discovery is published, scrutinised and analysed – only when philosophy makes the next great leap on behalf of all humankind will we know who the next genius is *(by which time of course, he or she could be long dead)*.

The challenge in the meantime for us, dear readers, is that we have to cope with our ever increasing frustrations, which inevitably arise due to the lack of ultimate answers for all our ultimate questions. Having read this entire book *(you're almost at the end, I promise)* you or I are no better off then when we started; maybe I should have told you from the offset that I was no genius!

The problems of God; consciousness; grasping reality; the infinite; time; human behaviour are all just as distant as they were. This frustration can give rise to a dire temptation. Since philosophy cannot provide answers to our ultimate questions; one of two misleading notions can be arrived at:

Firstly, that there are no answers; or that philosophy is the wrong medium to find those answers. Both, I believe, are patently wrong. Philosophy isn't about creating ideas. Rather it's about *living* particular ideas. Philosophy is living; not always thinking. Many of the answers to the ultimate questions are experiential and not intellectual.

I live philosophically.

Everything that I have discovered through the rabbit holes, I have tried to fuse it into my life. The answers to the ultimate questions cannot be verbalised – but can certainly be signposted. Since childhood, a day hasn't passed without my mind drifting onto the ultimate questions; the metaphysical puzzles surrounding all our existence.

In the first chapter I shared my childhood experiences that hurled me forward into the philosophical life, which will now be a lifelong quest. Since no fixed and final conclusions can be reached in this book I cannot round it off by reporting some great work of genius and solve any of the ultimate questions. Instead I should tell you where the philosophical life has taken me since my trip to India.

It's late 2008, and I've gone independent. Soon after arriving back home, I began to develop a personal coaching programme for young people, which I have since named the *Star Plus Programme*. The programme aims to introduce aspiring teenagers to the philosophical journey through exploring what's important to them – their academic progression. The course is a supplementary programme that people take on in the evenings once a week. It's designed to build the softer skills in people, and introduce them to the depth and opportunity that life has to offer. In 2005, I began with seven students. Presently, I have forty students enrolled onto the programme and got three fantastic individuals helping me market it. The issue of earning a wage is as real as ever, no matter where the rabbit hole takes you. Soon after the Star Plus Programmes were created, I began to develop a consultancy called WeComeOne Studio with a partner. Actually, its Asheeta's younger sister Bhavisha. WeComeOne Studio is essentially our creation.

Our Consultancy is underpinned by the premise that most of the marketing, which firms do and spend their valuable treasure on, is wasted, or at best has insignificant results. Marketing experts focus on the market – as you'd expect. We focus on the people. Essentially our consultants, which until last year were just Bhavisha and I, would go and carry out a through investigation of a firms marketing strategy, monitor it's spend levels, and witness successes and failures – all for free. Firms have little to no reason to deny us conducting this free analysis. Knowing full well that most firms overspend and have a scatty approach to marketing their products and services; we often end up producing a report highlighting how they could make their marketing strategy penetrating, psychologically speaking, and at the same time reduce their overall spend levels. We earn our money as a percentage of the money we end up saving them. So let's imagine a client spends £100 on marketing, and our analysis showed that they could reduce that level of spending to £80, and still build a better strategy than their existing model – our client clearly wins. They save £20; we win because we'll typically take 50% of all the money we end up saving them. Quite literally we put our money where our mouth is. It'll suffice to say here that so far our mouth has been on cue every time, and we've got many happy clients. Consequently our consultancy is growing.

Being self employed allows me to escape the dreary routines of working for someone else. Barely six months go by before a job offer arrives at my door from some bank or another. The money is good but I doubt the life style is. Freedom is something that for me at least, is invaluable. I enjoy the thrill of living on meagre wages, where I have to count the pennies I spend. I enjoy it because I do so out of choice. Spending a pound when you've earned it being self employed has a different feeling from earning it as a wage. The last three years have been a financial struggle; and have spent many nights thinking shall I just scrap all this independent palaver, and work. But, in the end the philosophical life always wins. I'm not allergic to material wealth you understand, rather while I'm young I want to live on the edge; I want to risk; live without restrictions; not join the rat race of owning a mortgage; and so on and on.

My hope is that the struggle I face now will expose me to Nietzsche's mountainous climb where one day I will be able to enjoy the views of life from the peak. I have no desire to make my life comfortable. I want it to be a challenge.

It's the challenge and the hardship that will propel me onto further philosophical truths. At least I hope so!

Ultimately however, I know that taking this route to making a living and marrying it up with the philosophical life will provide me with material wealth where I'll be able to, not only live well, but initiate fantastic projects, which I hope would add *real value to society*. I've enjoyed the entrepreneurial challenges; seldom a day goes by where I don't say "doh" – should have done this or that differently.

I have a wonderful, young, passionate, *but above all*, talented team surrounding me. It's they who flesh out my vision and ideas.

When Seeds begin to Sprout

It's been over three years since my journey across North-West India ended. Before, and soon after, I'd planted a few seeds. I've nurtured those seeds through emotional toil, patience and compassion. The first of these seeds is only now beginning to sprout, and this seed is called Bhavisha.

Bhavisha, as I've already mentioned is Asheeta's younger sister, and therefore, a few years younger than I. They look identical, except that Bhavisha is a little taller. Bhavisha symbolises *feminine strength*. When I first began to identify her potential, I realised that it was something that only I could see – her parents were oblivious to it; her sister was oblivious to it; and so were all her mediocre friends. By mediocre I don't mean to be derogatory, but rather that they were mediocre in every way imaginable – and they were content to be so! None of which makes them bad people; I'm just highlighting simple truths.

Bhavisha and I struck a cord quite quickly. Our relationship has grown exponentially ever since with the occasional dip; mostly when I've misjudged her mood. Bhavisha is indeed a deep and complicated character, something which I suspect will take a life time to understand. Whereas, Asheeta and I are no longer together *(of course we are still friends)*, Bhavisha, I suspect will most certainly be in my life for many more years. I've attempted to nurture her innate abilities, and psychologically build her competencies that were restricting her from flourishing. Slowly but surely, these psychological restrictive layers have fallen away. And with each layer that falls by the way side she flourishes with greater radiance.

Bhavisha now manages all our back end operations of the business. Barely a decision now gets made without her consent. I have no doubt or hesitation in saying that one day she'll be the *Chief*, and I'll become her counsel.

For me it's become important that I'm always developing the business model with someone else replacing me at one point or another firmly in my mind. This way I remain humble, as well as remaining unattached to fruits of my own labour. Essentially I'm creating businesses to give away to someone else – that someone being Bhavisha – my first seed to flourish, as well as my other Directors in waiting, with the likes of young Zima beginning to show the telltale signs of leadership.

As I nurture Bhavisha; so she is now helping me nurture all the other seeds we've collected. We both recognise the hidden talent that lies in these seeds that are yet to sprout. But a day shall arrive where the seeds have bloomed, who have germinated other seeds, which too would eventually flourish, and soon the barren garden that is today shall eventually become a ravishing garden tomorrow. Its beauty will be so majestic that the gardener, even though praised and remembered, will be sidelined *(and rightly so)* by all those that have arisen due to his toils. Once the first generation of seeds have successfully sprouted, nature will take her course, and then my toils will become enjoyment.

I have no doubt that Bhavisha (& Zima) will play a major role in my life; in which capacity and to what extent – I think this is a decision they'll be making – not me!

When curtains fall...

Perhaps this book ought to end in mid-sentence. There is no stopping point. Now that you have journeyed with me thus far, I shall continue to wonder and reflect, and do not expect to reach a natural end. The philosophical problems about which I might one day have something of substance to say are mostly connected to the limits of human understanding; and creating the ideal society, but that will at best be a subject for another book.

In this one my concern has been to show you the *philosophical life* – a life which has been far from perfect, but one which has had philosophy at its heart. The basic philosophical problems are presented to us by living, not by books or by the education factory. The pompous idea that one can only philosophise if they have studied philosophy is on a par with saying that one must have studied French to be able to communicate in France. The truth is that most tourists who visit France can barely speak a word beyond "bonjour" – yet most have quite an agreeable experience.

In this book I have tried to show how life hurled me into the rabbit hole time and time again, each time for me to be faced with mysteries of our everyday existence. I have tried to describe what I have experienced philosophically in my life – and how those experiences have shaped my actual living. Although this book has been predominantly about me, I do not intend to be the central theme – rather I have written it hoping that you'll connect with the philosophy underpinning everything that I've done.

Hopefully you would have struck a cord with much of what I've written and experienced, which ultimately I'm hoping will signpost you toward the entrance of your own rabbit hole!

My aim throughout my life has never been to prove anything, but rather to find out, to explore and discover the heart of the matter. All my life I have been absorbed by the metaphysics of our existence, and the meta-ethics of our morality.

This book tells my story; my story of the intellectual journey I have taken to arrive at wherever it is that I am. The simple truth is *I do not know* exactly where I am! The future is just as uncertain for me, as it is for the next person. The difference is that I believe I can face that uncertainty with uprightness, as well as a metaphysical conviction that I believe few ever develop.

Life has been kind. It continues to be.

www.ingramcontent.com/pod-product-compliance
Lightning Source LLC
Chambersburg PA
CBHW062157080426
42734CB00010B/1732